FR   S

COMPREHENSIVE TRAVEL GUIDE

MINNEAPOLIS &
ST. PAUL

4TH EDITION

by Lucille Johnsen Stelling
Assisted by Del Stelling

MACMILLAN • USA

About the Author

Although she was born in Brooklyn, NY, **Lucille Johnsen Stelling** has lived for more than four decades in the Twin Cities, where many of her travel articles have appeared in the *St. Paul Pioneer Press*. She taught literature and writing at Normandale Community College for 25 years and now develops Elderhostel programs for the University of Minnesota.

Macmillan Travel
A Prentice Hall Macmillan Company
15 Columbus Circle
New York, NY 10023

Copyright © 1988, 1990, 1993, 1995 by Simon & Schuster Inc.

All rights reserved. No part of this book may be reproduced or transmitted in any form or by any means, electronic or mechanical, including photocopying, recording, or by any information storage and retrieval system, without permission in writing from the Publisher.

Macmillian is a registered trademark of Macmillan, Inc.

ISBN 0-671-88374-7
ISSN 1051-6980

Design by Robert Bull Design
Maps by Ortelius Design

SPECIAL SALES

Bulk purchases (10+ copies) of Frommer's Travel Guides are available to corporations at special discounts. The Special Sales Department can produce custom editions to be used as premiums and/or for sales promotion to suit individual needs. Existing editions can be produced with custom cover imprints such as corporate logos. For more information write to: Special Sales, Prentice Hall, 15 Columbus Circle, New York, NY 10023.

Manufactured in the United States of America

CONTENTS

12 OTHER EASY EXCURSIONS FROM THE TWIN CITIES 168

LIST OF MAPS

This book is dedicated to

three honorary Minnesotans:

Molly Johnsen

Homer Johnsen

and

Bart Johnsen-Harris

WHAT THE SYMBOLS MEAN

 FROMMER'S FAVORITES—hotels, restaurants, attractions, and entertainments you should not miss

 SUPER-SPECIAL VALUES—really exceptional values

 FROMMER'S SMART TRAVELER TIPS—hints on how to secure the best value for your money.

IN HOTEL AND OTHER LISTINGS

The following symbols refer to the standard amenities available in all rooms:

A/C air conditioning   TEL telephone   TV television
MINIBAR refrigerator stocked with beverages and snacks

The following abbreviations are used for credit cards:

AE American Express   DISC Discover   MC MasterCard
CB Carte Blanche   ER enRoute   V Visa
DC Diners Club   EU Eurocard

INVITATION TO THE READERS

In researching this book, I have come across many wonderful establishments, the best of which are included here. However, I'm sure that many of you will also come across appealing hotels, inns, restaurants, guesthouses, shops, and attractions. Please don't keep them to yourself. Share your experiences, especially if you want to comment on places that I have covered in this edition. You can address your letters to me:

Lucille Johnsen Stelling
Frommer's Minneapolis & St. Paul, 4th Edition
c/o Macmillan Travel
15 Columbus Circle
New York, NY 10023

A DISCLAIMER

Readers are advised that prices fluctuate in the course of time, and travel information changes under the impact of the varied and volatile factors that affect the travel industry. The author and publisher cannot be held responsible for the experiences of the readers while traveling. Readers are invited to write the publisher with ideas, comments, and suggestions for future editions.

SAFETY ADVISORY

Whenever you're traveling in an unfamiliar city or country, stay alert. Be aware of your immediate surroundings. Wear a money belt and keep a close eye on your possessions. Be particularly careful with cameras, purses, and wallets, all favorite targets of thieves and pickpockets.

CHAPTER 1

INTRODUCING MINNEAPOLIS & ST. PAUL

When the largest shopping and entertainment complex in the United States opened in suburban Minneapolis-St. Paul in 1992, some observers were more surprised by its location in Bloomington than by its remarkable diversity of attractions. By now, huge numbers of people have come to the Twin Cities to see for themselves the beautifully landscaped, wholly enclosed Mall of America. Shopping is only part of what American and overseas visitors have experienced here. Children of all ages have enjoyed the merry-go-round, the roller coaster, the log chute, and other rides at a 7-acre theme park called Camp Snoopy. They've created a wide variety of brightly colored structures at the LEGO Imagination Center and have played the mall's 18-hole two-story miniature golf course, where hazards include waterfalls and streams.

Unlikely as the site of this unique shopping and entertainment complex may seem, those familiar with the Twin Cities were not surprised by the choice. Centrally located and readily accessible, the area has long been a major international destination with many other attractions.

The Mayo Clinic, home of the world's first and largest medical group practice, is just south, in Rochester, Minnesota. University Hospital, on the Minneapolis campus of the University of Minnesota, has also achieved world-wide recognition for pioneering procedures, including organ transplants. Supercomputers were born in the Twin Cities, bringing with them business travelers who had a way of coming back to vacation and sometimes to settle. Among the attractions they discovered here was an admirable quality of life, enhanced in part by the abundance of lakes—with more licensed fishing enthusiasts than anywhere else in the country. Also notable is the presence of world-class theaters, concert halls, museums, and educational institutions. And there's a remarkable variety of amenities for downtown visitors. Consider, for example, the Minneapolis

WHAT'S SPECIAL ABOUT THE TWIN CITIES

World-Class Theater

☐ Théâtre de la Jeune Lune, a bilingual theater company first formed in Paris in 1978 by Parisian and Twin Cities students.

☐ The Brave New Workshop, the oldest satirical theater company in the United States.

☐ The Tyrone Guthrie Theater helped initiate America's regional theater movement.

☐ Chanhassen Dinner Theatre, largest dinner theater in the United States—with four separate playhouses under one roof.

Major League Sports

☐ In baseball, the Twins—world champions in 1987 and 1991. In football, the Vikings—often one of the NFL's top teams. In basketball, the Timberwolves—one of the NBA's newer teams.

Spectacular Concert Halls

☐ Ordway Music Theatre, a European-style music hall, is itself a work of art.

☐ Orchestra Hall, the modernistic home of the Minnesota Orchestra and host to distinguished international performers.

City Parks

☐ St. Paul's Como Park, famous for its zoo and conservatory.

☐ Minneapolis's Lake Harriet Park, long known for its rose gardens and music band shell.

For the Kids

☐ The hands-on participatory Minnesota Children's Museum exhibits combine education and entertainment for children and grown-ups alike.

☐ The Children's Theatre, designed with young audience members in mind.

☐ At Fort Snelling children and their elders can relive 19th-century life.

Events and Festivals

☐ St. Paul Winter Carnival, an annual 12-day celebration, features ice sculpture, activities, and competitions.

☐ Minneapolis Aquatennial features sailboat races, milk-carton races, and a multitude of other summertime contests and activities.

Zoos

☐ Minnesota Zoo—find koalas, sharks, tropical birds, and luxuriant plant life; enjoy a bird's-eye view aboard the monorail.

☐ Como Zoo—a multitude of animals await you here, including the beloved trained seal, Sparky.

Shopping

☐ You can shop in the area for merchandise in virtually any price range in nationally known department stores and smaller outlets—especially at the huge Mall of America in suburban Bloomington.

and St. Paul skyway systems, which enable pedestrians to traverse miles of city blocks in climate-controlled comfort, whatever the weather outside.

1. GEOGRAPHY, HISTORY & BACKGROUND

GEOGRAPHY

Although every Minnesota license plate declares this the land of 10,000 lakes, there are really more than 12,000 lakes throughout the state, and that's only counting the ones that measure 10 acres or more. Thirty-one large lakes within the metropolitan area of Minneapolis and St. Paul offer a natural setting for year-round outdoor recreation: sailboating, canoeing, fishing, and swimming in the summertime; ice-skating, skiing, snowmobiling and ice sailing during the winter. Ice fishing, an important part of wintertime for many Minnesotans, was introduced to moviegoers in the popular made-in-Minnesota comedy *Grumpy Old Men* (1993), starring Walter Matthau, Jack Lemmon, and Ann Margret.

The 59 square miles that comprise Minneapolis are made up of relatively flat land interspersed with a number of lakes. St. Paul, surrounded by hills, has an area of 55 square miles, with several lakes within its city limits. Portions of the two cities are separated by the Mississippi River.

With an acre of city parkland for every 43 Twin Citians, joggers, walkers, skaters, and bikers do their thing amid picturesque settings throughout the cities. Public parks here maintain separate but equal paths for those on foot and those on wheels.

The suburbs offer outdoor attractions of their own: for example, in Apple Valley, cross-country skiers glide past elk, bison, and moose on authentically landscaped terrain at the Minnesota Zoo.

If your favorite sport is hand-to-mouth, you'll find picnic spots aplenty in the beautiful outdoors and, as a matter of fact, in the beautiful indoors as well. Consider the luxuriant glass-enclosed city park atop the shops and offices of St. Paul's Town Square. Here, among trees, shrubs, and cascading waterfalls, a classic carousel brings families from all over the Twin Cities to enjoy riding carefully restored ponies that many of today's parents and grandparents rode during its longtime residence at the Minnesota State Fair.

HISTORY

French explorers, traveling south from Canada, thought the Mississippi River might be their Northwest Passage toward the opulent East of which Marco Polo had written such

DATELINE

1654 French traders Pierre Radisson and sieur de Grosseilliers are the
(continue-

4 • INTRODUCING MINNEAPOLIS & ST. PAUL

DATELINE

first Europeans to reach Minnesota.

- **1680** Father Louis Hennepin is the first European to see the Falls of St. Anthony, the site of Minneapolis.
- **1763** Treaty of Paris, which ended the French and Indian War, cedes French territory east of the Mississippi River to England.
- **1803** Through the Louisiana purchase, U.S. President Thomas Jefferson acquires from Napoléon the part of Minnesota lying south and west of the Mississippi River.
- **1815** Lt. Zebulon Pike selects land at the junction of the Mississippi and Minnesota rivers as the site for Fort St. Anthony (established 1819; renamed Fort Snelling 1825). Pike pays 60 gallons of whiskey and $200 worth of trinkets.
- **1818** Convention of 1818 with England results in all present-day Minnesota coming under American flag.
- **1823** First steamboat arrives at Fort St. Anthony.
- **1836** Territory of Wisconsin organized to include the entire area of Minnesota. Joseph N. Nicollet
(continues)

tantalizing accounts. During the 17th century at least one of these adventurous souls, the self-confident Jean Nicolet, brought along on his expedition a change of clothes that he must have considered appropriate for the pomp and circumstance of his arrival in China. Imagine his chagrin and the open-mouthed astonishment of passing Dakota tribespeople when Nicolet stepped ashore in an intricately decorated robe "all strewn with flowers and birds of many colors."

Disappointed in their search for a new continent, these explorers may have found some consolation in the abundance of furs that awaited them here. Also waiting were Native Americans who were more than willing to exchange their beaver and muskrat pelts for blankets, knives, tobacco, tools, and other unfamiliar and intriguing items.

In time the Ojibwa from the east joined the Dakota, moving into this area in advance of the white men who had given them rifles, liquor, and other trappings of civilization. The name "Ojibwa" sounded like "Chippewa" to white men's ears, and that's the name by which the tribe is still known today. The Ojibwa disparaged the Dakota, calling them "Nadouessioux," or "little vipers," a name the white men shortened to "Sioux." Different from each other in language and customs, the Sioux and the Chippewa waged fierce warfare that threatened not only the white men's fur trade but also their own settlements.

French domination in the area ended in 1763, at the conclusion of the French and Indian War, when France surrendered to Great Britain all the land east of the Mississippi River. British rule was short-lived, however: Just 20 years later Britain relinquished the land to the newly formed United States of America, and in 1803, by terms of the Louisiana Purchase, Napoléon sold to the United States the territory that would one day include the state of Minnesota.

At this point President Thomas Jefferson sent army troops out to prepare for the construction of a "center of civilization" at the juncture of the Mississippi and Minnesota rivers. Fort Snelling became a refuge for traders, explorers, missionaries, and settlers, among them several Swiss families. Essentially squatters on land that had been ceded to the military by the Sioux, these families made their homes and livelihood in the protective shadow of the fort until a treaty with the tribes in 1837 officially opened new lands for settlement. The families then crossed the Mississippi to live and work on land that was to become St. Paul.

Awaiting the settlers when they arrived was an unsavory Canadian *voyageur,* Pierre "Pig's Eye" Parrant, who did a brisk business bootlegging rum to soldiers. The new settlement was known as "Pig's Eye" until 1841, when Father Lucien Galtier named his recently constructed log chapel in honor of St. Paul. Townspeople made that the name of their community as well.

NEW SETTLERS POUR IN

Until as late as 1848, many of the inhabitants of this area spoke only French, but when Minnesota became an American territory in 1849 settlers from the eastern United States began to arrive in large numbers. And then came more immigrants from elsewhere in Europe. During the decades between 1860 and the turn of the century, thousands of newcomers arrived from northern European countries, including Sweden, Norway, Denmark, and Germany, along with some from the British Isles, particularly Ireland. Pamphlets printed in various languages and distributed abroad offered deals that were impossible to refuse—reduced ship and railway rates and inexpensive food, clothing, and shelter while the newcomers searched for land.

St. Paul, now the port of entry to the frontier beyond, was also the acknowledged center of business and culture in the new territory. Incorporated as a city in 1854, St. Paul became the state capital in 1858.

Minneapolis, off to a somewhat slower start, didn't become a city until 1867. But in 1872 it absorbed the village of St. Anthony, whose waterfall powered the sawmills and flour mills that would make the "Mill City" a prosperous industrial center. By the end of the decade, Minneapolis was declaring itself superior to St. Paul in numbers as well as importance. Competition grew more and more intense, and finally, in 1890, sibling

DATELINE

begins explorations there.

• **1837** Treaties with Ojibway and Dakota lead way for white settlement in Minnesota.

• **1838** Franklin Steele establishes a claim at the Falls of St. Anthony, in what is now Minneapolis. Pierre Parrant builds a shanty on the present site of St. Paul. His small settlement is called "Pig's Eye," after his nickname.

• **1841** The Chapel of St. Paul is built, consecrated, and named by Father Lucien Galtier. It's on the site of the state capitol.

• **1848** The Stillwater Convention separates Minnesota from Wisconsin. Henry Hastings Sibley is elected as Minnesota's delegate to Congress.

• **1849** On March 3, Minnesota becomes a territory of the United States.

• **1851** University of Minnesota is chartered by the territorial legislature.

• **1853** First state capitol is constructed.

• **1854** St. Paul is incorporated as a city.

(continues

DATELINE

- **1855** The first bridge to span the main channel of the Mississippi links Minneapolis and St. Anthony.
- **1858** Minnesota becomes the 32nd state on May 11, third in size only to Texas and California.
- **1861** Under Gov. Alexander Ramsey Minnesota is first state to offer troops to Union as Civil War begins. The first Minnesota regiment leaves Fort Snelling on June 22.
- **1862** First railroad in Minnesota is opened, between Minneapolis and St. Paul. Also, Sioux uprising by Dakota frustrated by broken agreements with government.
- **1867** Minneapolis is incorporated as a city.
- **1870** Minneapolis becomes flour milling capital of the world.
- **1872** Minneapolis absorbs the village of St. Anthony.
- **1883** Minnesota is connected to the Pacific and Atlantic oceans by Northern Pacific Railroad.
- **1889** Mayo Clinic founded as St. Mary's Hospital opens in Rochester.
- **1898** Minnesota first state to re-

(continues)

rivalry erupted into internecine warfare when census results showed the population of Minneapolis to be 40,386 greater than that of St. Paul. Amid cries of foul play, a recount showed that both cities had substantially inflated their numbers. Both embarrassed, the cities' free-swinging antagonism toward each other gradually faded away.

MODERN ACHIEVEMENTS

At present, the region proudly boasts about the numerous modern trends it furthered. American regional theater got a big boost when the Tyrone Guthrie Theater first raised its curtain in Minneapolis in 1963. And enclosed shopping malls and pedestrian skyways also debuted here, as did the popular sports of waterskiing and roller-blading.

Through the years, Minneapolis and St. Paul have developed individual styles that complement rather than conflict with each other. More traditional than its younger sibling, St. Paul is often called "The last city of the East." And if St. Paul reminds you a bit of New England, then Minneapolis, "The first city of the West," may make you think of Los Angeles.

Which of the two will you prefer? That's a question that needn't be answered—or even asked. One of the best things about the Twin Cities is that you don't have to choose between them. With their downtown areas only 10 minutes apart, they combine to offer a remarkable diversity of activities and attractions, and that's what makes them such an extraordinary vacation value. It's two great destinations for the price of one when you visit Minneapolis and St. Paul.

2. FAMOUS MINNESOTANS

Eddie Albert (b. 1908), graduated from the University of Minnesota before gaining fame as an actor. Perhaps best known for his work in the TV series "Green Acres," he also appeared in many films and was nominated for an Oscar for roles in *Roman Holiday* and *The Heartbreak Kid*.

The Andrews Sisters Laverne 1915–1967, Maxine (b. 1918), and Patty (b. 1920), formed a harmony trio as girls growing up in Minneapolis and then went on to achieve stardom on radio and in films after recording their first hit, "Bei Mir Bist Du Schoen."

Patty Berg (b. 1918), one of the first women to become a professional golfer. In 1938, the Minneapolis native won the U.S. Women's National Amateur tournament; in 1946 she took first place in the U.S. Women's National Open.

F. Scott Fitzgerald (1896–1940), Famous Minnesota-born author who wrote his first novel, *This Side of Paradise*, while living on Summit Avenue in St. Paul.

Judy Garland (1922–1969), born Frances Gumm in Grand Rapids, gained early and enduring fame in films, notably as Dorothy in *The Wizard of Oz* (1939). As a teenager, she costarred with Mickey Rooney in a succession of musicals and as an adult appeared in such dramas as *A Star is Born* (1954) and *Judgment at Nuremberg* (1960).

Dr. Laurence Gould (b. 1896), geologist, explorer, and author, accompanied Adm. Robert Byrd to Antarctica (1928–30) and further explored the South Pole region in 1957. He was president of Carleton College, in Northfield, from 1945 to 1962.

James J. Hill (1838–1916), U.S. railroad magnate and financier, founded the Great Northern Railroad, which extended rail transportation from Chicago to the Pacific coast.

Hubert H. Humphrey (1911–1978), politician, began his career as a young reformist mayor of Minneapolis and later served as U.S. senator and U.S. vice president.

Garrison Keillor (b. 1942), author and radio personality, born in Anoka, Minnesota, and graduated from the University of Minnesota in 1966. He originated and hosted the radio show, "A Prairie Home Companion."

Frank B. Kellogg (1856–1937), U.S. senator from Minnesota (1917–1923) and later secretary of state under President

DATELINE

spond to U.S. President Grover Cleveland's call for volunteers for the Spanish-American War.

- **1905** Present state capitol is occupied.

- **1914** World War I begins. Some 123,300 Minnesota troops serve.

- **1918** Minnesota congressman Andrew J. Volstead authors the legislation that enforces Prohibition.

- **1920** Minnesota author Sinclair Lewis publishes *Main Street*, a satirical novel about life in small-town America. (Lewis awarded Nobel Prize in literature in 1931.)

- **1927** Minnesotan Charles A. Lindbergh makes the first solo transatlantic flight, from New York to Paris.

- **1930** Minnesotan Frank B. Kellogg, U.S. secretary of state, wins Nobel Prize for Kellogg-Briand Peace Pact (1928).

- **1942** 200 Japanese American soldiers begin study in the U.S. Army's Military Intelligence Service Language School, in Twin Cities suburb of Savage, then go on to
(continu

DATELINE

serve in Allied armies fighting Japan during World War II.

- **1958** Year-long celebration commemorates the first 100 years of Minnesota's statehood.
- **1959** St. Lawrence Seaway opens, making Duluth accessible to ocean vessels.
- **1965** Hubert H. Humphrey becomes U.S. vice president, under President Lyndon B. Johnson.
- **1977** Walter F. Mondale is sworn as U.S. vice president, under President Jimmy Carter. Mondale had been a U.S. Senator from Minnesota.
- **1987** Minnesota Twins win baseball's World Series.
- **1991** Twin Cities host International Special Olympics; Minnesota Twins again win World Series.
- **1992** Hubert H. Humphrey Metrodome in Minneapolis is site of pro football's Super Bowl; huge Mall of America opens in suburban Bloomington.

Calvin Coolidge. Awarded Nobel Peace Prize in 1929 for Kellogg-Briand Peace Pact outlawing war.

Sister Elizabeth Kenny (1886–1952), Australian nurse who came to Minnesota in 1940 to persuade doctors to use her method of treating poliomyelitis. The Sister Kenny Institute of Minneapolis is now a famous health center.

Sinclair Lewis (1885–1951), born and raised in Sauk Centre, Minnesota, he achieved national fame in 1920 with the publication of the novel *Main Street*. His other novels include *Babbitt* (1922), *Arrowsmith* (1925), *Elmer Gantry* (1927), and *Dodsworth* (1929). In 1927, he declined the Pulitzer Prize, but in 1930 he accepted the Nobel Prize in literature, becoming the first American to receive this prestigious award.

Charles A. Lindbergh, Jr. (1902–1974), raised on a farm near Little Falls, Minnesota, he gained fame in 1927 by making the first nonstop solo flight across the Atlantic.

Eugene J. McCarthy (b. 1916), born in Watkins, Minnesota, and served in U.S. House of Representatives (1949–59) and U.S. Senate (1959–71). He ran unsuccessfully for U.S. president in 1968 in an attempt to end the Vietnam War.

William Worral Mayo (1819–1911) and his two sons, Dr. Will Mayo (1861–1939) and Dr. Charlie Mayo (1865–1939), founded the world-famous Mayo Clinic in Rochester, Minnesota.

Walter [Fritz] Mondale (b. 1928), born in southern Minnesota, he served as U.S. senator and later as U.S. vice president under President Jimmy Carter and ambassador to Japan under President Bill Clinton.

General Lauris Norstad (1907–1988), graduated high school in Red Wing, Minnesota, and the U.S. Military Academy at West Point, before serving with the army in Africa during World War II; was supreme commander of the North Atlantic Treaty Organization (NATO) in Europe from 1956 to 1963.

Gordon Parks (b. 1912), noted photographer. He also as an artist, musician, author, and film editor. His popular raphy is *A Choice of Weapons*.

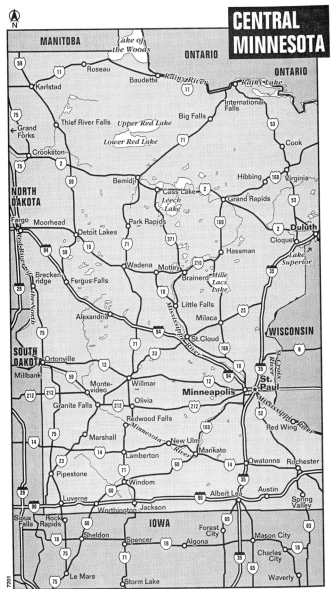

John S. Pillsbury (1827–1901), builder of one of the first flour mills in Minneapolis. He later served as governor of Minnesota from 1876 to 1882. As a regent of the University of Minnesota, he earned the unofficial title, "Father of the University."

Prince (Prince Rogers Nelson, b. 1958), born in Minneapolis, achieved international fame as a musician, actor, singer, and songwriter. He established a state-of-the-art recording complex called Paisley Park.

Charles M. Schulz (b. 1922), creator of the por

"Peanuts" comic strip, was born in Minneapolis, grew up in St. Paul, and began his cartooning career in the Twin Cities. His cartoon character Snoopy is featured at Camp Snoopy theme park at Mall of America.

Harold E. Stassen   (b. 1907), governor of Minnesota, who was later a member of the American delegation to the San Francisco conference (1945) that drafted the United Nations charter. He has frequently been a minor candidate for president of the United States.

C. C. Washburn   (1818–1882), built the first flour mill at the Falls of St. Anthony. Later joined with John Crosby (1829–1887) to form the Washburn-Crosby Milling Company, known today as General Mills.

3. ART, ARCHITECTURE & CULTURAL LIFE

ART

Art fanciers will find more than 100 galleries throughout Minneapolis and St. Paul and several major museums as well. The Minneapolis Institute of Art offers a comprehensive collection of art in all media from prehistoric times to the present. The Walker Art Center is devoted to 20th-century art, and the newly opened Frederick R. Weisman Art Museum at the University of Minnesota is a teaching museum with an emphasis on contemporary American painting. (It has been praised in the *New York Times* for "five of the most gorgeous galleries on Earth.")

Nationally known Twin Cities artists have distinguished themselves in a variety of forms, from the abstract prints and paintings of Steven Sorman to the installation art of Tom Rose. Rose's mixed-media work often combines drawings, photographs, and other individual pieces whose significance derives from his manner of assembling them. Other widely praised work by Twin Cities artists include the kinetic sculpture of Bruce Stillman and the surrealistic "flying houses" done in oil on canvas by Bruce Nygren.

ARCHITECTURE

Some observers fault Minneapolis for having razed a number of historic buildings in order to make way for newer structures. St. Paul, on the other hand, has chosen to restore old buildings for present-day use; for example, the 90-year-old Landmark Center, once a Federal Court House, now provides offices for arts and civic organizations; Landmark Center often serves as the site of important occasions as well.

The majestic Minnesota State Capitol and the Cathedral of St. Paul occupy the highest sites in the city of St. Paul while the highest point in downtown Minneapolis is the top of the Investors Diversified building, widely considered one of the finest works of contemporary architect Philip Johnson.

IMPRESSIONS

When I was born, St. Paul had a population of three persons, Minneapolis had just a third as many. The then population of Minneapolis died two years ago; and when he died he had seen himself undergo an increase, in forty years, of fifty-nine thousand nine hundred and ninety-nine persons. He had a frog's fertility.
—MARK TWAIN, *LIFE ON THE MISSISSIPPI* (1883)

In St. Paul's historic World Theatre, Garrison Keillor hosts his popular weekly radio show when it isn't on tour. Other touring companies perform frequently at the World as well, keeping this grand old building a very vital part of downtown St. Paul.

In both cities, at any time of year, you can walk from one end of downtown to the other with no concern for rain or snow or anything else our weatherpersons may forecast; our extensive skyway systems are absolutely weatherproof. In Minneapolis, the network of glassed-in second-story thoroughfares is the world's longest privately owned skyway system. St. Paul's skyway system is the world's largest publicly owned one.

Certainly mobility is one of the prime perks offered by these enclosed second-story glassed-in walkways. Another is the view they provide. In Minneapolis you'll be able to look down on the busy Nicollet Mall, surrounded by striking new structures like the Conservatory, the IDS Tower, and City Center. St. Paul has some impressive structures of its own for skyway viewing: the new World Trade Center and Town Square, among others. But nothing here can beat the St. Paul Skyway view of the Minnesota State Capitol and the Cathedral of St. Paul.

In both downtowns, architectural beauty is complemented by the natural beauty of the Mississippi, just a short walk away.

CULTURAL LIFE

Musical performances play a prominent role in Twin Cities cultural life, most notably at two world-class symphony halls: the elegant Ordway Music Theatre in St. Paul and the modern Orchestra Hall in Minneapolis. And there's music for the eye as well as the ear in downtown Minneapolis, where 32 windows of the Schmitt Music Center were bricked up on the parking-lot side of the building to accommodate a mammoth mural of a segment from the score of Maurice Ravel's *Gaspard de la Nuit.* Van Cliburn, in town for an appearance at Orchestra Hall, was so intrigued by the mural that he agreed to perform portions of the piece on a 9-foot Steinway that was pushed out into the parking lot for the occasion.

Perhaps, though, it's theater that has provided the Twin Cities' most significant contribution to culture. *Time* evidently thought so back in August 1973, when it highlighted the Tyrone Guthrie Theater in a cover story called "The Good Life in Minnesota." The article told the whole world about the remarkably rich quality of life in this area of superb natural beauty, where first-rate sports and recreation coexist amiably with some of the finest art, music, and theater to be found anywhere.

Probably no other major city in the United States besides New York City has more theaters per capita, and no city except New York spends more on the performing arts than the Twin Cities do. Since its opening in 1962, the Guthrie Theater has staged dozens of exciting productions, none more unique, though, than the Shakespearean History Cycle, which ushered in the 1990–91 season. In fact, by offering *Richard II*, *Henry IV*, parts 1 and 2, and *Henry V* in rotating repertory, the Guthrie made history of its own. This was the first time that a professional American theater company had ever performed these four Shakespearean history plays in a single season. But the Guthrie is only one of dozens of playhouses in and around Minneapolis and St. Paul.

Theater in the Round, near the University of Minnesota main campus, is one of the oldest continuously operating community theaters in the country; the Old Log, on the banks of Lake Minnetonka, houses the longest-lived theatrical stock company; and the Minneapolis Children's, adjoining the Institute of Art, is the largest of all American theaters for children; Great North American History Theater offers well-researched, well-written, and well-received original historical plays based on Minnesota events and people. And Curt Wollan's Troupe America stages small-cast comedies and off-Broadway musicals at theaters throughout the country, including three here in the Twin Cities.

Kid-style culture awaits at the hands-on Children's Museum in St. Paul where tomorrow's doctors and dentists, engineers and crane operators, service-station attendants, computer scientists, and TV personnel get to practice their future professions. The specially outfitted "habitot" offers fun and games to the even-younger set. (In early 1995, the Children's Museum will be growing up in a sense when it moves to a new home in downtown St. Paul at a site three times larger than the one it now occupies at Bandana Square.)

The Science Museum of Minnesota attracts audiences of all ages to attend films at its unusual Omnitheater, where panoramic adventures are displayed on a huge domed screen by the special 70-mm OmniMax movie projector. First, though, you have to get by that giant iguana at the museum's front door. A 16-year-old artist created this remarkable and celebrated reptile that sometimes serves as an extended bench for young museum goers. Popular as he is, no one has tried taking Iggy home, maybe because at 40 feet in length and 3,900 pounds in weight, this one-of-a-kind iguana is far from portable. Lighter but no less popular are the dinosaurs to be found inside the Science Museum, where, in the fascinating "dinosaur lab," visitors can watch the step-by-step reconstruction of these extinct reptiles.

For those who prefer sports culture, three professional major-league teams call the Twin Cities home. At the Hubert H. Humphrey Metrodome, 55,000 fans can watch the Minnesota Twins in action. When the Minnesota Vikings are in town, the dome contains a gridiron, with seats for 62,000 football enthusiasts. The Timber-wolves, an NBA expansion team, play in a large new downtown arena called Target Center.

4. RECOMMENDED BOOKS

ART & ARCHITECTURE

Coen, Rena. *Painting and Sculpture in Minnesota, 1820–1914* (University of Minnesota Press, 1976).
— *In the Main Stream: The Art of Alexis Jean Fournier* (North Star Press, 1983).
Gebhard, David. *A Guide to the Architecture of Minnesota* (University of Minnesota Press, 1977).
Torbert, Donald. *A Century of Arts and Architecture in Minnesota* (University of Minnesota Press, 1958).
History of Art and Architecture in Minnesota, ed. William V. O'Connor (University of Minnesota Press, 1958).
Homecoming: The Art Collection of James J. Hill (Minnesota Historical Society Press, 1991).

HISTORY

Blegen, Theodore. *Minnesota: A History of the State* (University of Minnesota Press, 1975).
Clark, Clifford E. *Minnesota in a Century of Change* (Minnesota Historical Society Press, 1989).
Folwell, William Watts. *The History of Minnesota* (University of Minnesota Press, 1956).
Gilman, Rhoda R. *The Story of Minnesota's Past* (Minnesota Historical Society Press, 1992).
Kunz, Virginia Brainard. *Saint Paul: The First 150 Years* (The Saint Paul Foundation, 1991).
Martin, Albro. *James J. Hill and the Opening of the Northwest* (Minnesota Historical Society Press, 1992).
Meyer, Roy W. *Everyone's Country Estate: A History of Minnesota's State Parks* (Minnesota Historical Society Press, 1992).
Stipanovich, Joseph. *City of Lake: An Illustrated History of Minneapolis* (Windsor Publications, Inc., 1982).
The WPA Guide to Minnesota (Minnesota Historical Society Press, 1985).

IMPRESSIONS

Minneapolis and St. Paul . . . are nicknamed the Twin Cities. They are divided by the Mississippi River, and united by the belief that the inhabitants of the other side of the river are inferior.
—TREVOR FISHLOCK, *AMERICANS AND NOTHING ELSE* (1980)

FICTION

Novels by Minnesota authors using Minnesota as a setting.

Hassler, Jon. *Grand Opening* (Morrow, 1987).
  —*A Green Journey* (Morrow, 1985).
  —*Dear James* (Ballantine, 1993).
  —*The Love Hunter* (Morrow, 1981).
  —*Simon's Night* (Atheneum, 1979).
  —*Staggerford* (Atheneum, 1977).
Keillor, Garrison, *Lake Wobegon Days* (Viking, 1985).
  —*Leaving Home* (Viking, 1987).
Lewis, Sinclair. *Babbitt* (Harcourt, Brace, 1922).
  —*Main Street* (Harcourt, Brace, 1920).
Powers, J. F. *Look How the Fish Live* (Knopf, 1975).
  —*Wheat that Springeth Green* (Knopf, 1988).
Weaver, Will. *Red Earth, White Earth* (Simon & Schuster, 1986).

YOUNG ADULT FICTION

Schwandt, Stephen. *Guilt Trip* (Atheneum, 1990).
  —*Holding Steady* (H. Holt, 1988).
  —*The Last Goodie* (Holt, Rinehart and Winston, 1985).

MISCELLANEOUS

Meier, Peg. *Bring Warm Clothes* (Minneapolis Tribune, 1981).
  Too Hot, Went to the Lake (Neighbors Publishing, 1993).
Meier, Peg, and Dave Wood. *The Pie Lady of Winthrop and Other Minnesota Tales* (Neighbors Publishing, 1985).
Toth, Susan Ann. *How to Prepare for Your High School Reunion and Other Midlife Musings* (Little, Brown 1988).
Wood, Dave. *My Mother the Arsonist: And Other Toasty Tales* (Waldman House, 1988).

PLANNING A TRIP TO MINNEAPOLIS & ST. PAUL

A little planning goes a long way toward the success of any venture, especially one involving travel. This chapter will answer some of your questions about a visit to the Twin Cities; it might even answer a few questions you hadn't thought to ask about how best to prepare before you leave home and about what you're likely to encounter after you've arrived here.

1. INFORMATION & MONEY

SOURCES OF INFORMATION

The **Minnesota Office of Tourism** (tel. 612/296-5029, toll free 800/657-3700, or Canada toll free 800/766-8687) is staffed with travel counselors who can answer your general questions and also key into a data base listing hotels, motels, and campgrounds offering specific amenities you desire.

Among the information you can get by phone or mail is listings of accommodations with no charge for children, weekend packages, senior citizen rates, pets permitted, babysitting and day care available, indoor pool, whirlpool, tennis, water beds, limousine and shuttle service, and scheduled entertainment. At your request the office will send you a travel newspaper, the *Minnesota Explorer,* and a variety of brochures.

For information on Minneapolis, contact the **Greater Minneap-**

olis Convention and Visitors Association, 4000 Multifoods Tower, 33 S. 6th Street, Minneapolis, MN 55402 (tel. 612/348-4313). For information concerning St. Paul, contact the **St. Paul Convention and Visitors Bureau,** 101 Norwest Center, 5th and Cedar, St. Paul, MN 55101 (tel. 612/297-6985). Additional visitor information sites in St. Paul are World Trade Center (main floor), Wabasha and 7th Place; Dayton's Department Store (main floor), Cedar Street near 6th Street; Landmark Center, 75 W. 5th St.; City Hall, 15 W. Kellogg; Science Museum of Minnesota, Wabasha and Exchange Streets; and the Minnesota State Capitol.

MONEY

Though prices in the Twin Cities are comparable with those in other U.S. metropolitan areas, there's no sales tax on apparel. Hence, you may pay considerably less for clothing here.

WHAT THINGS COST IN THE TWIN CITIES U.S. $

Taxi from airport to downtown Minneapolis	18.00
Taxi from airport to downtown St. Paul	14.00
Local phone call	0.25
Double at The Saint Paul Hotel (expensive)	154.00
Double at Thunderbird Motel (moderate)	77.00
Double at Days Inn/University (inexpensive)	60.00
Lunch for one at Gallivan's (moderate)	8.50
Lunch for one at Nora's (inexpensive)	5.00
Dinner for one, without wine, at Goodfellow's (very expensive)	29.00
Dinner for one, without wine, at Cocolezzone (moderate)	15.00
Dinner for one, without wine, at Lotus (inexpensive)	9.00
Cup of coffee	1.00
Roll of ASA 100 Kodacolor film (36 exposures)	5.45
Movie ticket, afternoon	3.75
Movie ticket, evening	6.00
Theater ticket (Guthrie Theater)	8.00–42.00
Theater ticket (Theater in the Round Players)	9.00–12.00
Concert ticket (Orchestra Hall)	2.00–45.00

2. WHEN TO GO — CLIMATE & EVENTS

CLIMATE

The Twin Cities enjoy four distinct seasons, with temperatures and precipitation that vary accordingly. The common perception of Twin Cities winters is that they're similar to those in outer Siberia or, closer to home, those in International Falls, the northernmost Minnesota town whose bone-chilling temperatures regularly make national news. Actually, weather in Minneapolis and St. Paul tends to be similar to that in other northern U.S. cities, except that for most of the year there's relatively little humidity, so you probably won't feel as cold (or warm) as the thermometer might indicate.

The winter ushers in a dry cold unlike in windy cities like Chicago or oceanside cities like New York. When the temperature really dips, the temptation is to stay indoors, but as often as not, proper clothing, including a hat and gloves, will enable you to enjoy the clean, crisp, invigorating outdoors. In any event, you'll be comfortable downtown because of the extensive skyway system.

The Twin Cities' Average Monthly Temperature and Rainfall

	Jan	Feb	Mar	Apr	May	Jun	Jul	Aug	Sep	Oct	Nov	Dec
Temp °F	11.2	17.5	29.2	46.0	58.5	68.1	73.1	70.6	60.6	49.6	33.2	19.2
Rainfall (inches)	.82	.85	1.7	2.05	3.20	4.07	3.51	3.64	2.50	1.85	1.29	.87

MINNEAPOLIS & ST. PAUL CALENDAR OF EVENTS

JANUARY/FEBRUARY

✪ ***ST. PAUL WINTER CARNIVAL*** *The largest winter celebration in the nation features ice sculptures, hot-air balloon races, ice-fishing contests, and other festivities. King Boreas, a mythical monarch, reigns over all of the merry proceedings.*

Where: *Events take place downtown and on various lakes.* ***When:*** *Usually the last Wednesday of January through the first Sunday of February.* ***How:*** *Call 297-6953 for specific dates and details.*

MARCH

☐ **St. Patrick's Day Celebration.** Every March 17 finds downtown St. Paul and Minneapolis hosting what are reportedly the largest celebrations outside of New York City. The pubs and bars are full of revelers, and the festivities culminate in parades in both St. Paul and Minneapolis.

APRIL/MAY

✪ *FESTIVAL OF NATIONS* *The St. Paul Civic Center plays host to a giant celebration of ethnic diversity that has been a local attraction for more than sixty years. Food, entertainment, and a wide variety of crafts for sale make this a particularly popular annual event.*
Where: St. Paul Civic Center, located downtown.
When: Last weekend of April or first weekend of May.
How: Tickets may be purchased at the door.

MAY

☐ **Cinco de Mayo.** The largest Hispanic celebration in the Midwest, this traditional affair features music, folk dancers, a craft fair, and a carnival. Food vendors sell tacos, tamales, tortillas, and salsa among other Mexican favorites. On the Saturday closest to May 5, participants parade down St. Paul's Concord Street, which is closed off to traffic for the occasion (tel. 222-6347).

☐ **Scottish County Fair.** The largest Scottish gathering in the upper Midwest features massed bands, bagpipe competitions, highland dancing, athletic heavy events, and other popular activities. Held the first Saturday in May at Macalester College, 1600 Grand Ave., St. Paul.

☐ **Syttende Mai.** Costumed participants celebrate Norwegian Constitution Day. A popular feature of this annual event is the parade on Nicollet Mall. Third week in May.

JUNE

☐ **Grand Old Day.** Grand Avenue hosts an annual St. Paul celebration with festivities that include music, food, and a variety of events. For more details, call 224-6959. First Sunday in June.

☐ **Svenskarnes Dag.** This annual celebration of the Twin Cities' Swedish heritage takes place each year at Minnehaha Falls Park in Minneapolis. Fourth Sunday in June.

JULY

☐ **Independence Day Celebration.** Costumed participants re-enact the 1827 Fourth of July celebration at Historic Fort Snelling. Call 726-1171 for details.

☐ **Taste of Minnesota.** An abundance of food and fun await celebrants next to the state capitol, as some of the area's best-known restaurants sell snack-size portions of their most popular dishes. Fireworks provide a fitting finale to the festivities. Usually held during the Fourth of July weekend.

☐ **Minneapolis Aquatennial.** A city-wide celebration of summer and the lake-related fun to be enjoyed in these parts. Call 377-4621 for further information. Usually the third week in July.

JULY/AUGUST

✪ *SOMMERFEST* *The great composers of Europe are saluted by the Minnesota Orchestra through a series of performances, and a wide variety of delectables are available, most of them European.*

   Where: Peavey Plaza, on the Nicollet Mall, between 11th and 12th streets. When: Usually mid-July to early August. How: Call 371-5656 for specific details and dates.

☐ **Concerts at the Minnesota Zoo.** Jazz is mostly what you'll hear on every Sunday during July and August at the picturesque Minnesota Zoo in the southern suburb of Apple Valley.

☐ **Uptown Art Fair.** The Midwest's largest outdoor arts-and-crafts festival takes place Friday, Saturday, and Sunday from 10am to dusk during the first weekend in August. Over 500 exhibitors from throughout the country offer everything from pottery to photography to wearable art. About 350,000 people generally attend. The central point is Hennepin Avenue at Lake Street, in Minneapolis.

☐ **Powderhorn Festival of the Arts.** Approximately 150 exhibitors from a five-state region display their works on the shores of Powderhorn Lake in Powderhorn Park at 34th Street and 15th Avenue South in Minneapolis. Booths are set up around Powderhorn Lake. Musical performances add to the festive nature of the event. Times and hours approximate those of the Uptown Art Fair.

AUGUST/SEPTEMBER

✪ *RENAISSANCE FESTIVAL* *This event re-creates the activities and atmosphere of 16th-century England with an assortment of events that involve visitors as well as costumed performers.*

   When: Every weekend from the middle of August to the end of September (including Labor Day). How: Tickets are available at the Renaissance Festival Office, located five miles south of Shakopee on Highway 169.

✪ *MINNESOTA STATE FAIR* *One of the largest state fairs in the nation, this annual get-together features*

*nationally known entertainers as well as a variety of
homegrown exhibitions, demonstrations, and
entertainments. Call 642-2200 for more information.*
   ***Where:** The Minnesota State Fairgrounds in St. Paul,
near the intersection of Snelling Avenue and Midway
Parkway.* ***When:** The 12-day event ends on Labor Day.*
***How:** Tickets are available at the front gate.*

SEPTEMBER

☐ **Burnsville Fire Muster.** Held in the southern suburbs, this
event includes a parade of fire trucks, a variety of outdoor musical
entertainment, games, block parties, and fireworks. Altogether it's
a very entertaining end-of-summer event. Second week in September.

OCTOBER

☐ **Twin Cities Marathon.** A 26.2-mile course through one of the
most picturesque marathon routes in the country takes runners
from downtown Minneapolis to the state capitol area in St. Paul.
First Sunday in October.

DECEMBER

☐ **Folkways of Christmas.** Forty-four historic homes comprise a
19th-century village called Murphy's Landing; Christmas is celebrated here in accordance with the various ethnic customs that
prevailed in the village from the 1840s to 1890s. Costumed
interpreters will lead you through kitchens in which you can
watch the preparation of old-time Christmas goodies.
   ***Where:** On Highway 101, about halfway between Savage and
Shakopee.* ***When:** Three weeks before Christmas.*

3. HEALTH INSURANCE & OTHER CONCERNS

Every traveler should have on hand whatever health-insurance
identification cards or documents are necessary for treatment that
might be required during an out-of-town trip. (Your local insurance
agent can inform you about additional short-term coverage that
might be appropriate.)
   In addition to checking your health coverage, you may want to
check your home and auto insurance as well to find out whether a
short-term complementary policy may be advisable during your trip.
   Diverse services are available to travelers through **United Way's
First Call for Help** (tel. 335-5000), where volunteers can meet
children or elderly travelers at their destinations or help them make

transportation connections. The organization can also provide interpreters for non-English-speaking travelers as well as help for people with visual and hearing impairments.

4. WHAT TO PACK

Although some restaurants require that men wear a jacket and tie for dinner, dress generally tends to be less formal here than in other large U.S. cities. Light clothing will see you through every warm-weather occasion, but remember that evenings tend to be cool, so bring along a light jacket or sweater.

During the winter you'll certainly want to bring boots to keep your feet dry in case of snow. In fact, here, as in metropolitan centers around the country, women's boots have become a fashionable wardrobe accessory. And don't forget your woolen hat and gloves. Then you'll be ready for anything that might transpire during our "theater of seasons."

5. TIPS FOR SPECIAL TRAVELERS

In 1990, the Department of Transportation (DOT) issued rules on nondiscrimination on the basis of handicap in air travel. In 1991, rules were signed into law as the Americans with Disabilities Act (ADA). These have already had a great impact on the quality of life for disabled passengers. For example, Northwest Airlines, whose national headquarters are located in the Twin Cities, provides on-board wheelchairs for in-flight use and wheelchair battery-packaging kits. You might want to phone the airline you'll be using to find out what accommodations have been made that will make your flight more comfortable.

Minnesota's commitment to accessibility is demonstrated in all parts of Minneapolis and St. Paul. Removable theater seats to make room for wheelchairs and infrared listening aids are available in many local theaters and music halls. Selected performances at the Guthrie Theater are interpreted in American Sign Language. Tours are available for sight-and-hearing impaired visitors to the Minneapolis Institute of Art. Few architectural barriers exist at the Metrodome in Minneapolis. Again, it's always wise to phone ahead to find out what facilities are available at the particular site you'll be visiting.

For all travellers—disabled, seniors, singles, families, and students—calling **911** leads to a quick response to an emergency of any kind. In addition, travellers to the Twin Cities can get help at any time for a wide variety of problems by telephoning **First Call for Help** at 335-5000. It operates under the auspices of the United Way.

6. GETTING THERE

Situated midway between the Atlantic and the Pacific, Minneapolis and St. Paul are readily accessible from anywhere in the world. All flights land at Minneapolis/St. Paul International Airport.

BY PLANE

THE MAJOR AIRLINES

Northwest Airlines (tel. toll free 800/225-2525) brings international visitors here daily from Europe, Asia, Mexico, and the Caribbean; its nonstop service includes flights from London, Amsterdam, and Tokyo. **Continental Airlines** (tel. toll free 800/525-0280) flies in daily from Paris, Madrid, and Frankfurt.

    United Airlines (tel. toll free 800/241-6522) also serves the Twin Cities, with flights from Paris, London, Amsterdam, Brussels, Tokyo and Sydney, among other international cities.

    American Airlines (tel. toll free 800/433-7300) and **KLM Royal Dutch Airlines** (tel. toll free 800/777-5553) are also among the nearly two dozen international, national, and regional airlines serving the Minneapolis–St. Paul airport.

BY TRAIN

Amtrak (tel. toll free 800/872-7245) offers round-trip fares to Minneapolis and St. Paul from New York for $218; from Chicago it's $82; and from Los Angeles it's $238. Amtrak also offers a Monday-through-Thursday 15% discount to travelers over 62 and an everyday 25% discount for handicapped passengers and military personnel.

 FROMMER'S SMART TRAVELER: AIRFARES

1. Shop all the airlines that fly to Minneapolis-St. Paul.
2. Always ask for the lowest-priced fare, not just a discount fare.
3. Be aware that some inexpensive fares depend on advance booking; don't let a deadline go by without making your reservation.
4. Airline price wars occur frequently. Newspaper ads and articles will keep you up-to-date on developments that can save you lots of money.
5. Keep calling the airlines to check fares. Availability of inexpensive seats changes daily, and as your departure date draws nearer, seats may be available at lower prices.
6. Ask about senior citizen discounts (usually 10%) or about seniors' coupon books that give you hefty discounts if you're willing to buy four or eight one-way tickets at one time.

BY BUS

Greyhound/Trailways offers a round-trip between Minneapolis-St. Paul and New York City for $225. Nonrefundable tickets must be purchased 14 days in advance. Round-trip tickets between Minneapolis–St. Paul and Chicago cost $90 if purchased 14 days in advance. Round-trip tickets purchased three days in advance are $102. Round-trip tickets from Minneapolis-St. Paul to Los Angeles are $136 if purchased 14 days in advance. Tickets are $270 if purchased three days in advance.

The Greyhound/Trailways terminal in Minneapolis is located at 29 N. 9th St.; in St. Paul, it's situated at 7th Street and St. Peter Street (tel. toll free 800/231-2222 for both).

BY CAR

As for highway accessibility, I-35, which extends from the Canadian border to Mexico, and I-94, which extends from the Atlantic to the Pacific, intersect in downtown Minneapolis and downtown St. Paul. Within the Twin Cities, I-35 divides, becoming I-35E in St. Paul and I-35W in Minneapolis. I-35E goes all the way through St. Paul, while I-35W goes north to south through Minneapolis. I-94 goes through both cities in an east-west direction. A Belt Line freeway system encircles the Twin Cities area, with I-494 extending through the southern and western suburbs and I-694 traveling through the eastern and northern suburbs. The Belt Line has interchanges with all the major highway routes.

A new interstate, I-394, now runs from the Lowry Hill tunnel off I-94 in Minneapolis west to I-494. Highway 169 extends through the western suburbs from U.S. 10 to I-494 and continues on to the southwestern part of the state.

CHAPTER 3

FOR FOREIGN VISITORS

Although American fads and fashions have spread across Europe and other parts of the world so that America may seem like familiar territory before your arrival, there are still many peculiarities and uniquely American situations that any foreign visitor will encounter.

1. PREPARING FOR YOUR TRIP

ENTRY REQUIREMENTS

DOCUMENT REGULATIONS   Canadian citizens may enter the United States without visas; they need only proof of residence.

Citizens of the United Kingdom, New Zealand, Japan, and most western European countries traveling on valid passports may not need a visa for fewer than 90 days of holiday or business travel to the United States, providing that they hold a round-trip or return ticket and enter the United States on an airline or cruise line participating in the visa-waiver program. Citizens of these visa-exempt countries who first enter the United States may then visit Mexico, Canada, Bermuda, and/or the Caribbean islands and then reenter the United States by any mode of transportation, without needing a visa. Further information is available from any United States embassy or consulate.

Citizens of countries other than those stipulated above, including citizens of Australia, must have two documents: a valid passport, with an expiration date at least six months later than the scheduled end of the visit to the United States, and a tourist visa, available without charge from the nearest U.S. consulate.

To obtain a visa, the traveler must submit a completed application form (either in person or by mail) with a 1½-inch square photo and demonstrate binding ties to a residence abroad. Usually you can obtain a visa at once or within 24 hours, but it may take longer during the summer rush from June to August. If you cannot go in person, contact the nearest U.S. embassy or consulate for directions on applying by mail. Your travel agent or airline office may also be able to provide you with visa applications and instructions. The U.S.

consulate or embassy that issues your visa will determine whether you will be issued a multiple- or single-entry visa and inform you of any restrictions regarding the length of yourstay.

MEDICAL REQUIREMENTS No inoculations are needed to enter the United States unless you are coming from, or have stopped over in, areas known to be suffering from epidemics, particularly of cholera or yellow fever.

If you have a disease requiring treatment with medications containing narcotics or pharmaceuticals requiring a syringe, carry a valid signed prescription from your physician to allay any suspicions that you are smuggling illegal drugs.

CUSTOMS REQUIREMENTS Every adult visitor may bring in free of duty one liter of wine or hard liquor; 200 cigarettes or 100 cigars (but no cigars from Cuba) or three pounds of smoking tobacco; $100 worth of gifts. These exemptions are offered to travelers who spend at least 72 hours in the United States and who have not claimed them within the preceding six months. It is altogether forbidden to bring into the country foodstuffs (particularly cheese, fruit, cooked meats, and canned goods) and plants (vegetables, seeds, tropical plants, and so on). Foreign tourists may bring in or take out up to $10,000 in U.S. or foreign currency with no formalities; larger sums must be declared to customs on entering or leaving.

INSURANCE

There is no national health system in the United States. Because the cost of medical care is extremely high, we strongly advise every traveler to secure health insurance before setting out.

You may want to take out a comprehensive travel policy that covers (for a relatively low premium) sickness or injury costs (medical, surgical, and hospital); loss or theft of your baggage; trip-cancellation costs; guarantee of bail in case you are arrested; costs of accident, repatriation, or death. Such packages (for example, "Europe Assistance" in Europe) are sold by automobile clubs at attractive rates, as well as by insurance companies and travel agencies.

MONEY

CURRENCY & EXCHANGE The U.S. monetary system has a decimal base—one American **dollar ($1)** = 100 **cents** (100¢).

Dollar bills commonly come in $1 ("a buck"), $5, $10, $20, $50, and $100 denominations (the last two are not welcome when paying for small purchases and are not accepted in taxis or at subway ticket booths). There are also $2 bills (seldom encountered).

There are six denominations of coins: 1¢ (one cent or "penny"), 5¢ (5 cents or "a nickel"), 10¢ (10 cents or "a dime"), 25¢ (25 cents or "a quarter"), 50¢ (50 cents or "a half dollar"), and the rare $1 piece.

TRAVELER'S CHECKS Traveler's checks denominated in U.S.

dollars are readily accepted at most hotels, motels, restaurants, and large stores. But the best place to change traveler's checks is at a bank. Do not bring traveler's checks denominated in other currencies.

CREDIT CARDS The method of payment most widely used is the credit card—**VISA** (BarclayCard in Britain), **MasterCard** (EuroCard in Europe, Access in Britain, Chargex in Canada), **American Express, Diners Club, Discover Card,** and **Carte Blanche.** You can save yourself trouble by using "plastic money" rather than cash or traveler's checks in most hotels, motels, restaurants, and retail stores. (A growing number of food and liquor stores now accept credit cards.) You must have a credit card to rent a car. It can also be used as proof of identity (often carrying more weight than a passport) or as a "cash card," enabling you to obtain cash from banks.

SAFETY

GENERAL While tourist areas are generally safe, crime is on the increase everywhere, and U.S. urban areas tend to be less safe than those in Europe or Japan. Visitors should always stay alert. This is particularly true of large U.S. cities. It is wise to ask the city's or area's tourist office if you're in doubt about which neighborhoods are safe. Avoid deserted areas, especially at night. Don't go into any city park at night unless there is an event that attracts crowds—for example, New York City's concerts in the parks. Generally speaking, you can feel safe in areas where there are many people and many open establishments.

Avoid carrying valuables with you on the street and don't display expensive cameras or electronic equipment. Hold on to your pocketbook and place your billfold in an inside pocket. In theaters, restaurants, and other public places, keep your possessions in sight.

Remember also that hotels are open to the public, and in a large hotel, security may not be able to screen everyone entering. Always lock your room door—don't assume that once inside your hotel you are automatically safe and no longer need be aware of your surroundings.

DRIVING Safety while driving is particularly important. Question your rental agency about personal safety or ask for a brochure of traveler safety tips when you pick up your car. Obtain written directions, or a map with the route marked in red, from the agency showing how to get to your destination. And, if possible, arrive and depart during daylight hours.

Recently more and more crime has involved cars and drivers. If you drive off a highway into a doubtful neighborhood, leave the area as quickly as possible. If you have an accident, even on the highway, stay in your car with the doors locked until you assess the situation or until the police arrive. If you are bumped from behind on the street or are involved in a minor accident with no injuries and the situation appears to be suspicious, motion to the other driver to follow you. *Never* get out of your car in such situations. You can also keep a premade sign in your car which reads: PLEASE FOLLOW THIS VEHICLE

TO REPORT THE ACCIDENT. Show the sign to the other driver and go directly to the nearest police precinct, well-lighted service station, or all-night store.

If you see someone on the road who indicates a need for help, do *not* stop. Take note of the location, drive on to a well-lighted area, and telephone the police by dialing 911.

Park in well-lighted, well-traveled areas if possible. Always keep your car doors locked, whether attended or unattended. Look around you before you get out of your car, and never leave any packages or valuables in sight. If someone attempts to rob you or steal your car, do *not* try to resist the thief/carjacker—report the incident to the police department immediately.

You may wish to contact the local tourist information bureau in your destination before you arrive. It may be able to provide you with a brochure on safety.

2. GETTING TO & AROUND THE U.S.

Travelers from overseas can take advantage of the **APEX** (Advance Purchase Excursion) fares offered by all the major international carriers. Aside from these, attractive values are offered by **Icelandair** on flights from Luxembourg to New York and by **Virgin Atlantic Airways** from London to New York/Newark.

Some large American airlines (for example, TWA, American, Northwest, United, and Delta) offer travelers on their transatlantic or transpacific flights special discount tickets under the name **Visit USA,** allowing travel between any U.S. destinations at minimum rates. They are not on sale in the United States, and must, therefore, be purchased before you leave your point of departure. This system is the best, easiest, and fastest way to see the United States at low cost. You should obtain information well in advance from your travel agent or the office of the airline concerned, as conditions attached to these discount tickets can be changed without notice.

The visitor arriving by air, no matter what the port of entry, should cultivate patience and resignation before setting foot on U.S. soil. Getting through immigration control may take as long as two hours on some days, especially summer weekends. Add the time it takes to clear customs and you'll see that you should make very generous allowance for delay in planning connections between international and domestic flights—an average of two to three hours at least.

In contrast, travelers arriving by car or by rail from Canada will find border-crossing formalities streamlined to the vanishing point. And air travelers from Canada, Bermuda, and some places in the Caribbean can sometimes go through customs and immigration at the point of departure, which is much quicker and less painful.

International visitors can also buy a **USA Railpass,** good for 15 or 30 days of unlimited travel on Amtrak. The pass is available through many foreign-travel agents. Prices in 1994 for a 15-day pass are $208 off-peak, $308 peak; a 30-day pass costs $309 off-peak, $389 peak. (With a foreign passport, you can also buy passes at some Amtrak offices in the United States, including locations in San Francisco, Los Angeles, Chicago, New York, Miami, Boston, and Washington, D.C.) Reservations are generally required and should be made for each part of your trip as early as possible.

Visitors should be aware of the limitations of long-distance rail travel in the United States. With a few notable exceptions (for instance, in the Northeast Corridor between Boston and Washington, D.C.), service is rarely up to European standards: Delays are common, routes are limited and often infrequently served, and fares are rarely significantly lower than discount airfares. Thus, cross-country train travel should be approached with caution.

The cheapest way to travel the United States is by **bus.** Greyhound, a nationwide bus line, offers an **Ameripass** for unlimited travel for 7 days (for $250), 15 days (for $350), and 30 days (for $450). Bus travel in the United States can be both slow and uncomfortable, so this option is not for everyone.

 FOR THE FOREIGN TRAVELER

Automobile Organizations Auto clubs will supply maps, suggest routes, guidebooks, accident and bail-bond insurance, and emergency road service. The major auto club in the United States, with some 955 offices nationwide, is the **American Automobile Association (AAA).** Members of some foreign auto clubs have reciprocal arrangements with AAA and enjoy its services at no charge. If you belong to an auto club, inquire about AAA reciprocity before you leave. The AAA can provide you with an **International Driving Permit** validating your foreign license. You may be able to join the AAA even if you are not a member of a reciprocal club. To inquire call toll free 800/336-4357. In addition, some automobile rental agencies provide similar services, so you should inquire about their availability when you rent your car.

Automobile Rentals To rent a car you need a major credit card. A valid driver's license is required, and you usually need to be at least 25 years old. Some companies rent to younger people but add a daily surcharge. Be sure to return your car with the same amount of gas you started with; rental companies charge excessive prices for gasoline.

Business Hours Many **banks** are open weekdays from 9am to 5pm, and there's 24-hour access to the automatic tellers (ATMs) at most banks and other outlets. Generally, **offices** are open weekdays from 9am to 5pm. **Stores** are open six days a week, with many open on Sunday too; department stores usually stay open until 9pm at least one day a week.

Climate See "When to Go" in Chapter 2.

Currency   See "Money" in "Preparing for Your Trip," above.

Currency Exchange   You will find currency-exchange services at major international airports. Elsewhere, exchange may be difficult to come by. In the Twin Cities the following banks will provide foreign-exchange service. **First Bank Minneapolis,** 120 S. 6th St., Minneapolis (tel. 973-1111); **First Bank St. Paul,** 332 Minnesota St., St. Paul (tel. 244-4646); **Norwest Bank,** 6th St. and Marquette Avenue, Minneapolis (tel. 667-5450); **Norwest Bank,** 55 E. 5th St., St. Paul (tel. 291-2211).

Customs   See "Preparing for Your Trip" in this chapter.

Electric Current   The United States uses 110 to 120 volts, 60 cycles, rather than 220 to 240 volts, 50 cycles, as in most of Europe. Besides a 100-volt converter, small appliances of non-American manufacture, such as hair dryers or shavers, will require a plug adapter with two flat parallel pins.

Embassies and Consulates   Embassies are located in Washington, D.C., the capital of the United States. Embassies for English-speaking foreign visitors include:

Australian Embassy, 1601 Massachusetts Ave. NW, Washington, DC 20036 (tel. 202/797-3000).

Canadian Embassy, 501 Pennsylvania Ave. NW, Washington DC 20001 (tel. 202/682-1740).

Irish Embassy, 2234 Massachusetts Ave. NW, Washington, DC 20008 (tel. 202/462-3939).

New Zealand Embassy, 37 Observatory Circle NW, Washington, DC 20008 (tel. 202/328-4800).

United Kingdom Embassy, 3100 Massachusetts Ave. NW, Washington, DC 20008 (tel. 202/462-1340).

The following countries maintain consulates in the Twin Cities area. **Austria,** World Trade Center, Suite 2490, 30 E. 7th St., St. Paul, MN 55101 (tel. 227-2052); **Belgium,** 800 Norwest Center, 55 E. 5th St., St. Paul, MN 55101 (tel. 227-9505); **Canada,** 701 4th Ave. S., Suite 900, Minneapolis, MN 55415 (tel. 333-4641); **Colombia,** 6800 Telemark Trail, Minneapolis, MN 55436 (tel. 933-2408); **Costa Rica,** 2400 Engergy Park Dr., St. Paul, MN 55108 (tel. 647-3618); **Denmark,** 7600 Parklawn Ave., Suite 444, Minneapolis, MN 55435 (tel. 893-1305); **Dominican Republic,** One Financial Plaza, Suite 1910, 120 S. 6th St., Minneapolis, MN 55402 (tel. 339-7566); **Finland,** 224 Franklin Ave. W., Minneapolis, MN 55114 (tel. 872-0014); **France,** 701 4th Ave. S., Suite 500, Minneapolis, MN 55415 (tel. 337-9557); **Germany,** 1910 One Financial Plaza, 120 S. 6th St., Minneapolis, MN 55402 (tel. 338-6559); **Guatemala,** 1728 Comstock Lane, Plymouth, MN 55447 (tel. 473-0110); **Honduras,** 20 Cygnet Place, Long Lake, MN 55356 (tel. 473-5376); **Iceland,** 3444 Edmund Blvd., Minneapolis, MN 55406 (tel. 729-1927); **Italy,** 24 Circle W., Minneapolis, MN 55436 (tel. 920-3330); **Japan,** 5318 Malibu Dr., Minneapolis, MN 55436 (tel. 933-9700); **Republic of Korea,** 2222 Park Ave., Minneapolis, MN 55404 (tel. 870-4400); **Luxembourg,** 2375 University Ave. W., St. Paul, MN 55114 (tel. 644-0942); **Malta,** Suite 2100, First National Bank Building, 332 Minnesota St., St. Paul, MN 55101 (tel. 228-0935); **The Netherlands,** 700 N. Lilac Dr., P.O. Box 1452, Minneapolis, MN 55422 (tel. 540-1210); **Norway,** 800 Foshay Tower, 821

Marquette Ave., Minneapolis, MN 55402 (tel. 332-3338); **Singapore,** 607 Marquette Ave., Suite 400, Minneapolis, MN 55402 (tel. 332-8063); **Sweden** (720 Baker Building, 706 2nd Ave. S., P.O. Box 2107, Minneapolis, MN 55402 (tel. 724-1841); **Switzerland,** 15500 Wayzata Blvd., Wayzata, MN 55391 (tel. 449-9767); and **Uruguay,** 743 Heinel Dr., Roseville, MN 55113 (tel. 625-7296; 484-8635).

Emergencies   By dialing **911,** you can reach police and the fire department or call an ambulance at any time of day or night. If you encounter problems such as sickness, accident, or lost or stolen baggage, call **Traveler's Aid,** an organization that helps travelers, foreign or American. Assistance is also available 24 hours a day at the United Way's **First Call for Help** (tel. 335-5000).

Gasoline [Petrol]   Prices vary, but at this writing you'll pay $1.05 to $1.25 in the Twin Cities for each U.S. gallon (about 3.75 liters) of regular unleaded gasoline. Higher-octane fuels are also available at gas stations for a slightly higher price. Taxes are included in the posted price. A majority of gas stations in the United States are "self-service." This means that patrons save money by pumping their own gasoline. Follow the directions on the station's gasoline pump.

Holidays   Banks, government offices, post offices, and many stores, restaurants, and museums are closed on the following national holidays: January 1 (New Year's Day); third Monday in January (Martin Luther King, Jr., Day); third Monday in February (Presidents' Day); last Monday in May (Memorial Day); July 4 (Independence Day); first Monday in September (Labor Day); second Monday in October (Columbus Day); November 11 (Veterans Day); fourth Thursday in November (Thanksgiving Day); and December 25 (Christmas). Every four years (1996 is next), the Tuesday following the first Monday in November is election day for U.S. president, a legal holiday.

Information   See "Information" in Chapter 2.

Mail   The **main post office** of Minneapolis is at 100 S. 1st St. (tel. 349-9100). St. Paul's main post office is at 180 E. Kellogg Blvd. (tel. 293-3099). **Postal rates** in the United States, at this writing, are 19¢ for postcards and 29¢ for letters up to one ounce. Rates to foreign countries vary; again at this writing, the cost is 40¢ for letters to Canada, 40¢ for postcards, and 50¢ per half-ounce for letters to most (but not all) other countries. Major city post offices are open Monday through Friday from 8am to 4pm, Saturday from 9am to noon; smaller communities often have more limited hours.

Mail receptacles   ("mailboxes"), generally located at intersections, are blue with a red-and-white logo and carry the inscription "U.S. MAIL." If your mail is addressed to a U.S. destination, don't forget to add the five-figure ZIP code after the two-letter abbreviation of the state to which the mail is addressed (MN for Minnesota).

If you want your mail to follow you on your vacation and you aren't sure of your address, your mail can be sent to you, in your name, c/o **General Delivery** at the main post office of the city or region where you expect to be. You must pick it up in person and produce proof of identity (driver's license, credit card, passport).

Newspapers & Magazines   There are two daily newspapers in the Twin Cities, the *Star Tribune,* published in Minneapolis, and the *St. Paul Pioneer Press.* Free weekly and semiweekly local newspapers are available at many supermarkets and banks. National daily newspapers like *USA Today* and *The Wall Street Journal* are sold at many newsstands. Newspapers published in New York, Chicago, Los Angeles, and other American cities are available at some bookstores (Barnes and Noble and B. Dalton among others) and at some supermarkets. *Minneapolis St. Paul Magazine* is a well-written monthly magazine which offers a wide variety of articles and events listings. **Shinder's** newsstands, at 8th St. and Hennepin in Minneapolis and on Wabasha St. between 5th and 6th streets in St. Paul, carry foreign newspapers and magazines.

Radio & Television   There are many radio and television broadcasters in the Twin Cities. Radio stations include WCCO at 830 on the AM dial, KSTP at 1500 on the AM dial, and KSJN at 99.5 on the FM dial. Among the television broadcasters are KSTP-TV, Channel 5; WCCO-TV, Channel 4; and KTCA-TV (PBS), Channel 2. In addition, most hotels provide cable television, with a wide variety of offerings, including CNN and MTV.

Sales Tax   In the Twin Cities, you'll pay a 6½% local sales tax on all items except food and apparel. There is no national value-added tax (VAT).

Telephone, Facsimile [Fax], Telegraph   The telephone system in the United States is run by private corporations, so rates, particularly for long-distance service and operator-assisted calls, can vary widely—especially on calls made from public telephones. Local calls in the United States usually cost 25¢. Note that all phone numbers with the area code 800 are toll free.

Hotel surcharges on long-distance and local calls can be astronomical. You are usually better off using a **public pay telephone,** which you will find clearly marked in most public buildings and hotels and other private establishments as well as along the street. Outside metropolitan areas, public telephones are more difficult to find. Stores and gas stations are your best bet.

Most **long-distance** and **international calls** can be dialed directly from any phone. For calls to Canada and other parts of the United States, dial 1 followed by the area code and the seven-digit number. For international calls, dial 011 followed by the country code, city code, and the telephone number of the person you wish to call. To avoid an excessive charge, determine the long-distance provider and its rate before placing your call.

For **reversed-charge** ("collect") **calls,** and for **person-to-person calls,** dial 0 (zero, *not* the letter "O") followed by the area code and number you want; an operator will then come on the line, and you should specify that you are calling collect or person-to-person or both. If your operator-assisted call is international, ask for the overseas operator.

For local **directory assistance** ("information"), dial 411; for **long-distance information,** dial 1, then the appropriate area code and 555-1212.

Like voice and fax service, **telegraph** service is provided by private corporations like ITT, MCI, and above all, Western Union.

You can bring your telegram in to the nearest Western Union office (there are hundreds across the country) or dictate it over the phone (a toll-free call, 800/325-6000). You can also telegraph money, or have it telegraphed to you, very quickly over the Western Union system.

Telephone Directory   There are two kinds of telephone directories. The general directory is the **White Pages,** in which private and business subscribers are listed in alphabetical order. The inside front cover lists the emergency number for police, fire, and ambulance and other vital numbers (like the Coast Guard, poison-control center, crime-victims hotline, and so on). The first few pages are devoted to community-service numbers, including a guide to long-distance and international calling, complete with country codes and area codes.

The second directory, printed on yellow paper (whence its name, **Yellow Pages**), lists local services, businesses, and industries by type of activity, with an index at the back. The listings cover not only such obvious items as automobile repairs by make of car, or drugstores (pharmacies), often by geographical location, but also restaurants by type of cuisine and geographical location, bookstores by special subject and/or language, places of worship by religious denomination, and other information that the tourist might otherwise not readily find. The *Yellow Pages* also include city plans or detailed area maps, often showing postal ZIP codes and public transportation routes.

Time   The United States is divided into four **time zones** (six, if Alaska and Hawaii are included). From east to west, these are: eastern time (ET), central time (CT), mountain time (MT), Pacific time (PT), Alaska time (AT), and Hawaii time (HT). Always keep changing time zones in mind if you are traveling (or even telephoning) long distances in the United States. For example, noon in New York City (ET) is 11am in Chicago (CT), 10am in Denver (MT), 9am in Los Angeles (PT), 8am in Anchorage (AT), and 7am in Honolulu (HT). **Daylight saving time** is in effect from the last Sunday in April through the last Saturday in October (actually, the change is made at 2am on Sunday), except in Arizona, Hawaii, part of Indiana, and Puerto Rico. Daylight saving time moves the clock one hour ahead.

Tipping   This is part of the American way; many service personnel receive little direct salary and depend on tips for most of their income. Here are some rules of thumb:

In **hotels,** tip bellhops at least $1 per piece of luggage ($2 to $3 if you have a lot of luggage) and tip the chamber staff $1 per day. Tip the doorman or concierge only if he or she has provided you with some specific service (for example, calling a cab or obtaining theater tickets).

In **restaurants, bars, and nightclubs,** tip service staff 15% to 20% of the check, tip bartenders 10% to 15%, tip checkroom attendants $1 per garment, and tip valet-parking attendants $1 per vehicle. Tip the doorman only if he provided a specific service (such as calling a cab). Tipping is not expected in cafeterias and fast-food restaurants.

Tip **cab drivers** 15% of the fare.

As for **other service personnel,** tip redcaps at airports or railroad stations at least 50¢ per piece ($2 to $3 if you have a lot of luggage) and tip hairdressers and barbers 15% to 20%.

Ushers in **cinemas** and **theaters** and **gas-station attendants** do not expect a tip.

Toilets Foreign visitors often complain that public toilets are hard to find in most U.S. cities. True, there are none on the streets, but the visitor can usually find one in a bar, restaurant, hotel, museum, department store, or service station—and it will probably be clean (although the last-mentioned sometimes leaves much to be desired). Note, however, a growing practice in restaurants and bars of displaying a notice that "toilets are for the use of patrons only." You can ignore this sign, or better yet, avoid arguments by paying for a cup of coffee or soft drink, which will qualify you as a patron. The cleanliness of toilets at railroad stations and bus depots may be more open to question, and some public places are equipped with pay toilets, which require you to insert one or more coins into a slot on the door before it will open.

AMERICAN SYSTEM OF MEASUREMENT

LENGTH

1 inch (in.)	=	2.54cm				
1 foot (ft.)	=	12 in.	=	30.48cm	=	0.305m
1 yard (yd.)	=	3 ft.	=	0.915m		
1 mile	=	5,280 ft.	=	1.609km		

To convert miles to kilometers, multiply the number of miles by 1.61. Also use to convert speeds from miles per hour (m.p.h.) to kilometers per hour (kmph).

To convert kilometers to miles, multiply the number of kilometers by 0.62. Also use to convert kmph to m.p.h.

CAPACITY

1 fluid ounce (fl. oz.)	=	0.03 liters		
1 pint	=	16 fl. oz.	=	0.47 liters
1 quart	=	2 pints	=	0.94 liters
1 gallon (gal.)	=	4 quarts	=	3.79 liters
	=	0.83 imperial gal.		

To convert U.S. gallons to liters, multiply the number of gallons by 3.79.

To convert liters to U.S. gallons, multiply the number of liters by 0.26.

To convert U.S. gallons to imperial gallons, multiply the number of U.S. gallons by 0.83.

To convert imperial gallons to U.S. gallons, multiply the number of imperial gallons by 1.2.

WEIGHT

1 ounce (oz.)	=	28.35g				
1 pound (lb.)	=	16 oz.	=	453.6g	=	0.45kg
1 ton	=	2,000 lb.	=	907kg	=	0.91 metric tons

To convert pounds to kilograms, multiply the number of pounds by 0.45.

To convert kilograms to pounds, multiply the number of kilograms by 2.2.

AREA

1 acre	=	0.41ha				
1 square mile	=	640 acres	=	259ha	=	2.6km²

To convert acres to hectares, multiply the number of acres by 0.41.

To convert hectares to acres, multiply the number of hectares by 2.47.

To convert square miles to square kilometers, multiply the number of square miles by 2.6.

To convert square kilometers to square miles, multiply the number of square kilometers by 0.39.

TEMPERATURE

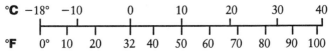

To convert degrees Fahrenheit to degrees Celsius, subtract 32 from °F, multiply by 5, then divide by 9 (example: 85°F − 32 × 5/9 = 29.4°C).

To convert degrees Celsius to degrees Fahrenheit, multiply °C by 9, divide by 5, and add 32 (example: 20°C × 9/5 + 32 = 68°F).

CHAPTER 4

GETTING TO KNOW MINNEAPOLIS & ST. PAUL

1. ORIENTATION
2. GETTING AROUND
- **FAST FACTS: MINNEAPOLIS & ST. PAUL**

The purpose of this chapter is to make you feel comfortable in the Twin Cities from the moment you arrive. I'll also familiarize you with some of the sights and services that await you here. Specific information about hotels, restaurants, things to do, and places to go will follow in succeeding chapters.

1. ORIENTATION

ARRIVING

BY PLANE

When your plane arrives in the Twin Cities, you'll be landing at **Minneapolis–St. Paul International Airport,** just 10 miles south of downtown Minneapolis and 8½ miles southwest of downtown St. Paul. After you leave your plane, you'll enter the upper level of Charles Lindbergh Terminal Building; baggage-claim carousels and ground-transportation desks are on the lower level.

GETTING TO & FROM THE AIRPORT On the lower level outside the terminal you'll see a line of waiting cabs. **Taxi fares** average about $18 to downtown Minneapolis and $14 to downtown St. Paul. At press time, a 10% discount is available from Airport Taxi (tel. 721-6566) if you phone for an assigned cab number after picking up your luggage. You'll be picked up by your designated taxi on the ground level beyond the baggage carousels near Door #4.

If you'd like **van service** to Minneapolis, you can arrange for it across from baggage carousel #10 on the lower level of the terminal at the limousine service desk (tel. 827-7777). Service to downtown Minneapolis is $10 one-way, $15.50 round-trip. For van service to St. Paul, go to the limousine service desk (tel. 726-5479) across from carousels #8 and #9. The fare to downtown St. Paul is $6 one-way, $9.50 round-trip.

The Metropolitan Transit Commission (tel. 349-7000) runs **buses** from the airport to Washington Avenue in downtown Minneapolis and to Robert Street in downtown St. Paul for $1 ($1.25 during rush hour). Bus #7 will take you to downtown Minneapolis at varying intervals throughout the day. Service to St. Paul is more limited. The #4 bus runs every 20 minutes throughout the day, less frequently at night. All MTC buses are marked with a large "T" on the side.

During the morning or afternoon rush hour, an **express bus** will take you to either Minneapolis or St. Paul for $1.60.

BY TRAIN

Amtrak passengers to the Twin Cities pull in to St. Paul at St. Paul/Minneapolis Minnesota Midway Station, 730 Transfer Rd., St. Paul (tel. toll free 800/872-7245), located about 10 minutes from downtown St. Paul and 20 minutes from downtown Minneapolis. Cab service from the Amtrak terminal is $1.20 to $1.30 per mile.

BY BUS

Greyhound Bus Lines maintains terminals in both St. Paul and Minneapolis. In Minneapolis, the address is 29 N. 9th St. (tel. 371-3320); the St. Paul terminal is at 7th Street and St. Peter Street (tel. 222-0509).

TOURIST INFORMATION

The **St. Paul Convention and Visitors Bureau** (tel. 297-6985) maintains a Visitor Information Booth on the street level of Town Square, at 7th Street and Cedar Avenue, with plenty of brochures to help tourists get acquainted with the city. Hours are Monday through Friday from 8am to 5pm.

The **Greater Minneapolis Convention and Visitors Association** at 33 S. 6th St., Minneapolis, MN 55402 (tel. 348-4313), dispenses brochures and information Monday through Friday from 8am to 5pm. If requested, it will mail a tourist packet to you.

The **Greater Minneapolis Chamber of Commerce,** 81 S. 9th St., Suite 200, Minneapolis, MN 55402-3223 (tel. 370-9132) has a **Tourism Hotline** (tel. 370-9103), which can send you a brochure and detailed street map of the Twin Cities region.

CITY LAYOUT

In the south, Minneapolis and St. Paul are largely separated by the Mississippi River.

In Minneapolis, avenues generally run north and south while streets run east and west. Main arteries are Hennepin Avenue, Nicollet Avenue, Lyndale Avenue, Park Avenue, Portland Avenue, and University Avenue.

In St. Paul, the main arteries are Summit Avenue, Grand Avenue, Selby Avenue, Marshall Avenue, University Avenue, Wabasha Street, Robert Street and West 7th Street (Fort Road).

NEIGHBORHOODS IN BRIEF

Downtown Minneapolis In recent years this section has become a somewhat prestigious address for young business and professional people as well as for retirees. Just a short walk from Nicollet Mall and Hennepin Avenue, high-rise condominiums and handsome town houses stand amid cultural centers like Orchestra Hall and the Guthrie Theater. Gaviidae Common, the Conservatory, and City Center await with some of the finest shopping in this part of the country.

Uptown Minneapolis   The area near the intersection of Lake Street and Hennepin Avenue, some three miles south of downtown Minneapolis, has long been considered one of the trendiest parts of town. Home to a very diverse population—creative and commercial, artistic and academic, the neighborhood is great for people watching. There are also lots of small specialty shops, foreign film theaters, and all kinds of ethnic restaurants.

Downtown St. Paul   Near the beautiful and majestic state capitol complex and the Cathedral of St. Paul, this area is home to many condominiums. Also in the neighborhood is the "Cultural Corridor" that connects some truly astonishing centers of music, art, and theater. On three sides of tiny Rice Park, you'll find the exquisite Ordway Music Theatre, the historic Landmark Center, and the distinguished St. Paul Public Library. Just two blocks away is the Minnesota Museum of American Art.

Grand Avenue   This is St. Paul's answer to uptown Minneapolis. Filled with small distinctive shops and a variety of ethnic restaurants, it's a stimulating and often trend setting part of town. Its special style and spirit is captured each June in Grand Old Day, the largest 1-day street festival in the Midwest.

2. GETTING AROUND

BY BUS

Thanks to the Metropolitan Transit Commission's **Quarter Zone,** a mere 25¢ will take you to most offices, restaurants, and businesses in the downtown area.

For longer MTC expeditions, you can get maps, pocket schedules, and tokens in St. Paul in the American National Bank Skyway, Minnesota Street between 5th and 6th streets. In Minneapolis, you'll find them at the MTC Transit Store, 719 Marquette Ave.

Bus fares range from $1 to $1.25, depending on the time of day and distance traveled. You'll need the exact change when you board unless you've purchased a token or a commuter ticket. (They won't reduce the cost of your ride, but will save you from scrounging for change.)

For Metropolitan Transit Commission information, phone 349-7000.

BY TAXI

Cab fares range from $1.20 to $1.30 per mile (depending on the taxi company). Cab companies include **Airport Taxi** (tel. 721-0000),

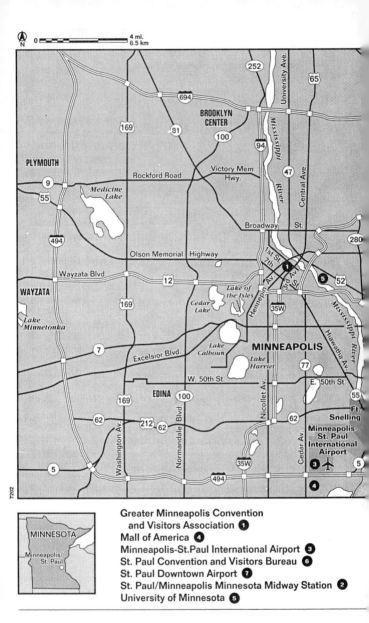

0 ⟝⟝⟝⟝ 4 mi.
6.5 km
N

Greater Minneapolis Convention
and Visitors Association ❶
Mall of America ❹
Minneapolis-St.Paul International Airport ❸
St. Paul Convention and Visitors Bureau ❻
St. Paul Downtown Airport ❼
St. Paul/Minneapolis Minnesota Midway Station ❷
University of Minnesota ❺

Suburban Taxi (tel. 884-8888), and **St. Paul Yellow Cab** (tel. 222-4433). You may want to inquire about fares in advance.

BY CAR

Unless you plan to spend all your time downtown, you'll want to rent a car for at least part of your visit to the Twin Cities. Otherwise you'll miss some of the many exciting attractions and activities in the

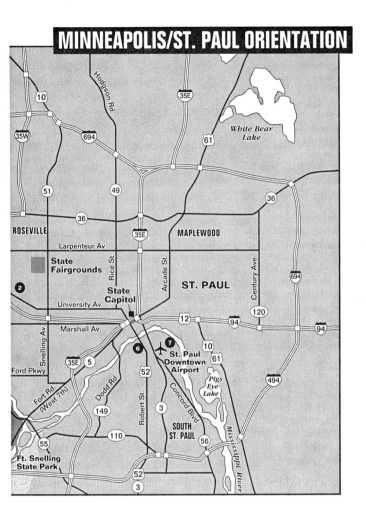

MINNEAPOLIS/ST. PAUL ORIENTATION

environs. Local car-rental companies include **Budget Rent-a-Car** (tel. 727-2000), **Hertz Rent-a-Car,** (tel. 726-1600), **National Car Rental** (tel. toll free 800/227-7368), and **Avis Rent-a-Car,** all located at Minneapolis–St. Paul International Airport (tel. 726-5220). Some also have downtown locations.

PARKING Downtown parking is viewed by many Twin Citians as a good reason to shop in the suburbs. There's no lack of parking lots, but the rates can be high. In general, rates vary depending on location, time of day, and length of stay.

DRIVING RULES   Unless posted otherwise, the urban speed limit is 30 mph, and the limit on major highways and in rural areas is 55 mph. State law permits a right-hand turn on red unless there's a sign indicating such a turn is not allowed.

SAFETY BELT LAW   State law requires that persons in the front seat of a car and all children under age 11 use a safety belt. Children under age four must be securely fastened in protective seats.

BY BICYCLE

Bike and pedestrian paths run parallel in Twin Cities' parks so folks on foot and those on wheels don't compete for the same space. If you're interested in renting a bike, call **The Bike Shop,** 213 S.E. Oak St. (tel. 331-3442), and **Calhoun Cycle,** 1622 W. Lake St. (tel. 827-8231), both in Minneapolis, or **Bennett's Cycle, Inc.,** in the Minneapolis suburb of St. Louis Park (tel. 922-0311) or in St. Paul (tel. 633-3019). In Excelsior, try **Area Wide Cycle** (tel. 474-3229).

FAST FACTS MINNEAPOLIS & ST. PAUL

Airport   See "Orientation" in this chapter.

American Express   In St. Paul, the **Amex** office (tel. 291-7081) is located in the St. Paul Center, 30 E. 8th St. In Minneapolis, the office (tel. 343-5500) is located in the Pillsbury Center, 200 S. 6th St. To report a lost or stolen card, dial toll free 800/528-2121.

Area Code   The telephone area code throughout the Twin Cities area is **612.**

Babysitters   The concierge at your hotel or the desk clerk should be able to make arrangements for you.

Business Hours   **Government offices** usually open at 8am and close at 4:30 or 5pm. **Stores** tend to open at 9:30 or 10am; those downtown or in the suburbs usually stay open until 9pm. **Banks** usually open at 9am and remain open until 3 or 4pm, with extended hours on Friday afternoon and on Saturday morning.

Car Rentals   See "Getting Around" in this chapter.

Climate   See "When to Go" in Chapter 2.

Dentist   Call the **Dental Referral Service** at 932-6000.

Doctor   The **Physician's Referral Service** can be reached at 932-6000.

Driving Rules   See "Getting Around" in this chapter.

Drugstores   In Minneapolis, try **Dahl Pharmacy,** 1200 Nicollet Mall (tel. 333-4205), or **Loop Drug,** 933 Marquette Ave. (tel. 333-2481). In St. Paul, drugstores include **Carlson Pharmacy,** 356 St. Peter St. (tel. 222-8594), **Moudry Apothecary Shop,** 364

St. Peter St. (tel. 222-0571), and **Walgreen Drugstore,** 425 Wabasha St. (tel. 222-0120).

   Emergencies   Call **911** for fire, police, or ambulance.

   Eyeglasses   Stores in Minneapolis include **Moss Optical** (tel. 332-7907), 10 S. 8th St., and **Vision World** (tel. 332-6656), 733 Marquette Ave. In St. Paul, try **Christy Optical** (tel. 222-4970), 355 Wabasha St.

   Hairdressers/Barbers   In Minneapolis try **Crossings Skyway Barber** (tel. 341-2462), 250 2nd Ave. S., and **Beauty Loft** (tel. 338-1763), 12 S. 6th St. In St. Paul there's **Ken's Barber Shop** (tel. 224-4242), 275 E. 4th St., and **Park Avenue Salon** (tel. 227-6677), 378 St. Peter St.

   Hospitals   **Abbott Northwestern Hospital** (tel. 863-4095) offers 24-hour telephone consultations. Prescription medicine, emergency-room visits, or hospital care can be provided as needed, and specialist referrals can also be arranged at competitive fees. VISA, MasterCard, and personal checks are accepted.

   Information   See "Information" in Chapter 2.

   Laundry/Dry Cleaning   In Minneapolis, try **White Way Cleaners** (tel. 333-7995), 800 Marquette Ave. In St. Paul, try **Lala and Keefe's** (tel. 227-3777), 469 Wabasha St.

   Libraries   The **Minneapolis Public Library** (tel. 372-6500) is at 300 Nicollet Mall. The **St. Paul Public Library** (tel. 292-6311) is at 90 W. 4th St.

   Liquor Laws   The legal drinking age in Minnesota is 21. Identification is required in nightclubs and bars.

   Newspapers/Magazines   The Minneapolis newspaper is the *Star Tribune,* which is published daily. The *St. Paul Pioneer Press* is also a daily.

   Photographic Needs   There are now several 1-hour color-print developing and printing companies in the Twin Cities. Many in shopping centers operate seven days a week. **Proex** (tel. 228-9608), one of the best, redevelops without charge any photos that customers find unsatisfactory.

   Police   Call **911** to summon the police in an emergency.

   Post Office   The **main post office** in Minneapolis is located at South 1st Street and Marquette (tel. 349-4970); in St. Paul it's at Kellogg Boulevard and Jackson Street (tel. 293-3011). There's 24-hour postal service available at the airport.

   Radio   Program listings appear in the daily newspaper. WCCO, 830 on the AM dial, broadcasts news, sports, and popular music. On KSTP, 1500 on the AM dial, you'll hear talk shows, news, and popular music. For classical music and news, tune in to KSJN, 99.5 on your FM dial.

   Religious Services   In Minneapolis, the **First Baptist Church** (tel. 332-3651) is located at 1021 Hennepin Ave. The **St. Olaf Catholic Church** (tel. 332-7471) is at 215 S. 8th St. The **Hennepin Avenue United Methodist Church** (tel. 871-5303) is found at 511 Groveland Ave. **Temple Israel** (tel. 377-8680) is at 2324 Emerson Ave.

   St. Paul's houses of worship include the **Central Baptist Church** (tel. 646-2751), 420 N. Roy St.; **Cathedral of St. Paul** (tel. 228-1766), 239 Selby Ave.; **Central Presbyterian Church** (tel. 224-4728), 500 Cedar St., and **Mount Zion Temple** (tel. 698-3881), 1300 Summit Ave.

Safety   You'll feel relatively safe in the Twin Cities, but remember that whenever you're traveling in an unfamiliar city or country you should stay alert. Be aware of your immediate surroundings. Wear a money belt and keep a close eye on your possessions. Be particularly careful with cameras, purses, and wallets, all favorite targets of thieves and pickpockets.

Shoe Repairs   In Minneapolis, try **Tony's Shoe Repair** (tel. 339-8302), 200 S. 5th St., or **Heels Plus** (tel. 338-1486), 625 Marquette Ave. In St. Paul, **Endicott Shoe Repair** (tel. 224-7173), 141 E. 4th St., or **Heels Plus** (tel. 222-2758), Town Square, will get your shoes back in shape.

Taxes   The Minnesota **6½% sales tax** does not apply to clothing, prescription drugs, and food purchased in stores. At hotels, restaurants, and bars within the city limits of Minneapolis and St. Paul you'll pay an additional ½% tax on the same items that are subject to the state 6½% sales tax.

Taxis   See "Getting Around" in this chapter.

Television   There are six broadcast TV channels available here: Channels 2 (PBS), 4 (CBS), 5 (ABC), 9 (independent), 11 (NBC), 17 (independent), and 29 (Fox). In addition, cable services offer a wide variety of programmers.

Time   Minnesota is in the central time zone, one hour behind the East Coast and two hours ahead of the West Coast. (If it's 8pm in New York, it's 7pm in the Twin Cities, 6pm in Denver, and 5pm in San Francisco.)

Transit Info   For Metropolitan Transit Commission information, phone 349-7000.

Weather   The **National Weather Service** can be reached at 725-6090.

TWIN CITIES ACCOMMODATIONS

Businesspersons and vacation travellers have long found Minneapolis-St. Paul a primary travel destination, but since the 1992 opening in Bloomington of the Mall of America, there's been a notable increase in the number of visitors to the Twin Cities, and this has caused occasional shortages in accommodations. As a result, some Twin Cities hotels and motels no longer provide printed rate sheets, preferring instead to quote prices on an individual basis, depending on the specific days of the week and season of the year as well as the specific corporate or organizational discounts involved.

Over the course of time, two types of accommodations have developed in the Twin Cities: large, expensive, rather formal hotels in downtown Minneapolis and St. Paul and smaller, more casual, more moderately priced hotels and motels in the suburbs along "strips" of highway that link them to Minneapolis–St. Paul International Airport. Generally hotels and motels on the Bloomington strip are 10 minutes or less from the airport, 20 minutes or less from downtown Minneapolis and St. Paul.

Recently, larger and pricier hotels have begun making their appearance beyond the city limits, but in general it's safe to say that you'll pay more for accommodations downtown than in the suburbs, and more in Minneapolis than in St. Paul.

If you're going to spend most of your time in either Minneapolis or St. Paul and will be without a car for most of your stay, you may be better off in one downtown or the other, where you can get around by foot or by bus to many popular local attractions. Destinations that lie outside downtown areas are readily accessible by cab. Shuttle service to the Mall of America from both cities is available free or at a small cost, depending on the accommodations you select.

On the other hand, if you will have the use of a car, you might consider heading for the I-494 strip, where hotels and motels offer free parking and easy access to the network of belt lines, freeways, and interstates that connect the cities and suburbs. If you're here on business, you'll find that many of the corporate offices in the Twin Cities are located in suburban rather than downtown areas.

I've selected hotels and motels in three price categories:—

expensive, charging $120 and up per night for a double Monday to Friday; **moderate,** charging $65 to $120; and **inexpensive,** charging less than $65. Most downtown hotels charge for parking; hotels in Bloomington and other suburbs generally offer free parking. Some hotels and motels offer packages that include one or more meals and other items for which you'd otherwise pay separately. Don't hesitate to ask about discounts when you're making reservations. Age and affiliation often make a big difference in your total tab. As a rule, special senior rates apply to persons age 55 and older; sometimes the minimum age is 60.

The **Minnesota Office of Tourism,** 100 Metro Square, 121 7th Place E., St. Paul, MN 55102-2112 (tel. 612/296-5029 or toll free 800/657-3700) will prepare a customized printout for you of hotels and motels offering the kinds of amenities you desire.

Note: For hotels near Mall of America, see also Chapter 11.

1. MINNEAPOLIS

EXPENSIVE

HOLIDAY INN—CROWNE PLAZA NORTHSTAR, 618 2nd Ave. S., Minneapolis, MN 55402. Tel. 612/338-2288 or toll free 800/THE-OMNI. Fax 612/338-2288. 24 rms, 3 suites. A/C TV TEL

$ Rates: Weekday $150 single, $165 double; weekend $79–$165 single or double. **Parking:** $10 Sun–Thurs; $7.95 Fri–Sat.

Twin Citians out for a special evening or event are apt to come to the handsome Northstar Hotel because of its fine restaurant, the Rosewood Room. Live entertainment is offered nightly in the restaurant and in the popular Rosewood Lounge.

The lobby is decorated in muted shades of beige and peach, and guest rooms feature browns and beiges. A drive-up area makes for convenient arrivals; facilitated by 24-hour uniformed doormen.

Facilities: International Fitness Center at nearby YMCA, $5 per visit.

HYATT REGENCY MINNEAPOLIS, 1300 Nicollet Mall, Minneapolis, MN 55403. Tel. 612/370-1234 or toll free 800/228-9000. Fax 612/370-1463. 533 rms, 21 suites. A/C MINIBAR TV TEL

$ Rates: $168 single; $193 double; weekend $89 single or double; suites from $290. AE, DISC, ER, MC, V. **Parking:** $8.

Luxury abounds at the downtown Hyatt Regency Minneapolis. A handsome fountain sculpture is the focal point of a large, decorative lobby where there's plenty of comfortable seating for prime people watching. All rooms enjoy delightful views of the city and provide in-house pay movies, complimentary HBO and cable news, and AM/FM clock radios. Female travelers often ask for the rooms outfitted with hair dryers and lighted cosmetic mirrors.

Dining/Entertainment: Two of the most popular eating spots in town adjoin the main lobby of the Hyatt Regency: Taxxi, an American bistro, features casual dining with everything from hamburgers to prime ribs, halibut to walleye, and a choice of three pasta dishes daily. At Spike's Sports Bar and Grille, you'll find pool tables, dart boards, and minibasketball courts, along with a wide variety of appetizers, soups, salads, sandwiches, and main courses.

Services: Room service, concierge.

Facilities: Nonsmoking floors, large swimming pool; Greenway Athletic Club ($8.50 per visit), with weight lifting, racquetball, tennis, squash, running track, sauna, Jacuzzi.

MINNEAPOLIS HILTON AND TOWERS, 1001 Marquette Ave. S., Minneapolis, MN 55403. Tel. 612/376-1000. Fax 612/397-4875. 763 rms, 51 suites. A/C TV TEL **Directions:** 35W to the 5th Ave. exit. Turn left at 11th St. and proceed four blocks to Marquette Ave. Turn right on Marquette and drive one block to hotel.

$ Rates: $115–$190 single; $135–$210 double. AE, CB, DC, DISC, JCB, MC, V. **Parking:** $15.

At this writing, the Minneapolis Hilton and Towers is the newest and the largest hotel in the Twin Cities. It's also the one with the most endearing statuary. As you enter the imposing lobby, you'll find a family of bronze instrumentalists representing *The Joy of Music.* The figures, two adults and three children, are a lovely acknowledgment of the area's long-standing commitment to the performing arts. In fact, this hotel has become an extension of Orchestra Hall, located a short skyway away. Suppers at the Hilton before a performance or dessert and coffee afterward have become a custom among many locals.

Guests at the Hilton have access to a complimentary health club and spa, an indoor pool, and a sauna. Many who stay here have come to town to attend a convention or other professional meeting, and rooms have been outfitted accordingly with double phone lines and personal voice mail. But individuals and families often arrive for a getaway and find here a variety of programs, some with children in mind. Check out "Vacation Station," which provides a welcoming gift for youngsters and the opportunity for them to check out a wide variety of games through the concierge during their stay.

MINNEAPOLIS MARRIOTT, 30 S. 7th St., Minneapolis, MN 55402. Tel. 612/349-4000 or toll free 800/228-9290. Fax 612/349-9223. 584 rms, 22 bi-level suites. A/C TV TEL

$ Rates: $145 single; $165 double; weekend $69 single or double. Seniors 10% discount. AE, DC, MC, V. **Parking:** $10 weekday; $3.50 weekend.

If you enjoy shopping, you'll be well situated at the Minneapolis Marriott. Rising above the three-level City Center downtown shopping mall, this luxury hotel is located barely a stone's throw away from Nieman Marcus, Saks Fifth Avenue, and Dayton's, one of the area's most distinguished department stores. There's a diversity of fine specialty shops accessible by skyway as well (see Chapter 9). But that's only part of the fun of staying at this sleek, modernistic 32-story triangular tower.

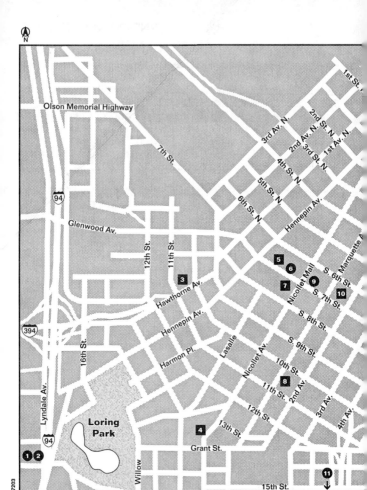

ACCOMMODATIONS:

Days Inn/University 15
Gopher Campus Motor Lodge 16
Holiday Inn Crown Plaza
　Northstar 10
Holiday Inn Metrodome 14
Hyatt Regency Minneapolis 4

Minneapolis Hilton 8
Minneapolis Marriott 5
Normandy Inn 12
Radisson Plaza Hotel Minneapolis 7
Regency Plaza Best Western 3

The decor in the Marriott's public places is stunning throughout and guest rooms are luxurious; many boast upholstered chairs and matching ottomans, built-in oak desks, and oversize beds. Also notable is the lighting provided by illuminated wall coves, which casts a soft glow over rooms that look out on beautiful cityscapes.

　　Dining/Entertainment: The hotel boasts two fine restaurants, Gustino's, featuring northern Italian cuisine, and Papaya's, a more

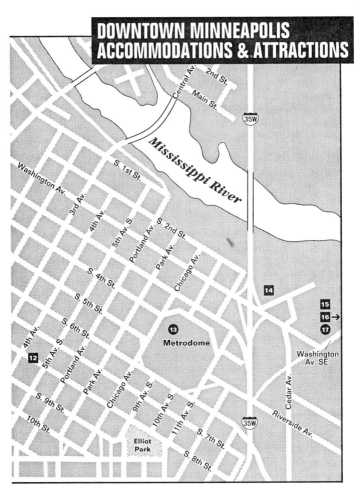

DOWNTOWN MINNEAPOLIS ACCOMMODATIONS & ATTRACTIONS

ATTRACTIONS:
City Center **6**
Gaviidae Common **9**
The Guthrie Theater **1**
Humphrey Metrodome **13**
James Ford Bell Museum
  of Natural History **17**

Minneapolis Institute of Art **11**
The Walker Art Center and
  the Minneapolis Sculpture
  Gardens **2**

---

casual family restaurant popular for hamburgers and other standard American fare. The tunes of Gustino's singing servers add a musical touch from time to time, as do the piano melodies from the lobby lounge below.

Services: Room service, concierge.

Facilities: Nonsmoking floors, well-equipped health club, with whirlpool and sauna.

**RADISSON PLAZA HOTEL MINNEAPOLIS, 35 S. 7th St.,
Minneapolis, MN 55402. Tel. 612/339-4900** or toll free
800/333-3333. Fax 612/337-9766. 357 rms, 30 suites. A/C TV
TEL

$ Rates: $169 single or double; weekend $89 single or double.
Senior citizen weekday rate $93. AE, DC, DISC, MC, V. **Park-
ing:** $10 weekday; free weekend.

A long-standing Twin Cities tradition was renewed in 1987
with the opening of the Radisson Plaza Hotel Minneapolis.
Since 1909 there's always been a Radisson Hotel on this site,
but many qualms were expressed when the decision was made in
1981 to tear down the old familiar structure and replace it with a
bigger and better one.

The Radisson Plaza Minneapolis is now the flagship of the
Minneapolis-based chain with over 200 hotels and affiliates world-
wide. The hotel occupies one of the most centrally located sites in the
Twin Cities: across the street from City Center, half a block from the
Nicollet Mall, and attached by skyway to downtown shops, offices,
and restaurants.

The first thing you'll notice is the elegant recessed entryway; the
second is the main lobby's 1,200-pound marble pedestal, on which a
huge 2,750-pound marble ball floats on half an inch of water. (It's 65
pounds of water pressure that keeps the ball suspended, in case you
wondered—I did.)

The effort here has been to contrast the elegance of the public
spaces with the residential feeling of the guest rooms. The colors
throughout the hotel combine teal and mauve. The French provincial
and Chippendale furnishings have an old-world look but offer
modern convenience: The mahogany armoires have color TV sets
hidden inside. Each bathroom has a TV speaker and telephone. Large
desks are provided for business travelers.

Dining/Entertainment: The Festival Restaurant is popular
for its Minnesota cuisine—walleye, steak, and wild rice. In the
less formal Café, you'll find soups, sandwiches, and other hearty
fare.

Services: Room service, concierge.

Facilities: State-of-the-art fitness center with daily aerobics
classes, computerized rowing and treadmill equipment, and a cross-
country ski machine.

MODERATE

**HOLIDAY INN METRODOME, 1500 Washington Ave. S.,
Minneapolis, MN 55454. Tel. 612/333-4646** or toll free
800/448-3663. Fax 612/333-7910. 265 rms. A/C TV TEL

$ Rates: $109.50 single; $119.50 double; weekend $79.50. Sen-
iors receive 20% discount. AE, DC, DISC, MC, V. **Parking:** $7
for 24 hours.

One of the most central locations in the Twin Cities is offered
by the Holiday Inn Metrodome. Situated on the eastern edge
of downtown Minneapolis, with the University of Minnesota
campus on one side and the Hubert H. Humphrey Metrodome on
the other, this hotel stands in the hub of the Seven Corners area,

known for its top-notch ethnic restaurants and bars. A Grandma's Restaurant is right next door, famous for its eclectic decor and its varied American menu. You're also right in the heart of the West Bank theater district here, with the popular Hey City Theatre and Restaurant located just next door and Theater in the Round across the street. In the lobby, as well as in the guest rooms, you'll find decor that's been described as "subtle art deco."

Dining/Entertainment: In addition to a bar, there's the Restaurant Grill Room, which offers everything from sandwiches and burgers to seafood and steaks. Children under 12 dine free of charge.

Services: Free shuttle service within a 3-mile limit, depending on availability.

Facilities: Indoor pool, whirlpool, sauna, exercise room.

NORMANDY INN, 405 S. 8th St., Minneapolis, MN 55405. Tel. 612/370-1400. Fax 612/370-0351. 160 rms. A/C TV TEL

$ Rates: $66 single; $70 double; weekend $59.50 single or double. AE, DC, DISC, MC, V. **Parking:** $5 Mon–Fri; free weekends.

For decades, visitors to the Twin Cities have been welcomed at the Normandy Inn. The rustic, French-chalet-type exterior of this four-story building stands in sharp contrast to the high-rise structures that have grown up around it. The interior has a country look, with dark woodwork, marble tile floors, and a graceful central fountain. Guest rooms are done in earth tones of rust and beige.

The Normandy has a moderately priced coffee shop and restaurant with a full menu and a reputation for delicious high-rise popovers, beer-cheese soup, and pecan pie. There is a swimming pool.

REGENCY PLAZA BEST WESTERN, 41 N. 10th St., Minneapolis, MN 55403. Tel. 612/339-9311 or toll free 800/423-4100. Fax 612/339-4765. 193 rms, 7 suites. A/C TV TEL

$ Rates: $66–$72 single or double; suites $95. Seniors receive a 10% discount. AE, DC, DISC, MC, V. **Parking:** Free.

A winning combination of downtown location and suburban rates is available at this newly remodeled three-story hotel located at the end of Highway 12 on the edge of downtown Minneapolis.

Wood paneling and marble give the lobby a classical look, as does the library beyond. The rooms are large and pleasant, many of them enhanced by the beautiful prints of Les Kouba, a popular Minnesota nature painter. A raspberry and royal-blue color combination prevails in all the rooms, along with light-oak furnishings. Each room contains free in-house movies.

Dining/Entertainment: The Regency Café serves breakfast, lunch, and dinner from 6:30am to 7pm weekdays and from 7:30am to 5:30pm on weekends. Harrigan's Dining Room offers burgers, steaks, seafood, and other American fare from 5 to 10pm. The Hub Cap Pub doles out soup, sandwiches, and dinner entrées; happy hour runs from 3 to 6pm.

Facilities: Large indoor swimming pool, children's wading pool, whirlpool.

Services: Free shuttle service to any downtown destination.

FROMMER'S SMART TRAVELER: HOTELS

1. Take advantage of the 30% to 50% discounts available during weekends.
2. If you're going to spend a week in Minneapolis or St. Paul, try to find a hotel offering weekly rates, which are cheaper.
3. Ask if parking or breakfast is included in the hotel rates.
4. Ask if there's a charge for local calls or a surcharge for long-distance calls.
5. Does the hotel have a free airport shuttle service? This can save you the cost of a taxi.
6. Ask about summer discounts, corporate rates, and special packages. Many hotels don't tell you about promotional rates unless you inquire.

INEXPENSIVE

DAYS INN/UNIVERSITY, 2407 University Ave. S.E., Minneapolis, MN 55414. Tel. 612/623-3999 or toll free 800/325-2525. Fax 612/331-2152. 130 rms. A/C TV TEL

$ Rates (including continental breakfast): $54 single; $60 double. Seniors discount available. AE, CB, DC, DISC, MC, V. **Parking:** Free.

Located at University and Washington avenues, this hotel is six blocks east of the University of Minnesota's Minneapolis campus. Guest rooms, done in earth tones of rust, brown, and orange, offer two large chairs, a desk, and a credenza; most have a vanity area separate from the bath. There are no restaurants on the premises but there is a branch of the Embers chain right across the street. Free local phone calls, free shuttle service to local hospitals, and two nonsmoking floors are also offered here.

GOPHER CAMPUS MOTOR LODGE, 925 S.E. 4th St., Minneapolis, MN 55414. Tel. 612/331-3740. 44 rms. A/C TV TEL

$ Rates: $39 single; $49 double. Weekly rate $234 single; $276 double; $246 room with kitchenette. Seniors receive a 10% discount. AE, DISC, MC, V. **Parking:** Free.

Low-cost weekly accommodations are available near the University of Minnesota at the Gopher Campus Motor Lodge. Thirty years after it first opened its doors, the Gopher Campus Motor Lodge remains a clean and comfortable place to stay. Brick walls in the guest rooms are a reminder of earlier times. Furnishings are simple and spare, as is the price structure.

BED & BREAKFASTS

BRASIE HOUSE, 2321 Colfax Ave. S., Minneapolis, MN 55405. Tel. 612/377-5946. 3 rms.

$ Rates: $49–$70.

This interesting Craftsman-style house, built in 1913 by inventor Frank Brasie, is quite unlike the frequently ornate Victorian mansions that so often serve today as bread-and-breakfast establishments. The lines here are simple and square, the atmosphere decidedly informal. Some of the details, surprising by contemporary standards, lend themselves admirably to bed-and-breakfasting; most notably, perhaps, mammoth walk-in closets, each with its own window, separate the bedrooms and thereby prevent noise transmission between common walls. Proprietor Mari Griffin serves as a resident concierge. When guests register by phone, she asks about their entertainment preferences and, in time for their arrival, secures information about team schedules, performance times, and store hours. She also regularly checks menus at restaurants within easy walking distance. The three second-floor guest rooms share a large bathroom. Each guest is offered a continental breakfast buffet which can be enjoyed on the porch or patio or in the dining room. Bus service to city attractions is available at the front door.

HEATHERWOOD BED & BREAKFAST, 2008 Pillsbury Ave. S., Minneapolis, MN 55404. Tel. 612/870-4610.
$ Rates: $65–$150.

Luxury abounds at this 1905 Victorian mansion, conveniently located about midway between uptown and downtown Minneapolis. Weddings, graduations, holiday parties, birthdays, and other important events are regularly celebrated here in a setting resplendent with intricate woodwork, carved fireplaces, and exquisite antiques.

Overnight guests are pampered with down comforters, feather pillows, and luxurious towels and robes. Those occupying the spacious two-room Bordeaux Suite can enjoy a marble Jacuzzi illuminated by a gleaming crystal chandelier. A more contemporary note is struck by the presence on the back deck of a spacious hot tub.

Gourmet breakfasts feature fresh juice and fruit, croissants, and items like French Toast Étouffé, thick slices of French bread stuffed with cream cheese and raspberries and topped with maple syrup, Grand Marnier, and whipped cream. Proprietors Michelle and Terry Hannun hope all who enter will feel as though they're being indulged throughout their stay, and it's hard to imagine guests not feeling that way.

LEBLANC HOUSE, 302 University Ave. NE, Minneapolis, MN 55413. Tel. 612/457-1434 or 379-2570. 3 rms.
$ Rates: $75–$95.

William LeBlanc was an engineer with the riverfront lumber mills when he built his home here in 1896. You'll be reminded of this fact as you admire the beautiful woodwork and wooden furnishings throughout this establishment, named in his honor by proprietors Barb Zahasky and Bob Shulstad. Located across Hennepin Ave. bridge from downtown Minneapolis, the LeBlanc House is within walking distance of some of the city's most popular sightseeing and shopping.

Guests have high praise for the comfort of the accommodations and for the outstanding breakfasts prepared by Zahasky and Shulstad. The gardens around the house are noteworthy too.

2. SOUTH SUBURBAN MINNEAPOLIS

EXPENSIVE

EMBASSY SUITES HOTEL, 2800 W. 80th Street, Bloomington, MN 55431. Tel. 612/884-4811 or toll free 800-EMBASSY. Fax 612/884-8137. 219 suites. A/C TV TEL

$ Rates: Weekday $129 for one person, $10 for each additional person; weekend $149 for up to four people in room with king-size and hide-a-bed or up to four people in room with two double beds and 1 hide-a-bed. AE, DC, DISC, MC, V. **Parking:** Free.

This Spanish-style hotel has an 8-story central courtyard, enhanced by towering palm trees and lush flowering plants, which is the setting each morning (6–9:30am) for a full cooked-to-order complimentary breakfast and each evening (5:30–7:30pm) for two hours of free cocktails.

Guests stay in comfortable two-room suites, decorated in tones of blue and mauve, which offer all the comforts of a well-appointed home. Each bedroom has a king-size bed or two double beds and a vanity area separate from the bathroom. The "parlor," separated by a door from the other part of the suite, features a kitchenette with refrigerator, freezer, stove, sink, and coffee maker for which coffee packets are provided. There's also a table and four chairs here along with a second TV and telephone. The sofa in the parlor converts into a sleeper.

Also on site is Chez Daniel, a fine French bistro that serves lunch and dinner each day. Free shuttle service is available to the airport and Mall of America.

MODERATE

BEST WESTERN BRADBURY SUITES, 7770 Johnson Ave., Bloomington, MN 55437. Tel. 612/893-9999 or toll free 800/423-4100. Fax 612/893-1316. 126 suites. A/C TV TEL

$ Rates: $64.95 single; $69.95 double. Seniors $58.25 single, $62.95 double. AE, DC, MC. **Parking:** Free.

Here, for the price of one room, you'll be staying in a two-room suite with a small refrigerator and two TV sets. The suites, all done in shades of green and mauve, are comfortable and spacious enough for an evening "at home," with dinner delivered by Lincoln Deli, T.G.I. Friday, or some other local restaurant.

Services: Shuttle service within 1-mile radius to local restaurants and to airport.

Facilities: Free admission to nearby U.S. Swim and Fitness Club; whirlpool and exercise bike.

BEST WESTERN SEVILLE PLAZA HOTEL, 8151 Bridge Rd., Bloomington, MN 55437. Tel. 612/830-1300. Fax 612/830-1535. 250 rms. A/C TV TEL
$ Rates: $55 single; $63 double. Seniors $56.70 double. AE, DC, MC, V. **Parking:** Free.

You'll find the ambience of romantic Old Spain at the large and lovely Seville Plaza. Orange, brown, and yellow dominate the large lobby, while guest rooms are decorated in softer earth tones of beige and brown. Located right on I-494, the Seville is about 20 minutes from the airport and 30 minutes from downtown Minneapolis and St. Paul. You're also close to fine suburban shopping at the nearby Southtown Center.

The dining facility here is Antonio's Steak and Pasta; there is also a bar. Facilities include a swimming pool, a sauna, and a whirlpool. There is also free shuttle service to and from the airport.

COMFORT INN, 1321 E. 78th St., Bloomington, MN 55420. Tel. 612/854-3400 or toll free 800/228-5150. Fax 612/854-2234. 276 rms, 4 suites. A/C TV TEL
$ Rates: Weekdays $60 single, $67 double; weekends $80 single or double. Seniors 10% discount. AE, CB, DC, DISC, ER, MC, V. **Parking:** Free.

Located on the Bloomington strip just five miles from the airport, the Comfort Inn offers the convenience of a motel and the pleasing decor of a hotel. Rooms are attractively furnished in a variety of styles, and if you order king-size accommodations, you'll find a leisure recliner waiting along with the standard furnishings. Each of the rooms in this five-story complex offers free HBO.

Facilities: Exercise room, indoor heated pool.
Services: 24-hour shuttle service to and from airport.

HOLIDAY INN AIRPORT 2, 5401 Green Valley Dr., Bloomington, MN 55437. Tel. 612/831-8000 or toll free 800/ HOLIDAY. Fax 612/831-8426. 258 rms. A/C TV TEL
$ Rates: $63 single; $70 double; weekend $70 single, $78 double. Executive wing $77 single, $86 double. Seniors receive 10% discount. AE, DC, DISC, MC, V. **Parking:** Free.

Just 7½ miles from the Minneapolis–St. Paul International Airport, this six-story Holiday Inn does a lot of fly-and-drive business: If guests stay for at least one night, they can leave their cars in the parking lot and take advantage of the free 24-hour airport shuttle service, thereby saving the cost of airport parking. Shuttle service is also available to nearby shopping malls and nearby restaurants. The two on-site restaurants to choose from here are Marti's and the Coffee Shop—both serve three meals daily from 7am to 10pm. The cocktail lounge is open from 8pm until 12:30am.

Facilities: Large swimming pool, whirlpool, sauna.

HOLIDAY INN EXPRESS, 814 E. 79th St., Bloomington, MN 55420. Tel. 612/854-5558 or toll free 800/HOLIDAY. Fax 612/854-4623. 142 rms. A/C TV TEL

$ Rates: $65 single; $73 double. Seniors $58.50 single, $66.50 double. AE, DC, DISC, MC, V. **Parking:** Free.

You'll feel welcome at once in the attractive lobby here, with its sunken sitting room, brick-walled fireplace, and comfortable burgundy-and-beige seating. Like many other moderate and economy-priced motels, the Holiday Inn Express (formerly Dillion Airport Inn) has no restaurant of its own; but it's connected to Denny's and is only a few steps away from several informal and popular eating places. You can choose a room with a king-size bed, a water bed, or two double beds. All rooms contain a pair of upholstered chairs and a small desk; some have a balcony.

Services: Complimentary coffee around the clock; free shuttle service to and from airport from 5am to midnight.

RADISSON HOTEL SOUTH AND PLAZA TOWER, 7800 Normandale Blvd., Minneapolis, MN 55439. Tel. 612/835-7800 or toll free 800/333-3333. Fax 612/893-8431. 562 rms, 13 suites. A/C TV TEL **Directions:** West on I-494 to Bush Lake Rd. exit. Turn right and proceed north to the first intersection. Turn right and drive east for two blocks, then turn left into the hotel parking lot.

$ Rates: Weekday $95–$139; weekend $79–$139; no charge for children under 17. AARP members room rate $79 on availability. AE, DC, DISC, ER, MC, V. **Parking:** Free.

There are more conventions held at this hotel than at any other Radisson nationwide, and that may account for some of the amenities in the rooms. Double telephone lines in every room make it possible to put one caller on hold while you speak to another. Voice messaging enables guests to receive timely and detailed messages. Computer ports permit personal computer use. This hotel is popular with families as well. One package includes two free hours at a local "kids' club," where children can amuse themselves with computer games and other activities.

There's plenty here to keep adults occupied too. In the Captains Quarter, a companionable lounge, grown-ups find morning complimentary coffee and newspapers from all over the country; later in the day they can gather for billiards, checkers, cards, and conversation. A large swimming pool and whirlpool occupy the handsome garden court. There are two popular restaurants right in the hotel, the Shipside specializing in seafood and the Café Stuga serving three

---

IMPRESSIONS

I have lived in Minnesota . . . for thirteen years, a western Scandinavia where the birds sing in Swedish, the wind sighs its lullabyes in Norwegian, and the snow and rain beat against the windows to the tune of a Danish dirge.
—ANONYMOUS (1925)

meals each day in Scandinavian style if not substance. (You will, though, always find herring among the dinner offerings.) Adjoining the premises you'll find two restaurants, T.G.I. Friday and Embers, and the hotel van will take you to Southdale, an elegant nearby shopping mall with more in the way of food and drink.

INEXPENSIVE

FRIENDLY HOST INN, 1225 E. 78th St., Bloomington, MN 55425. Tel. 612/854-3322 or toll free 800/341-8000. Fax 612/854-0245. 47 rms. A/C TV TEL

$ Rates: $40–$55 single or double. Seniors receive $3 discount. AE, DC, DISC, MC, V. **Parking:** Free.

If you're interested in economical accommodations with cooking facilities, you'll be glad to learn about the Friendly Host Inn. They have single-bed rooms with a two-burner stove, a small sink, and a refrigerator. The much larger two-bed rooms contain a four-burner stove; a small refrigerator, and double cupboards.

Decor varies here, but the rooms are all attractive and comfortable. The motel is well located, one mile from Mall of America and just five miles from the airport. An indoor pool and whirlpool are available on the premises.

HOPKINS HOUSE HOTEL, 1501 Hwy. 7, Hopkins, MN 55343. Tel. 612/935-7711 or toll free 800/328-6024. Fax 612/933-3621. 164 rms. A/C TV TEL

$ Rates: $39 single; $49 double; $65 room with hot tub. AE, DISC, MC, V. **Parking:** Free.

 FROMMER'S COOL FOR KIDS: HOTELS

Best Western Kelly Inn (see p. 58) has a swimming pool reserved for children.

Mall of America Grand Hotel (see p. 160) contains a video arcade room, where children will find pinball machines as well as air hockey and driving games.

Minneapolis Hilton and Towers (see p. 45) features "Vacation-Station" counselors, on duty in an office near the swimming pool from noon to 8pm to provide innertubes, beach balls, and supervision for water volleyball and other activities. Children can also borrow a variety of board games from this office.

Sheraton Airport Inn (see p. 161) offers pinball machines and other electronic entertainments in a game room located to the left of the front desk.

Ⓢ You'll find attractive, inexpensively priced accommodations at the suburban Hopkins Hotel. Located about 10 miles from Lake Minnetonka and 20 minutes from downtown Minneapolis, this seven-story complex offers an indoor pool, sauna, exercise room, and table tennis. The color scheme features shades of rose and blue, starting with the deep-rose cushioned couches and soft-blue table lamps in the lobby. Oak end tables and a brass ceiling punctuated with modern open globe lights complete the bright, cheery lobby decor. Your own room will doubtless be decorated in combinations of rose and blue as well, and if you like, it can also contain a heart-shaped water bed; just ask for a "happy-tub room." You'll find basic cable color TV here plus free HBO and ESPN sports.

3. ST. PAUL

EXPENSIVE

CROWN STERLING SUITES, 175 E. 10th St., St. Paul, MN 55101. Tel. 612/224-5400 or toll free 800/433-4600. Fax 612/224-0957. 210 suites. A/C TV TEL

$ **Rates:** $112 single; $122 double. $99 weekend triple or quad. Seniors $89. AE, DC, DISC, MC, V. **Parking:** Free (based on availability).

Ⓢ ★ If you're familiar with Crown Sterling Suites hotels, you'll be glad to know that there are three of them here in the Twin Cities: one in downtown St. Paul as cited above; one in downtown Minneapolis at 425 S. 7th Street (tel. 612/333-3111 or toll free 800/433-4600; fax 612/333-7984); and one near the airport at 7901 34th Ave. S., Bloomington, MN 55420 (tel. 612/854-1000; fax 612/854-6557).

These value-packed hotels have effectively countered the old admonition: "If you want the comforts of home, stay home." Actually, the comforts awaiting you here may rival what you've left at home: not one but two handsomely furnished rooms with a TV and a phone in each, a kitchenette whose facilities include a microwave oven, and decor to suit your individual preference, with whole floors devoted to rooms decorated in tones of mauve, green, or blue. Just choose your floor and you choose your color.

A full cooked-to-order breakfast is yours each morning, and at the end of each day you can have your favorite drinks at the 2-hour cocktail party held in the attractive courtyard. Here, brick pillars, tile floors, fountains, and even a waterfall will remind you of your last visit to the Mediterranean, or of the visit you've yet to make. Facilities include a pool, a sauna, a whirlpool, and a steam room. There is also a free airport shuttle.

RADISSON HOTEL ST. PAUL, 11 E. Kellogg Blvd., St. Paul, MN 55101. Tel. 612/292-1900 or toll-free 800/333-3333. Fax 612/224-8999. 465 rms, 10 suites. AC TV TEL

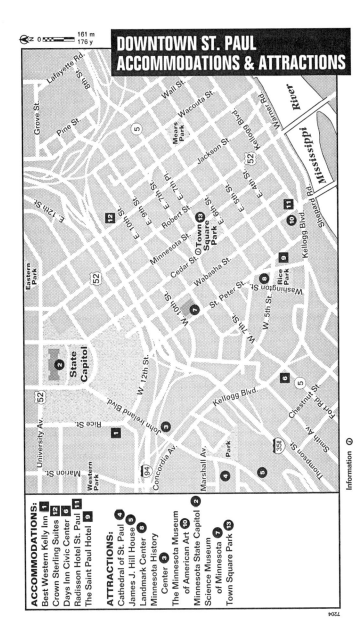

DOWNTOWN ST. PAUL ACCOMMODATIONS & ATTRACTIONS

ACCOMMODATIONS:
Best Western Kelly Inn **1**
Crown Sterling Suites **12**
Days Inn Civic Center **6**
Radisson Hotel St. Paul **11**
The Saint Paul Hotel **9**

ATTRACTIONS:
Cathedral of St. Paul **4**
James J. Hill House **5**
Landmark Center **8**
Minnesota History Center **3**
The Minnesota Museum of American Art **10**
Minnesota State Capitol **2**
Science Museum of Minnesota **7**
Town Square Park **13**

$ Rates: Weekday $99 single, $120 double; weekend $71 single or double. $150 suite. Seniors $68 if available.

Overlooking the Mississippi River and just 20 minutes from the Minneapolis-St. Paul International Airport and Mall of America, this handsome hotel is the largest in St. Paul. Connected by skyway to downtown businesses, shops, and entertainment, it is also conveniently close to the state capitol, the Civic Center Auditorium, the Ordway Music Theatre, and the Minnesota Museum of Art.

Facilities here include an indoor garden court, a pool, a fitness center, and four executive floors that offer, among other amenities, a full breakfast, a coffeepot in every room, and telephone lines that accept laptop personal computers.

Particularly popular is the commanding view from Carousel, the Twin Cities' only revolving restaurant, located on the 22nd floor.

THE SAINT PAUL HOTEL, 350 Market St., St. Paul, MN 55102. Tel. 612/292-9292 or toll-free 800/292-9292. Fax 612/228-9506. 223 rms, 31 suites. AC TV TEL
$ Rates: Sun–Thurs $139 single, $154 double; Fri–Sat $94 single or double; $169–$650 suite. AE, DC, DISC, V.

You'll find a beautiful blend of the old and the new at the downtown Saint Paul Hotel. In 1910 this was St. Paul's premier hotel, and now it has taken its place once more as a distinguished grand old hotel for those who expect and appreciate the best. Facing Rice Park and the Ordway Music Theatre, the Saint Paul Hotel is situated between the beautiful St. Paul Public Library and the Landmark Center, the restored Old Federal Courts Building.

But if The Saint Paul Hotel maintains close ties with the city's past, it's also an integral part of St. Paul's burgeoning present. Situated at one end of an extensive skyway system, it offers guests climate-controlled access to 38 downtown blocks of shops, banks, restaurants, and varied forms of entertainment.

Accommodations are appropriately elegant. Once past the lobby, with its antique crystal chandeliers, turn-of-the-century love seats and chairs, and large oriental screen, you'll be equally pleased with the guest rooms. Each is decorated uniquely, but all have either a king-size bed or two double beds, along with two comfortable chairs and an ample table. Deluxe rooms are outfitted with a love seat in place of the two chairs.

MODERATE

BEST WESTERN KELLY INN, 161 St. Anthony, St. Paul, MN 55103. Tel. 612/227-8711. 125 rms. TV TEL
$ Rates: $63 single; $73 double. Weekend specials available. AE, DISC, MC, V.

Located within easy walking distance of the Minnesota State Capitol and the Cathedral of St. Paul, this recently remodeled hotel overlooks downtown St. Paul with its shops, museums and other popular tourist attractions and is only 10 minutes away from the airport, the Metrodome and other downtown Minneapolis attractions. Amenities include an on-site restaurant, a lounge, an indoor pool, a whirlpool, sauna, and children's pool.

DAYS INN CIVIC CENTER, 175 W. 7th St., St. Paul, MN 55102. Tel. 612/292-8929 or toll free 800/635-4766. Fax 612/292-1749. 202 rms, 3 suites. A/C TV TEL **Directions:** I-94 to Kellogg. Turn right on Kellogg and proceed two blocks to Days Inn on your right.

$ Rates: $55 single; $63 double. No charge for children under age 18. AE, CB, DISC, MC, V. **Parking:** Free.

Long popular with participants and spectators of events taking place just across the street at the St. Paul Civic Center Auditorium, this popular budget hotel offers easy accessibility to other Twin Cities attractions as well. Located just two blocks from the Minnesota History Center, it's four blocks from the Ordway Music Hall and the World Trade Center and eight blocks from the Science Museum of Minnesota. There's free transportation to the Mystic Lake Casino. MTC buses stop in front of the door for those interested in going to the Mall of America. ($1.65 during peak hours, $1.35 other times. Seniors' rates available.) On-site dining at Jazzmin's 24-hour restaurant and complimentary parking, newspaper, and cable TV with HBO combine to make this a comfortable as well as an economical place to stay.

HOLIDAY INN EXPRESS, Bandana Sq., 1010 Bandana Blvd. W., St. Paul, MN 55108. Tel. 612/647-1637. Fax 612/647-0244. 109 rms. A/C TV TEL
$ Rates: $69 single; $75 double. Seniors $54. AE, DC, DISC, MC, V.
Connected by skyway to the Bandana Square shopping-and-dining complex, Holiday Inn Express offers an indoor pool, whirlpool, sauna and a wading pool. The two-story inn is a former railroad repair shop; the lobby retains a rustic quality with its wood-beamed ceiling and benches.

SHERATON INN MIDWAY, I-94 and Hamline Ave., St. Paul, MN 55104. Tel. 612/642-1234 or toll free 800/535-2339. Fax 612/642-1126. 200 rms. AC TV TEL
$ Rates: $83 single; $93 double; weekend $60. Senior weekday rates $62. AE, DC, DISC, MC, V.
Conveniently located about 10 minutes from downtown Minneapolis, and 5 minutes from downtown St. Paul, the Sheraton Inn Midway boasts Minnesota's largest sauna along with a popular swimming pool and whirlpool. The public space here is striking—a tasteful blend of natural plantings, polished brass, and gleaming glass. You're sure to find the rooms clean and comfortable.

BED & BREAKFASTS

CHATSWORTH BED AND BREAKFAST, 984 Ashland Ave., St. Paul, MN 55104. Tel. 612/227-4288. 5 rms.
$ Rates: $60–$105 single; $65–$115 double.
This large comfortable Victorian home is located just two blocks from the governor's mansion on elegant Summit Avenue and three blocks from the shops and restaurants of trendy Grand Avenue. Many Chatsworth guests come to the Twin Cities for business and professional reasons; others come here because their children are students at one of the many nearby colleges and universities. Inn-keepers Donna and Earl Gustafson raised eight children and hosted foreign students in this home before turning it into a

bed-and-breakfast with a distinctly international flavor. Only two rooms, the Oriental Room and the Scandinavian Room, share a bathroom, but they also share a unique Japanese soaking tub, only four-feet wide and unusually deep. There's a pedestal sink in the Victorian Room and an adjoining private bath with shower. That leaves the African-Asian Room and the Four-Poster Room, each of which contains a double whirlpool bath. "Continental Plus" is the term the Gustafsons use to describe their daily breakfast, which includes a combination of some of the following: fresh fruit and juices, muffins, cold cereal, yogurt, and, of course, coffee and tea.

THE GARDEN GATE BED AND BREAKFAST, 925 Goodrich Ave., St. Paul, MN 55105. Tel. 612/227-8430 or toll-free 800/967-2703. 3 rms (shared bath).
$ Rates $50–$60.

This large newly redecorated Victorian duplex is owned by Mary and Miles Conway, who report that fully half their guests have come to St. Paul to visit sons and daughters at nearby Macalester College. Many other guests have been referred here by friends and family members of neighbors in this pleasant part of St. Paul. Located a short distance from the shopping and dining attractions of Grand Avenue, this neighborhood enjoys easy access to downtown Minneapolis and St. Paul. (Transportation for guests can be arranged by the Conways.) Hot mineral baths are popular here and so too, for a $35 charge, are therapeutic massages administered by Mary Conway, a professional nurse and masseuse. Bikes are available for use without additional charge.

4. SUBURBAN ST. PAUL

INEXPENSIVE

COUNTRY INN BY CARLSON, 6003 Hudson Rd., Woodbury, MN 55125. Tel. 612/739-7300 or toll free 800/456-4000. Fax 612/731-4007. 159 rms, 4 suites. A/C, TV TEL **Directions:** I-94E to Century Ave. exit.
$ Rates (including continental breakfast): $69 standard room; $79 executive-wing room; Children under 18 free in parents' room. $135 whirlpool room. AE, CB, DC, DISC, MC, V.

This is the largest of the 40 Country Inns by Carlson, attractive and comfortable accommodations, related through Minnesota's Curt Carlson to his larger and more expensive Radisson Hotels. Located four miles east of downtown St. Paul, in close proximity to the headquarters of 3M and the Fortas Benefits Insurance Company, this comfortable two-story motel serves primarily a business clientele. *Note:* There's no elevator to the second floor.

Children have their own game room featuring appropriate video games. All guests are offered a complimentary continental breakfast. Those in standard rooms find a coffee maker waiting for them, while guests in the executive wing find, in addition, a microwave oven, refrigerator, hair dryer, and an invitation to complimentary canapés

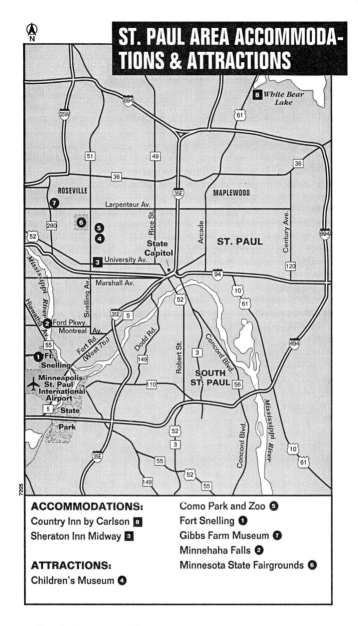

ACCOMMODATIONS:

Country Inn by Carlson **8**

Sheraton Inn Midway **3**

ATTRACTIONS:

Children's Museum **4**

Como Park and Zoo **5**

Fort Snelling **1**

Gibbs Farm Museum **7**

Minnehaha Falls **2**

Minnesota State Fairgrounds **6**

and cocktails Monday through Thursday from 5 to 7pm. There's an indoor pool on the premises along with a fitness center and a Green Mill Restaurant which serves three meals each day. A complimentary shuttle provides transportation to downtown St. Paul and anywhere else within a 5-mile radius.

CHAPTER 6

TWIN CITIES DINING

There's something in the Twin Cities to suit every taste and every budget. Far from being the land of *lefse* and *lutefisk,* Minneapolis and St. Paul are remarkable for the variety, the quality, and the cosmopolitan nature of their restaurant cuisine. Actually, they're a little short on Scandinavian dining places, but there's plenty of good British, French, German, Greek, Italian, Chinese, Japanese, Vietnamese, Afghani, and African fare to be found here. And there are fine eating spots that have a special way with basic American steaks, chops, and seafood.

A number of Twin Cities restaurants have won national and international awards, and they'll be called to your attention, along with those that have become favorites among knowledgeable local folks. Many of the places listed here, in fact, are the ones to which local hosts generally bring their own out-of-town guests.

I'll let you in on the not-to-be-missed restaurants in various parts of the cities and suburbs. They'll be listed in each area from the most expensive to the least expensive. Bear in mind that geographically some areas are relatively confined—the downtown Minneapolis, Warehouse, and Mill districts, for example. Others, like South Suburban Minneapolis, are rather spread out. Use the maps in this book to get oriented before you set out.

I've categorized restaurants by the typical cost of a meal for one without wine. Those charging more than $25 are considered **very expensive;** those charging $20 to $25, **expensive;** those charging $10 to $20, **moderate;** and those charging less than $10, **inexpensive.** Note that some restaurants serve strictly à la carte, with a separate charge for virtually every item, while others include soup, salad, vegetables, and other items with the price of the main course. Be aware, too, that even the fanciest eating spots tend to be moderately priced for lunch. Thus, you can enjoy the finest in ambience, cuisine, and presentation for a relatively modest cost. On the whole, you'll find that prices in Twin Cities restaurants tend to be lower than in other U.S. metropolitan areas.

1. MINNEAPOLIS

VERY EXPENSIVE
DOWNTOWN

AZUR RESTAURANT, 651 Nicollet Mall, Minneapolis. Tel. 342-2500.
Cuisine: FRENCH MEDITERRANEAN. **Reservations:** Recommended.

$ Prices: Appetizers $5.50–$8.50; main courses $18.50–$24; fixed-price three-course dinner $19–$28; lunch $6–$13.50. AE, DC, MC, V.

Open: Lunch Mon–Fri 11:30am–2pm; dinner Mon–Fri 5:30–9pm, Sat 5:30–10pm. **Closed:** Sun.

Among its many laurels, Azur was named one of the best new restaurants of 1990 by *Esquire* magazine. The handsome decor was designed by Richard D'Amico in shades of black, purple, and green; the ambience is bustling and upbeat, thanks in part to the French rock-and-roll music that provides a spirited background. Service is correct but unpretentious.

Featured here is chef Jay Sparks's version of the cooking you'd find in southern France's Côte d'Azur. Olive oil, roasted garlic, leeks, and fennel play an important part in Sparks's recipes. Popular dinnertime appetizers range from grilled tomato bread to crab and avocado tian with bell peppers. Favorite main courses include sautéed grouper with stewed artichokes and potato purée as well as steak Diane with porcini mushrooms and truffled asparagus.

There's an extensive wine list and a delightful variety of apéritifs and digestives. Entertainment by the Mandala Trio featuring Latin jazz is offered Friday and Saturday evenings. Complimentary valet parking is available in the Gavidae Common Parking Ramp.

GOODFELLOW'S, 800 Nicollet Mall, Minneapolis. Tel. 332-4800.
Cuisine: AMERICAN. **Reservations:** Recommended.

$ Prices: Dinner appetizers $8–$10; main courses $18–$28; lunch main courses $9–$14. AE, DC, DISC, MC, V.

Open: Lunch Mon–Fri 11:30am–2:30pm; dinner Mon–Thurs 5:30–9pm, Fri–Sat 5:30–10pm.

For a special occasion, you can't do better than Goodfellow's. Located on the top floor of the Conservatory, one of downtown Minneapolis's most unabashedly upscale shopping centers, Goodfellow's wide windows provide a dramatic view of the Nicollet Mall. The restaurant is accessible by skyway to major hotels and department stores, including Dayton's.

Goodfellow's has maintained its reputation for impeccable service, cuisine, and ambience. Prices here are relatively high, but the value is second to none. The menu changes seasonally with the availability of ingredients, but game, including venison, is available year-round. Particularly popular are appetizers like grilled lamb tenderloin with spinach-and-warm-goat-cheese salad and fried egg-plant, and fettuccine with grilled shrimp, oven-dried tomatoes, and basil sauce. Main-course favorites include braised pork tenderloin with wild rice cake and tomatillo-shallot sauce and grilled veal chop with herb cheese lasagne and roasted pepper sauce. Desserts are all tempting, but my personal favorite is the delectable lace cookie cup filled with raspberries, cream, and caramel.

The wine list here is widely and justifiably admired and includes over 400 selections, all of them American except for the champagne. (While most of the wines hail from California, a few are from the Finger Lakes of New York.) There's a wide variety of nonalcoholic wines and beers as well.

And then there's Goodfellow's vegetarian menu, devised with characteristic attention to detail. Vegetarians will be pleased with dinners featuring roast corn soup with cumin-seared tomatoes and cilantro, mixed green salad with red beet vinaigrette and parmesan cheese, fennel-and-pine-nut-stuffed phyllo leaves with white beans and grilled vegetables, and a choice of desserts or fresh fruit.

GUSTINO'S, in Minneapolis Marriott, 30 S. 7th St., Minneapolis. Tel. 349-4075.
    Cuisine: NORTHERN ITALIAN. **Reservations:** Recommended.
$ Prices: Appetizers $6–$9; main courses $17–$24. AE, DC, MC, V.
    Open: Dinner Mon–Thurs 6–10pm, Fri–Sat 6–11pm.

If you enjoy music in the foreground as well as the background when you dine, don't miss Gustino's. A talented group of singing servers are on hand here seven nights a week to bring you a beautiful blend of musical and culinary fare. Gustino's caters to the diverse performing schedules of these singers, who regularly appear in local operatic and musical-comedy productions.

There's a feast for the eye, as well, in this handsome art deco room with its panoramic view of downtown Minneapolis and, from March through October, spectacular Twin Cities sunsets. As you're led to your table through a glass alcove, you'll pass a white grand piano and a floor-to-ceiling triangular glass wine "cellar" displaying more than 200 bottles of Italian wine.

Veal is a specialty of the house and you can choose from veal scaloppine, veal in marsala sauce, breaded veal scallops with ham, mozzarella, and fresh tomatoes or a delectable roast veal with the stuffing and sauce of the day. Gustino's offers fine Italian seafood and chicken too, with each dish served with polenta or risotto and vegetables. You really can't go wrong with any of the soups, salads, pizzas, or pasta on the menu here, but do save room for a slice of pepperoni bread and one of the "painted desserts" concocted daily by the chef. The three-level *torre di pisa* is an extravaganza of assorted antipasti selections. Wine lovers will enjoy the "wines of the month," two selections that can be ordered by the glass that are ordinarily available only by the bottle.

MANNY'S, in Hyatt Regency Hotel, 1300 Nicollet Mall, Minneapolis. Tel. 339-9900.

FROMMER'S SMART TRAVELER:
RESTAURANTS

1. Eat your main meal at lunch, when prices are lower. You can eat at some of the Twin Cities' best restaurants for substantially less than what it would cost at dinner.
2. Choose set lunches and dinners when possible—many represent a 30% saving over à la carte menus.
3. Look for the daily specials on any à la carte menu; they're often cheaper than the regular listings.
4. Watch how much alcohol you drink; a lot of wine, beer, or liquor can run up your tab.
5. Some expensive restaurants offer pasta dishes that are priced much lower than most other main courses.
6. Ask if the main dish comes with a side dish like a vegetable or potato (this may be all you need to order).

Cuisine: STEAK HOUSE. **Reservations:** Required.

$ Prices: Appetizers $4.95–$7.95; main courses $13.95–$23.95. AE, DC, DISC, MC, V.

Open: Dinner Mon–Thurs 5:30–10pm, Fri–Sat 5:30–11pm, Sun 5:30–9pm.

One of the first things you'll notice at Manny's, along with the bright lighting and the hardwood floors, is the absence of centerpieces on the tables. Manny's makes no apologies for this omission. What's important here, they explain, is what's on the plate; and what's on the plate has kept the phones ringing since Manny's first opened in June 1988.

When you do get a table at Manny's, you'll discover that everything is à la carte, and everything is large—your waiter will suggest you consider sharing a baked potato, an order of french fries, or a portion of creamed garlic spinach. And he won't be surprised if you ask to share your main course as well. Splitting portions is encouraged at Manny's, where there's no charge for an extra plate.

Although steak is what Manny's is mainly about, there are many other choices as well. Try lamb chops at $21.95, pork chops at $16.95, or lemon pepper chicken at $13.95. And if you're a shrimp fancier, be advised that the shrimp, lemon peppered and grilled, are king-size and utterly delicious. But steak, of course, is the most frequently ordered item, and you'll have a choice among memorable New York strip steak for $23.95, filet mignon at $21.95 or $23.95, or porterhouse at $23.95. If you want to go all the way, consider the 48-ounce double porterhouse steak that goes for $47.90. Maybe you can share the cost as well as the portion with a partner, but in any case keep in mind that the doggie bags, like everything else at Manny's, are supersize.

MORTON'S OF CHICAGO, 655 Nicollet Mall, Minneapolis. Tel. 673-9700.

Cuisine: STEAK HOUSE. **Reservations:** Required.

$ Prices: Appetizers $4.25–$8.95; main courses $15.95–$28.95. AE, DC, MC, V.

Open: Lunch Mon–Fri 11:30am–2:30pm; dinner Mon–Sat 5:30–11pm, Sun 5–10pm.

Like all Morton's of Chicago steak houses across the country, this one is situated one floor below street level. If you've left your car in the underground garage at the Neiman Marcus end of Gaviidae Common, be sure to have your parking ticket validated at Morton's for complimentary dinnertime parking.

As you enter Gaviidae Common from the garage, you'll see Morton's to your right. To gain access to the dining room, just open the large mahogany door and walk right in. You can also enter Morton's by descending a staircase just inside Neiman Marcus's 6th Street entrance. A welcoming canopy with Morton's name on it will tell you you've come to the right place. Take time on your way down the stairs to look at the interesting black-and-white photographs on the wall. Collected from the Minnesota Historical Society, they depict the Twin Cities during bygone days.

Signature features at Morton's of Chicago steak houses are the open kitchens and the servers who provide you with a comprehensive show-and-tell presentation before taking your order. Tempting beef, lamb, chicken, veal, and fish, wrapped in plastic, will be displayed and discussed; a live lobster will be introduced as well. The portions, when they arrive, are easily large enough to share. (There's no charge for an extra plate.) The jumbo shrimp cocktail ($8.95) and broiled sea scallops wrapped in bacon with apricot chutney on the side ($7.50) are particularly popular appetizers. The Caesar salad ($4.95) and spinach salad ($4.75) are favorites as well. Among the main dishes, shrimp Alexander ($18.50) and lemon oregano chicken ($16.95) rank high, but if you came for steak, you really can't go wrong with any of the choices, from the New York sirloin ($29.95) to the double filet mignon ($27.95) or the tenderloin brochette ($18.95). To accompany your main course, consider sautéed fresh spinach and mushrooms ($3.95) or steamed fresh broccoli ($4.25) or asparagus ($6.50), both with hollandaise sauce. If you'd like a light and luscious soufflé for dessert, tell the waiter when you order; Mark Laurin, the gifted chef, requires 30 minutes preparation time.

THE NEW FRENCH CAFE, 128 N. 4th St., Minneapolis. Tel. 338-3790.

Cuisine: FRENCH. **Reservations:** Recommended.

$ Prices: Appetizers $4–$9; main courses $21–$26; lunch $8.95–$12.95; breakfast $5.75–$8.25; Sat–Sun brunch $8.85–$10.95. AE, DC, MC, V.

Open: Breakfast Mon–Fri 7–11am; lunch Mon–Fri 11:30–1:30pm; dinner Mon–Thurs 5:30–9:30pm, Sat–Sun 5:30–10pm; late-night supper Fri–Sat 10pm–midnight; brunch Sat–Sun 8am–2pm.

The New French Café, with its whitewashed brick walls and exposed wooden beams, is considered one of the smartest dining and drinking spots in the Twin Cities. This is the location of choice for that important breakfast meeting, the perfect spot for a casual lunch or a special dinner, and the place where many local artists get together late at night. It was the New French Café that began the transformation of Minneapolis's run-down warehouse district into a Soho on the Mississippi where nearby art galleries attract crowds every week.

The cuisine features classic and contemporary French selections including ragoût of goose with red wine, crème fraîche, mushrooms, turnips, carrots, and leeks served with Savoyard potatoes. Desserts and bread, baked on the premises, are a specialty here, including favorites like eclairs and fresh fruit tarts.

NORTHEAST

JAX CAFE, 1928 University Ave. N.E., Minneapolis. Tel. 789-7297.

Cuisine: AMERICAN. **Reservations:** Recommended.

$ Prices: Appetizers $3.95–$10.95; main courses $10.95–$31.95; Sun brunch $12.95 adults, $5.95 children under 10. AE, CB, DC, DISC, MC, V.

Open: Lunch Mon–Sat 11am–3pm; dinner Mon–Thurs 3–10pm, Fri–Sat 3–11pm, Sun 3:30–9pm; buffet brunch Sun 10am–3pm.

When lawyer/legislator Joseph Kozlak and his wife Gertrude decided to open a Minneapolis restaurant back in 1943, they were able to seat 56 diners. Today, the much-enlarged Jax, owned and operated by the founders' son Bill and his wife Kathy, can seat 300 people on each of its two floors, with room for 50 or so more on the beautifully landscaped patio. The handsome restaurant is known widely as a special-occasion place, where proms, weddings, anniversary celebrations, and other festive goings-on are enhanced by dark woods, soft lighting, and impeccable service. You can enjoy piano music here on Thursday, Friday, and Saturday evenings from 6:30 to 10:30pm and at Sunday brunch.

The dessert temptations are many, but do consider the Bailey's Irish Cream banana torte, which won first prize in a cities-wide competition and a place on the menu of the annual gala Symphony Ball. Before dessert, though, there are other choices to be made: "classic cut" tenderloin, chicken marinara, broiled filet of walleye pike—the list is long and varied. Main courses are served with soup or salad and rice, pasta, potato, or vegetable. At lunch, dishes run from $6.95 to $12.95.

WAREHOUSE DISTRICT

D'AMICO CUCINA, 100 N. 6th St., Minneapolis. Tel. 338-2401.

Cuisine: ITALIAN. **Reservations:** Required.

$ Prices: Appetizers $7.50–$9.50; main courses $18.75–$25; pastas $8–$10.

Open: Dinner Mon–Thurs 5:30–10pm, Fri–Sat 5:30–11pm, Sun 5–9pm.

No restaurant in the Twin Cities has proved more popular with the public and the press than D'Amico Cucina. Situated across the street from the Target Arena, D'Amico Cucina has been an unqualified winner since it was opened in September 1987 by the D'Amico brothers and their colleague, Steve Davidson. It is a handsome, casually sophisticated restaurant where the cuisine is imaginative, the service impeccable, and the atmosphere everything you could desire. The restaurant's brick wall and wood-beamed ceilings hearken back to the building's warehouse days, while the blend of peach and gray in the marble floor and the wall coverings is accented by steel and black leather chairs.

The menu choices here are varied and eminently tempting. The wine list, also, is extensive. Appetizers include the miniature thin-crusted pizza of the day, timbale of prosciutto, and charcoal grilled eggplant. Other notable items are the potato gnocchi with tomato, basil, thyme, and romano cheese and the savory *quadrucci* with chicken, walnuts, and sage.

Of the main courses, favorites include pork tenderloin with garlic, red beans, and smoked bacon; and grilled lamb with crispy lentils and black olives. The menu changes several times a year. Daily specials here are always worthy of careful consideration, and so are the pastries, custards, gelati, and sorbetti, all prepared on the premises.

EXPENSIVE

DOWNTOWN

510 RESTAURANT, 510 Groveland Ave., Minneapolis. Tel. 874-6440.

Cuisine: CONTINENTAL. **Reservations:** Recommended.

$ Prices: Appetizers $4–$8; main courses $13–$20; three-course fixed-price dinner $19 and $29. AE, CB, DC, DISC, MC, V.

Open: Mon–Sat 5:30–10pm.

After many years as one of the most expensive restaurants in the Twin Cities, the premiere special-occasion place where lawyers, architects, and businesspeople conferred with their peers and recruited new members for their firms, 510 took a more moderate turn early in 1993 when it changed its decor, menu, and price range. The challenge was to retain the loyalty of longtime diners, women and men of considerable affluence and influence, while at the same time broadening their appeal to people for whom cost was a more important consideration. The transformation has been accomplished with remarkable success. As the elegance of floor-length blue-gray draperies gave way to shorter, warmer peach-toned draperies, the seven- or eight-course fixed-price tasting dinners have been replaced by a choice between two considerably less expensive three-course fixed-price dinners. Steak remains a popular item here, but at $19.95 the grilled filet mignon, served on wild mushrooms and slow cooked garlic with a cabernet glace, represents a real value. So do braised lamb shank and sautéed breast of chicken stuffed with brie on herbed polenta. Fine California wines are featured here at prices just $1 over average retail price.

KIKUGAWA, Riverplace, 45 Main St. S.E., Minneapolis. Tel. 378-3006.

Cuisine: JAPANESE. **Reservations:** Recommended.

$ Prices: Appetizers $3.25–$9.50; main courses $8.50–$17.50; fixed-price dinner $24.50; lunch $5–$10. AE, CB, DC, DISC, JCB, MC, V.

Open: Lunch Mon–Fri 11am–2pm, Sat noon–2pm, Sun 12–2:30pm; dinner Mon–Thurs 5pm–10pm, Fri–Sat 5–11pm, Sun 4:30–9:30pm.

Japanese cuisine, both traditional and contemporary, is featured at Kikugawa. Owner-operator John Omori recalls that since sushi first appeared on the menu during the early eighties, the raw-fish delicacy has gone from less than one-tenth of his food orders to about one-half. A full sushi bar is one of the features of his handsome restaurant with its pale-wood pillars and beams. *Nabemono* table cookery is available throughout the different dining rooms. Particularly popular are the tatami rooms, where diners leave their shoes at the door and experience traditional Japanese dining. There is also a main dining room and a room facing the river.

A favorite menu choice is beef shabu, paper-thin slices of filet mignon cooked for two or three seconds in hot shabu broth. Currently a favorite in Japan, the dish is particularly popular with the growing number of local residents who have visited the country. Omori has also introduced a yakitori bar, a broiling station for skewered chicken, beef, seafood, and vegetables. Other items you might try are sukiyaki and the nabemono table-prepared dishes, including shabu shabu (Japanese fondue). For haute cuisine Japanese style, try the combination tempura made of seafood, chicken, beef, and seasonal vegetables. There's a delicious selection of desserts here, including two inspired intercontinental inventions—tempura ice cream and green-tea ice cream.

MURRAY'S, 26 S. 6th St., Minneapolis. Tel. **339-0909.**

Cuisine: AMERICAN. **Reservations:** Recommended.

$ Prices: Appetizers $6.25–$8.95; main courses $14.50–$25.95; steaks $19.50–$48.95; lunch $4.75–$11.95; afternoon tea à la carte $2.25–$6.50. AE, MC, V.

Open: Lunch Mon–Fri 11am–3pm; tea Mon–Fri 2–3:30pm; dinner Mon–Thurs 4–10:30pm, Fri–Sat 4–11pm, Sun 4–10pm.

For more than four decades Twin Citians have headed to Murray's. Butter-knife steak is the specialty of this handsome, family-managed restaurant, but you needn't live by beef alone at Murray's. The menu features broiled filet of walleye pike and T-bone veal steak, among other favorites. There are vegetarian selections as well.

Murray's has somehow managed to retain its intimacy after being enlarged a few years ago. Mirrored walls, dusty-rose draperies and valances, and wrought-iron chandeliers and balustrades provide the same warm and gracious setting that Art and Marie Murray cultivated back in the forties. Their grandson Tim, who now runs the restaurant, also kept the popular piano and violin accompaniment to the evening's dining experience.

Dinners here are in the expensive-but-worth-it category, but the ever popular downtowner menu, served from 4 to 6pm every day, features a full dinner including potato or vegetable and salad along with Murray's famous bread basket for $7.95 to $12.50.

MODERATE

DOWNTOWN

BRIT'S PUB & EATING ESTABLISHMENT, 1110 Nicollet Mall, Minneapolis. Tel. 332-3908.

Cuisine: BRITISH. **Reservations:** Not accepted.

$ **Prices:** Appetizers $4–$6; main courses $6–$14. AE, DC, MC, V.

Open: Mon–Fri 11am–1am, Sat 8–1am, Sun 8am–midnight.

Situated directly across Nicollet Avenue from Orchestra Hall, Brit's is a relatively recent addition to downtown dining. It could hardly be more welcome. The proprietor, the cuisine, and the decor are all decidedly British, and the clientele is as eclectic as can be. Concertgoers in minks mingle affably with sports fans in jeans. Others come in not for a meal, but for a few pints and a game of darts or pool. Owner-manager Nigel Chilvers has imported an assortment of beers, as many if not more, he says, than are available in London. But, as in London, beer here is served at 54 degrees, which, he explains, enables a beer to best express its flavor.

The cuisine at Brit's is as delightful as the conviviality. Chilvers has shown that British food is not necessarily disappointing: the steak-and-kidney pie is a real treat. For dessert, try the Thames River mud cake with crème à l'anglaise or the thoroughly British trifle.

BUCA, 1204 Harmon (12th St. at Harmon Place), Minneapolis. Tel. 638-2225.

Cuisine: ITALIAN. **Reservations:** Accepted only for groups of 8 to 16.

$ **Prices:** Appetizers $4–$12; pizzas $10–$15; pasta $8–$18; main courses $13–$20; desserts $5–$8. AE, DC, MC, V.

Open: Mon–Thurs 5–10pm, Fri 5–11pm, Sat 4:30–11pm, Sun 4–10pm.

This bustling basement restaurant will remind you more of an American Little Italy than of the southern Italian places so closely identified with robust red-sauce cuisine. Portions at Buca are mammoth and meant to be shared, a fact that makes posted prices a bit misleading. (There's no extra charge for extra plates, of course, in this supremely congenial setting.) The ambience tends to be festive if not frenetic, and the informality veers toward the unconventional. Table settings are a case in point. Don't be surprised if the flatware and dishes on your table are hopelessly mismatched. Note too that on the map of Italy that decorates your placemat, northern Italy is nowhere to be seen.

Buca offers a wide variety of main dishes, pizzas, pastas, and salads whose flavor is anything but timid. Individual preferences can be readily accommodated, though, because everything's made from scratch. Along with tasty traditional meatballs and spaghetti, you'll find delectable seafood dishes like linguine frutta di mare with mussels, clams, and calamari. Vegetarians find much here to gladden their hearts and palates, and even carnivores enjoy pizza *rustica* with a topping of eggplant, escarole, onions, tomatoes, artichokes, broccoli, and provolone cheese. Consider as well the eggplant parmigiana and homemade goat-cheese ravioli. If you find yourself among those waiting for a table, be advised that a portable blackboard with bells and a long handle will notify you when you're about to be seated. The ringing of the bells prompts you to look at the blackboard, where your name will appear when your table is ready. Meanwhile take the time to look at the abundance of museum-quality pictures and artifacts on display; most of them were purchased at flea markets in Italy. Although reservations are accepted only for groups of 8 to 16, smaller parties can phone in advance to have their names placed on the waiting list one hour before their arrival time.

KAPOOCHI'S, 815 Nicollet Mall (Second Level), Minneapolis. Tel. 339-1011.

Cuisine: CONTEMPORARY EUROPEAN/JAPANESE. **Reservations:** Recommended.

$ Prices: Appetizers $3.50–$7.50; main courses $9.50–$16.50. AE, DC, DISC, MC, V.

Open: Breakfast Mon–Fri 7am–10am; lunch Mon–Fri 11am–2pm; dinner Sun–Thurs 5:30–10pm, Fri–Sat 5:30–11pm.

How to describe what awaits you at Kapoochi's? Founder and maitre d' Michael Kutscheid describes the cuisine here as "modern European—prepared, presented, and spiced in a more traditional Japanese fashion." There's a lot of searing, steaming, and stir-frying of meats, seafood, and vegetables with sauces that are held together by natural juices instead of fat. Kutscheid is a lawyer who made money waiting tables while he earned his degree at William Mitchell College of Law in St. Paul. It wasn't until after graduation that he realized he didn't want to give up restaurant work. But his academic training wasn't wasted, he declares. It taught him to think and to organize, and these abilities served him well during his years as maitre d' at several fine Twin Cities dining places. His training in research techniques also helped him work out every detail of the beautiful and functional decor in this large skyway-level space. It has been turned into a series of small settings, with limited sight lines imparting a sense of coziness and intimacy. "Anyone with a library card could have done it," Kutscheid says of the architectural research that led to some of the more surprising elements of Kapoochi's decor, including the bar with its keyboard design and the stage whose curving shape captures the sound of the nightly musical entertainment.

Heading the kitchen staff is chef Greg Westcott, who, like Kutscheid, has had a long and auspicious career in the Twin Cities. The menu changes biweekly, Kutscheid explains, so that the chefs can keep their creative juices flowing. Typical of the atypical items you'll find on the menu here are potato and smoked salmon lasagne and beef tender wonton ravioli. Kutscheid reports that children of 9 or 10 seem to have a fine time at Kapoochi's: "They might not recognize the food by appearance, but they love the way it tastes." That goes for the grown-ups too.

The wines here are as unique as the food and come from small boutique wineries in New Zealand, Australia, Chile, Spain, Italy, and France as well as from California, Oregon, and other diverse locations. "Anyone can find a great expensive bottle of wine," Kutscheid states. "For me it's exciting to find a great wine at one-tenth the price."

PALOMINO, 825 Hennepin Ave., Minneapolis. Tel. 339-3800.
Cuisine: FRENCH/MEDITERRANEAN. **Reservations:** Required.
$ Prices: Appetizers $4.50–$8.50; main courses $6.95–$21.95. AE, DC, DISC, MC, V.
Open: Lunch Mon–Sat 11:15am–2:30pm; dinner Mon–Thurs 5–10pm, Fri–Sat 4–9pm. Bar menu Mon–Sat 11:15am–1am, Sun 4pm–midnight.

Located in LaSalle Plaza, an escalator ride above the historic State Theatre and a short distance from the Target Arena, Palomino opened in October 1991, intending to provide a special-occasion environment at moderate prices. They've accomplished that and a whole lot more. This is one restaurant in which the majority of diners tend to dress more formally in the daytime than at night. That's because the businesspeople who come for lunch often stop in during the evening as well, but much more casually clad.

Described as a "metropolitan bistro," Palomino features a south European cuisine that's predominately French, Italian, Greek, and Spanish. It also features one of the largest open kitchens you're likely to see anywhere. As you're led to your table in the beautiful two-level dining room, you'll pass an exhibition cooking area and see preparations of everything from spit-roast garlic chicken to oven-fired pizza, Roman style. Menus are printed daily or weekly here, depending on the availability of fresh items.

The dining rooms are at once elegant and comfortable. Marble dining tables, a large Matisse, and gleaming blown-glass fixtures combine with the mauve, purple, and black decor to make these rooms appropriate for all sorts of occasions. The handsome adjoining bar provides a pleasant alternative, including a menu of its own and a no-reservations policy. The bar, by the way, offers the largest grappa selection in the Midwest along with a large selection of ports and, among other favorites, the Pallini champagne and the peach schnapps that have become so popular here during spring and summer. Whether you come in for a meal or only for a pick-me-up, do consider one of the luscious desserts. The tiramisù is universally praised and for very good reason. Also be sure to try the house bread—baked by Baldinger's Bakery, with a mixture of seasonings devised by Palomino, with thoroughly delectable results. Many Twin Citians are thoroughly addicted to it.

PING'S, 1401 Nicollet Ave. S., Minneapolis. Tel. 874-9404.

Cuisine: CHINESE. **Reservations:** Recommended.

$ Prices: Appetizers $4–$6; main courses $7–$15; lunch buffet Mon–Fri $6.95; Sun buffet $9.95. AE, DC, DISC, MC, V.

Open: Mon–Thurs 11am–10pm, Fri 11am–midnight, Sat noon–midnight, Sun noon–9pm.

One of the best bargain buffets in the Twin Cities is found at Ping's, Monday through Friday from 11:30am to 2pm. Even more lavish buffets are available on Sunday. Pink Chinese kites contrast with gray walls and pillars in this attractive informal dining room, and a pink tile bar is the focal point of the lower of two dining levels. Chef Minh Tran's selections attract downtown businesspeople, local residents, and theatergoers from the adjoining Music Box Theatre who savor the spicy Szechuan dishes that are featured here. One of the most renowned specialties is the crispy flavorful Peking duck. Complimentary valet parking.

TEJAS, 800 Nicollet Mall, Minneapolis. Tel. 375-0800.

Cuisine: SOUTHWESTERN. **Reservations:** Recommended.

$ Prices: Appetizers $6–$9; main courses $10–$16. AE, DISC, MC, V.

Open: Mon–Thurs 11am–9pm, Fri–Sat 11am–10pm.

The cuisine at Tejas is not Tex-Mex; it's decidedly southwestern. That means what you'll be tasting in this handsome dining room is a unique blend of Mexican and southwestern-Native-American foods and flavors. The dining area is decorated in shades of peach, deep rose, and sea-foam green and accented with Indian pottery. The meticulously arranged foods, many of them presented on plates "painted" with subtly seasoned sauces, are a treat for the eye. Visitors from as far away as California have been known to stop in the Twin Cities overnight in order to dine at Tejas. Reviews in the *New York Times, Esquire,* and *USA Today* have helped spread the word further yet.

The menu changes four times a year, but certain signature items are a permanent part of the offerings, such as tortilla soup with chicken, avocado, smoked tomato, and Jack cheese; Caesar salad with cayenne croutons and cumin-tamarind dressing; smoked shrimp enchilada with creamy barbecue sauce and jicama relish; smoked chicken nachos with Jack and Asiago cheeses and avocado and tomato salsas. For dessert, choices include flourless dark chocolate-*ancho* cake with Mexican vanilla sauce and warm upside-down pineapple skillet cake with rum-caramel sauce. Try any of these dishes and you'll understand what all the fuss is about.

If you're interested in take-out orders, Tejas will deliver anywhere in the downtown area. And one last bit of information—all the juices here are fresh squeezed, which accounts for the popularity of Tejas's lemonade and margaritas. I suspect this is Cilantro City

WAREHOUSE DISTRICT

MONTE CARLO BAR & GRILL, 219 3rd Ave. N., Minneapolis. Tel. 333-5900.

Cuisine: AMERICAN. **Reservations:** Recommended.

$ Prices: Appetizers $3.95–$7.95; main courses $6.95–$18.95. Sun breakfast $4.95. AE, DC, DISC, MC, V.

Open: Mon–Sat 11am–11:45pm, Sun 10am–10:45pm; Sun brunch 11am–4pm.

There's some question as to whether this popular art deco hangout is a restaurant with a bar or a bar with a restaurant. When the tin ceiling first went up some 70 years ago, the Monte Carlo was exclusively a drinking spot, and that's what it remained until the Warehouse District became chic back in the seventies. Now it has broadened its clientele, serving chicken soup, burgers, steaks, chops, and more at lunch and dinner to office workers, antiques dealers, sales clerks, and shoppers. The best deal of all is the extended brunch, 10am to 4pm on Sunday: all the scrambled eggs, Canadian bacon, sausage, toast, and hash browns you can eat for $4.95.

The copper bar is still the focal point of Monte Carlo, with shelves of more than 500 bottles reaching up to the ceiling. Drinks are served club style—the mixer in a large tumbler, liquor in shot glasses, garnishes at the side. There's free parking in an adjoining lot. There's a relatively quiet front room off to the right as you enter Monte Carlo, preferred by those who find the rest of this lively restaurant a bit rambunctious.

UPTOWN

FIGLIO'S, 3001 Hennepin Ave., Minneapolis. Tel. 822-1688.
Cuisine: NORTHERN ITALIAN/AMERICAN. **Reservations:** Recommended.
$ Prices: Appetizers $4–$6; main courses $7–$15; lunch $5–$10. AE, MC, V.
Open: Sun–Thurs 11:30am–1am; Fri–Sat 11:30am–2am; brunch Sun 11:30am–2am.

Figlio's is a gem of an Italian restaurant, albeit one with a California accent. One of Figlio's dining rooms overlooks busy Lake Street, which has some of the best people watching hereabouts. The other, larger room has a view of the busy kitchen with its built-in wood-burning oven flanked by brick walls.

The northern Italian cuisine is overseen by executive chef Rex Retneyer, who is famous locally for his version of carpaccio—paper-thin slices of raw beef tenderloin marinated in olive oil, shallots, capers, and herbs and topped with thinly sliced parmesan cheese and placed on Italian bread, with three kinds of mustard at the ready.

Another specialty is something called *morto nel cioccolato,* "death by chocolate," of which happy locals contentedly declare, "What a way to go!" Do consider a portion of this extravagantly rich and utterly delicious concoction composed of alternating layers of chocolate cake and chocolate-amaretto gelato and served with a thick chocolate sauce.

The rest of the menu is a wide assortment of Italian and American favorites, from fettuccine Alfredo and stuffed tortellini to grilled swordfish and 10-ounce burgers.

There are a lot of nice touches to the service here, including the heated plates that keep your selection piping hot. Outdoor dining on Lake Street, take-out service, and Sunday brunch are some of the features that keep Figlio's popular.

LUCIA'S RESTAURANT, 1432 W. 31st St., Minneapolis. Tel. 825-1572.
Cuisine: CONTINENTAL/AMERICAN. **Reservations:** Recommended.
$ Prices: Appetizers $4.25–$4.95; main courses $7.95–$15.95. MC, V.
Open: Lunch Tues–Fri 11:30am–2:30pm; dinner Tues–Thurs 5:30–9:30pm, Fri–Sat 5:30–10pm, Sun 5:30–9pm; Sat–Sun brunch 10am–2pm.

Lucia Watson has been cooking since she was a small child growing up in Minneapolis, so her family and friends weren't surprised when she opened a small restaurant in 1985. What proved surprising about Lucia's new enterprise, though, was how fast it grew. A small room with a handwritten menu has now become a two-room restaurant with a bar. The handwritten menus have remained, though, adding a personal touch. And flexibility is something that Lucia considers important, especially for diners with dietary restrictions. "We're always open to special orders," she declares.

There are always two fresh soups on the menu, a choice of salads, a vegetarian dish (usually pasta), as well as a fish dish, a poultry dish, and a meat dish. And among the tantalizing selection of desserts, there's always a variety of choice. The honey crushed-wheat bread is one of Lucia's own creations. The bar menu, popular for an afternoon snack or after attending a performance at night, features fresh pastries, cheese-and-fruit plates, pastas, salads, and soups. Prices range from $3.25 to $8.95.

NORTHEAST

YVETTE, in Riverplace, 1 Main St. S.E., Minneapolis. Tel. 379-1111.
Cuisine: FRENCH/AMERICAN. **Reservations:** Recommended for indoor dining, not accepted for outdoor dining.
$ Prices: Appetizers $3.95–$6.95; main courses $9–$19; lunch $5–$11; Sun brunch $5–$11. AE, DC, MC, V.
Open: Lunch Mon–Sat 11am–3pm; dinner Mon–Thurs 5pm–10pm, Fri–Sat 5–11:45pm. Sun lunch 11am–3pm, dinner 5–9pm (May through Dec; closed on Sun Jan–April).

A dimly lit dining room tastefully decorated in warm shades of mauve and gray. Sound romantic? It is, and it's part of what brings diners back again and again to Yvette. There's much to recommend this lovely restaurant that overlooks the Mississippi and historic St. Anthony Falls.

The dry-aged beefsteak here is among the best you'll find in the Twin Cities, and the daily seafood specials feature a mouth-watering selection flown in from Boston each day. Dinner main courses are served with potato and vegetable. Desserts are another specialty, with the top draw being the chocolate velvet cake, baked on the premises. The wine selection ranges in price from a house wine for $18 to a Château Mouton Rothschild Pauillac 1897 for $4,000.

There's live jazz here every Tuesday through Saturday and a jam session each Monday night when Yvette's singer-pianist is joined by other musicians who are performing in other spots around town. When weather permits, there's outdoor dining on a flower-bordered terrace.

SOUTH

BLACK FOREST INN, 1 E. 26th St., Minneapolis. Tel. 872-0812.

Cuisine: GERMAN. **Reservations:** Recommended.

$ Prices: Appetizers $1.50–$5; main courses $6–$16; lunch $3–$6. AE, DC, DISC, MC, V.

Open: Lunch Mon–Sat 11am–5pm; dinner Mon–Sat 5–11pm, Sun noon–10pm; late menu Mon–Sat 11pm–midnight.

An extensive selection of domestic and imported beers and wines are served here amid the dark woods and stained glass of an authentic German "gasthaus." Luncheon main courses include Wiener Schnitzel and Sauerbraten, as well as chicken wings and corned beef on rye. The more comprehensive dinner menu includes German favorites like Schweinbraten (roast pork with apple dressing and red cabbage) and *gefuellte krautrolle* (stuffed cabbage with rice); dishes are served with a vegetable and often a potato pancake or *spaetzel*. The Black Forest features a long list of German, French, and California wines, plus a variety of liqueurs, brandies, and cognac.

RUDOLPH'S BAR-B-QUE, Franklin and Lyndale Aves., Minneapolis. Tel. 871-8969.

Cuisine: AMERICAN. **Reservations:** Recommended.

$ Prices: Appetizers $2.95–$4.95; main courses $7.95–$16.50; lunch $4.95–$5.50; Sun brunch $9.95. AE, CB, DC, MC, V.

Open: Mon–Thurs 11am–11pm, Fri–Sat 11am–2am, Sun 10am–11pm.

Wit, whimsy, and wonderful ribs are what you'll get at Rudolph's, which uses the steamy 1920s matinee idol as its theme. The barbecue sauce here has won innumerable national awards. If you're not a devotee of barbecued ribs, there are plenty of other dishes, ranging from Greek-style chicken to New York steak. Save room for the desserts; peach Melba is a real treat. On your way out, take a look at some of the wonderful vintage Hollywood photos that line the walls.

The other two Rudolph's are located at 815 E. Hennepin Ave., Minneapolis (tel. 623-3671), and 366 Jackson St., Galtier Plaza, St. Paul (tel. 222-2226). Hours vary by location, so call for specifics.

LORING AREA

LORING CAFE, 1624 Harmon Place, Minneapolis. Tel. 332-1617.

Cuisine: CONTINENTAL/AMERICAN. **Reservations:** Recommended.

$ Prices: Appetizers $5–$7; pasta $8–$11; main courses $11–$15; Sat–Sun brunch $5–$9; lunch $7–$11. MC, V.

Open: Lunch Mon–Fri 11:30am–2:30pm; dinner Mon–Thurs 5:30–10pm, Fri–Sat 5:30–midnight, Sun 5–10pm.

You can have your choice of ambience at the Loring Café. Owner/manager Jason McLean has provided a variety of spaces, indoors and out, to suit a wide variety of tastes. This restaurant, bar, and arts center is located in a converted automobile showroom that dates back more than 50 years. Dine on the main floor, in the loft, or, in the summertime, in the courtyard, one of the best outdoor settings in town. From time to time a saxophonist appears on the roof of an adjoining building, playing some of the sweetest dinner music you'll ever hear. During less balmy times, other kinds of music are offered at the Loring Café—jazz, blues, folk, and classical music in the coffeehouse/bar.

During off-hours, the bar becomes a large studio available to painters, dancers, writers, and other artists. And in July 1991, the Loring Café launched the Loring Playhouse, which presents theater and dance performances. An example of the work here was the 1991 presentation of Sartre's *No Exit* with a dance interpretation by a company known as Ballet of the Dolls.

But it's the culinary achievements of the Loring Café that have made everything else possible. Appetizers like *focaccia* served with roasted garlic bulb and French goat cheese are perennially popular. Main courses range from fresh vegetable sauté to veal loin chops with caramelized apples and calvados. And don't overlook the excellent pasta and pizza selections, the imaginative salads, and the long and excellent wine list.

INEXPENSIVE

DOWNTOWN

LOON CAFE, 500 1st Ave. N., Minneapolis. Tel. 332-8342.
  Cuisine: AMERICAN/MEXICAN. **Reservations:** Recommended.
  $ Prices: Appetizers $3–$7; main courses $4–$9. AE, DC, MC, V.
  Open: Mon–Sat 11am–1am, Sun 11am–midnight.
Downtown office workers and shoppers find this a good place for a quick lunch. The oblong burger served on a sourdough bun is popular, and so are the "championship chilis." There's also a selection of soups, salads, and sandwiches.

Primarily, though, this is a bar that sells food, not a restaurant that sells drinks, and the Loon really comes into its own in the evening, when it's one of the busiest, noisiest spots in this chic neighborhood. Taped music, overpowering when you walk in, soon subsides into the general din and somehow doesn't inhibit conversation. Celebrities, local and national, wander in from time to time: Bob Dylan, Morgan Fairchild, and others have been sighted at the Loon.

UPTOWN

LOTUS, 3037 Hennepin Ave., Minneapolis. Tel. 825-2263.
  Cuisine: VIETNAMESE. **Reservations:** Recommended.
  $ Prices: Appetizers $2.15–$3.85; main courses $5–$10. No credit cards.
  Open: Sun–Thurs 11am–10pm, Fri–Sat 11am–11pm.
Budget dining doesn't get any better than at Lotus. Don't be put off by the minimal decor at this casual, congenial spot. The white Oriental lamp shades are about as far as Le and Hieu

Tran went in 1983 when they decorated the first of what would become four busy neighborhood eating places.

Because sharing is encouraged, you can try a number of savory, nutritious dishes; everything from beginners' fare like chicken or beef with vegetables to less familiar selections such as curried mock duck sautéed with onion, garlic, and lemongrass and served in a spicy coconut gravy. The chow mein here is delectable—a hearty mixture of chicken, beef, and shrimp with crunchy slabs of cabbage, carrots, celery, onion, and broccoli that in no way resembles the gelatinous mound you find in many Chinese restaurants. The menu indicates which items are hotter than others, but the dishes can be adjusted to taste. You may have to wait for a table at the Lotus restaurants, but you'll be rewarded by the food.

You'll find other locations at 313 Oak St., Minneapolis (tel. 331-1781); 3907 W. 50th St., Edina (tel. 922-4254); 1917 E. Hwy. 13, Burnsville (tel. 890-5573); and 867 Grand Ave. in St. Paul (tel. 228-9156). Hours vary with each restaurant.

SOUTH

THE MALT SHOP, 809 W. 50th St. at Bryant, Minneapolis. Tel. 824-1352.

Cuisine: AMERICAN/INTERNATIONAL. **Reservations:** Not accepted.

$ **Prices:** Appetizers $2.50; main courses $3.95–$6.25. AE, DC, DISC, MC, V.

Open: Mon–Thurs 11am–10:30pm, Fri 11am–11pm, Sat 8:30am–11pm, Sun 8:30am–10:30pm.

Famous for its hamburgers and ice-cream desserts, The Malt Shop also offers an array of international specialties—everything from bird's-nest salad to feta salad. All soups, dressings, and sauces are made by The Malt Shop. "Gourmet hamburgers" come in many variations. Daily specials, served with soup or salad and a grilled onion roll, change every day. Popular box lunches include a sandwich, potato chips, fruit or feta salad, a chocolate-pecan cookie, and condiments and utensils for $5.45. Breakfast is served daily at another Malt Shop, at 1554 Concordia Ave., St. Paul (tel. 645-4643). A third Malt Shop is at Hwys. 7 and 101 in Minnetonka (tel. 474-2758).

MUD PIE VEGETARIAN RESTAURANT, 2549 Lyndale Ave. S., Minneapolis. Tel. 872-9435.

Cuisine: VEGETARIAN. **Reservations:** Accepted for 5 or more.

$ **Prices:** Salads $2.50–$8; main dishes $3–$10. MC, V.

Open: Mon–Thurs 11am–10pm, Fri 11am–11pm, Sat 8am–11pm, Sun 8am–10pm.

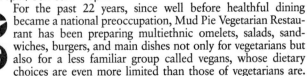

For the past 22 years, since well before healthful dining became a national preoccupation, Mud Pie Vegetarian Restaurant has been preparing multiethnic omelets, salads, sandwiches, burgers, and main dishes not only for vegetarians but also for a less familiar group called vegans, whose dietary choices are even more limited than those of vegetarians are.

But more and more during recent years, a growing number of other diners have discovered Mud Pie too, people who very much enjoy the flavor of the food they find in this small two-room restaurant with a mellow southwestern ambience; there's outdoor dining as well when weather permits. Featured dishes here include Arabic felafel sandwiches and tabbouleh salads along with Vietnamese mock duck and Indian rotti. And then there's the signature item, Mud Pie Veggie Burgers, now available in the freezer sections of groceries throughout the area. The comprehensive and surprisingly interesting Mud Pie menu uses symbols to indicate which items have had lactose-free soy sauce substituted for regular cheese and which can't be prepared without dairy products. The menu also notes that "vegetarian" is derived from the Latin word meaning "to enliven." Those wishing to enliven groups of folks can order whole pans of Mud Pie lasagne, cakes, and other foods.

NORA'S, 3118 W. Lake St., Minneapolis. Tel. 927-5781.
> **Cuisine:** AMERICAN. **Reservations:** Recommended.
> **$ Prices:** Appetizers $1.50–$2; main courses $5–$9. DISC, MC, V.
> **Open:** Daily 7am–10pm.

Among the perennial favorites at this popular restaurant are the homey decor, the remarkably low prices, and the attentive service. Fried chicken, fresh roast turkey, and tenderloin filets are only three of Nora's many claims to fame. Everything is made from scratch; specialties include popovers and real mashed potatoes. Fresh vegetables are served with every dish. You'll find a bountiful breakfast buffet here seven days a week from 7am to 11am. A second Nora's is at 2117 E. Lake St. (tel. 729-9353).

2. SOUTH SUBURBAN MINNEAPOLIS

EXPENSIVE

KINKAID'S, 8400 Normandale Lake Blvd., Bloomington. Tel. 921-2255.
> **Cuisine:** STEAK/SEAFOOD. **Reservations:** Recommended.
> **$ Prices:** Appetizers $5.50–$7.50; main courses $13.95–$26.95; Sun brunch $7.95–$13.95. AE, DISC, MC, V.
> **Open:** Lunch Mon–Sat 11am–2:30pm; dinner Mon–Thurs 5–9:30pm, Fri 5–10:30pm, Sat 4:30–10:30pm, Sun 5–9pm; Sun brunch 10am–2pm.

This beautifully appointed steak-and-seafood house is an elegant assemblage of marble, brass chandeliers, and cherry-wood furnishings. Kinkaid's offers a choice of top-notch steaks, chops, and mesquite-grilled fish, along with pasta, soups, and desserts.

Luncheon main courses, served with vegetable and herb bread, range from $7.50 for fish-and-chips to $12 for boneless New York steak. The dinner menu, which includes a lengthy wine list, carries a money-back guarantee that your steaks, chops, and roasts will be moist, flavorful, and tender. An elegant back bar has a dining area of its own, and a separate bar features fresh oysters flown in daily from the East Coast, West Coast, Canada, and New Zealand. Desserts are delicious too.

MODERATE

COCOLEZZONE, 5410 Wayzata Blvd., Golden Valley. Tel. 544-4014.

Cuisine: NORTHERN ITALIAN. **Reservations:** Recommended.

$ Prices: Appetizers $4–$8; main courses $7–$27; pizza $5–$8. AE, DC, MC, V.

Open: Lunch Mon–Fri 11am–5pm, Sat 11am–1pm, Sun 11am–2:30pm; dinner Mon–Thurs 5–10pm, Fri–Sat 5–11pm, Sun 5–9:30pm.

The next best thing to a trip to Italy is a meal at CocoLezzone. Named for a popular trattoria in Florence, this large, lively, and very beautiful spot was an instant success when it opened in June 1985. With marble floors and a plenitude of imported artifacts, CocoLezzone is an altogether delightful place.

Because northern Italian fare is featured here, be prepared to see, along with the usual tomato-laden toppings, such relatively unfamiliar sights as seafood pizza and pizza with spinach, cheese, and a cooked egg in the center.

Dining here can be very expensive or inexpensive, depending on how you approach the lengthy à la carte menu. Sharing is encouraged by the helpful waiters, who will explain the traditional succession of the Italian courses. The lunchtime menu lists a variety of antipasti, or you may prefer to select your own assortment from the tempting display case. Next comes the pizza, followed by soups, *primi* (a selection of pastas), meat, fish, and, finally, salad—for reasons of digestion, you'll be told.

DA AFGHAN, 929 W. 80 St., Bloomington. Tel. 888-5824.

Cuisine: AFGHANI. **Reservations:** Recommended.

$ Prices: Appetizers $4.25–$7.95; main courses $7.95–$16.95; lunch $4.50–$10.95. MC, V.

Open: Lunch Mon–Fri 11am–2:30pm; dinner Mon–Thurs 5–9:30pm; Fri–Sat 5–10:30pm.

You're in for a wide diversity of tastes at Da Afghan. Although many of the dishes feature shrimp, beef, lamb, and chicken, vegetarians will find a lot to enjoy as well. An appetizer listed as *pakawra*—potatoes, eggplant, and zucchini fried in a specially seasoned batter—is particularly delicious. Among the main courses, served with or without meat, try *bahnjean bouranee,* eggplant cooked with tomatoes and spices, served in *korma* sauce, topped with homemade garlic, yogurt sour-cream sauce, and dry mint. In addition to main courses, you'll have a wide choice here among sandwiches and kebabs, along with Afghani-style pizza and a large tossed salad featuring homemade Afghani cheese. The ambience here is noteworthy too—colorful rugs, serving trays, and costumes hang on the wall; soft Middle Eastern music provides a

FROMMER'S COOL FOR KIDS: RESTAURANTS

Lake Elmo Inn *(see p. 91)* Each child gets a celophane-wrapped four-pack of crayons as well as a choice of placemats on which to color or connect the dots. The popular junior menu features hamburgers, cheeseburgers, and corn dogs, all accompanied by French fries.

Marie Callender's Restaurant & Bakery *(see below)* Balloons await children as they arrive here, although some parents prefer to have their kids pick a balloon as a going-away present after dining. There's a good choice of hamburgers and cheeseburgers as well as a salad bar that kids enjoy. They also have fun using the placemat and crayons that accompany all children's meals.

W. A. Frost and Company *(see p. 89)* Children are welcome to choose among a wide variety of coloring books and crayons for use on the premises. Children's menu items include corn dogs, pasta, and, of course, soda pop.

pleasant background. Da Afghan can be difficult to find, so call ahead for directions.

MARIE CALLENDER'S RESTAURANT & BAKERY, 50 E. County Rd. 42 at Nicollet Ave. Tel. 435-2880.
   Cuisine: AMERICAN. **Reservations:** Recommended for large parties, especially on Sun.
$ Prices: Appetizers $4–$6.50; main courses $7–$13 (including soup-and-salad bar). AE, MC, V.
   Open: Mon–Thurs 11am–10pm, Fri 11am–11pm; Sat 9am–11pm, Sun 9am–10pm; brunch Sat–Sun 9am–2pm. **Closed:** Christmas.

You'll find Minnesota's only Marie Callender Restaurant & Bakery located in suburban Burnsville, not far from Cobblestone Court, Burnsville Marketplace, and Burnsville Shopping Center. Designed inside and out to resemble a comfortable country home, this attractive restaurant is busy seven days a week, as its crowded parking lot indicates. The waiting time, though, tends to be brief, and the food well worth waiting for. Hand-carved turkey, served in three ways, is a special favorite here. Choose a traditional oven roasted turkey lunch or dinner, served with stuffing, gravy, mashed potatoes, and vegetable; or, if you prefer, select turkey Caesar salad or a turkey sandwich on focaccia. A delicious assortment of homemade soups, pasta dishes, and burgers, along with comfort food like meat loaf, pot roast, and fish-and-chips, makes it difficult to save room for the baked goods that first started this 16-state network of restaurant/bakeries. Reportedly it was her Long Beach, California, neighbors who, in the mid-1940s, persuaded

Marie Callender to market the pies she'd shared with them at local get-togethers. Marie Callender's fruit pies are still baked in California and shipped nationwide for sale in restaurants and groceries. Particularly popular hereabouts is Marie's razzleberry pie, a mix of raspberries and blackberries. Kahlúa cream pie is a favorite too. And so, of course, are the other baked goods for sale on the premises.

Wines and drinks are available from a full bar in the back of the restaurant. And there's an ample salad bar as well. Children have a menu of their own, and grown-ups with small appetites can order half a portion for slightly more than half the price.

MINNESOTA STEAKHOUSE, 13050 Aldrich Ave. S., Burnsville. Tel. 890-4350.
  Cuisine: AMERICAN. **Reservations:** Accepted for 8 or more.
$ **Prices:** Appetizers $4.45–$6.95; main courses $8.95–$18.95. (Early dining specials $7.95–$8.95.) AE, DC, DISC, MC, V.
  Open: Dinner Sun–Thurs 4–10pm, Fri–Sat 4pm–midnight.
  Closed: Thanksgiving Day and Christmas.

The hours are limited in this popular steak house, but the enthusiasm of local diners for the food and drink awaiting them here is apparently unlimited. From 4pm each day, the parking lot of the Minnesota Steakhouse is filled with the automobiles of habitués who know that the later they arrive, the more likely they are to wait for a table. (A 4 to 7pm two-for-one Happy Hour may also be a factor in the early arrivals.)

There's a Minnesota North Woods ambience here, the sort of setting in which the legendary lumberjack Paul Bunyan would have felt at home. The first Minnesota Steakhouse in the country was opened here in September 1991 by Doron Jensen, whose clergyman father was widely known as radio host for Lutheran Vespers. (The grandfather of Doron and his younger brother Derek, who manages the kitchen and trains personnel, had owned and operated a restaurant in Fremont, Nebraska; in this family, choosing a career as a restaurateur skipped a generation.)

While prime rib, ranging in price from $10.95 to $16.95, is the most frequently ordered item here, filet mignon and top sirloin steak come close. Also popular are walleye pike and grilled chicken. First though you might want to consider an appetizer, for example an onion named for Paul Bunyan; it resembles a huge crysanthemum and has a dish containing a special secret sauce set in the middle of the "petals." Within the first two years of its opening, the Minnesota Steakhouse in Burnsville had been joined by two others in the suburban Twin Cities as well as by one in Duluth and two in upstate New York at Buffalo and Niagara Falls. There are, of course, plans to expand even farther. (The other suburban Minnesota Steakhouses are at 16396 Wagner Way, Eden Prairie (tel. 937-7629), and Snelling Avenue at County Road B, Roseville (tel. 628-0350).

THE OLIVE GARDEN, 1451 W. County Rd. 42, Burnsville. Tel. 898-4200.
  Cuisine: ITALIAN. **Reservations:** Recommended.
$ **Prices:** Appetizers $3.45–$5.50; main courses $7.25–$11.95; pasta $6.50–$9.95; lunch $3.95–$6.25. AE, DC, DISC, MC, V.

Open: Lunch daily 11am–4pm; dinner Sun–Thurs 4–10pm, Fri–Sat 4–11pm.

If you liked the Olive Garden restaurants you've encountered before, chances are good that you'll be pleased with the ones you visit in the Twin Cities. The one in Burnsville is a particular favorite with folks living south of the Minnesota River and with shoppers at the nearby Burnsville Shopping Center. The manager of this branch, Tim Hall, reports that veal piccata, chicken marsala, and chicken Florentine are particular favorites, along with cannelloni and lasagne. At lunchtime, one of the best buys here would have to be the specialties that include a main course—everything from spaghetti with tomato sauce to pasta and seafood—and a choice of soup or salad and garlic breadsticks for $3.95 to $5.85. Desserts are worth mentioning too: Try the scrumptious cannoli, a pastry shell filled with cream and topped with powdered sugar.

STEAK AND ALE, 2801 Southtown Dr., Bloomington. Tel. 884-0124.

Cuisine: AMERICAN. **Reservations:** Recommended.

$ Prices: Appetizers $4–$5; main courses $10–$19.

Open: Lunch Mon–Sat 11am–2:30pm; dinner Mon–Thurs 4:30–10pm, Fri–Sat 4:30–11pm, Sun noon–10pm.

Consistency is one of the main virtues of Steak and Ale, a local landmark since 1976. During all these years, this handsome dining place, overlooking I-494 from its vantage point on a rise in suburban Bloomington, has been consistent in the quality and variety of fine fare offered at surprisingly moderate prices. Reminiscent in decor and cuisine of the British pubs that served generations of Britons, Steak and Ale remains the site of choice for business and social get-togethers. By now a second generation of local folks gather here to celebrate graduations, weddings, anniversaries, and other stellar events. Prime rib remains high among favorite dishes and French onion soup and baked stuffed mushrooms are among the most popular starters. Other popular selections include flavorful beef and seafood combinations such as lobster tails and top sirloin ($18.95); blackened snapper ($9.95) and Hawaiian chicken served in two sizes ($7.95 and $9.95) are among relatively recent favorites. Most main dishes come with vegetable, warm bread, baked potato or rice pilaf, plus choice of Caesar salad or the ample salad bar. There are seven dining rooms and a lounge where entertainment is offered from Wednesday to Saturday evenings. Children have their own menu, and grown-ups their own wine and beer list. Desserts are for everybody, particularly perhaps the do-it-yourself 3-Step Brownie Blowout.

INEXPENSIVE

OLD COUNTRY BUFFET, 9 E. 66th St., Richfield. Tel. 869-1911.

Cuisine: AMERICAN. **Reservations:** Accepted only for large groups.

$ Prices: Breakfast $5.30; lunch $5.25; dinner $6.80. No credit cards.

Open: Mon–Sat 7am–9:30pm, Sun 9am–7pm.

Pearson's features the kind of down-home cooking that many Minnesotans grew up with. Brothers Paul and Marston Pearson, the second-generation owners, share responsibility for the restaurant which their parents opened in 1973 as a coffee shop. That small diner has since been joined by the Oak Room and the Oak Room West, two elegant, handsomely paneled dining rooms with large stone fireplaces and brass chandeliers.

Local families enjoy Pearson's because the menu is varied enough so that everyone can find something to his or her liking, including the basic hamburger, omelets, or salads. Breakfasts are well under $5, and most lunches and dinners are under $10. Swedish meatballs, baked chicken, and roast prime rib rank high among the favorites here; and the pastries, soups, salad dressings, and dinner rolls all deserve high marks.

3. ST. PAUL & ENVIRONS

EXPENSIVE

DOWNTOWN

GREAT NORTHERN SUPPER CLUB, Galtier Plaza, 175 E. 5th St., St. Paul. Tel. 224-2720.
   Cuisine AMERICAN. **Reservations:** Recommended.
$ Prices: Appetizers $5.95–$7.95; main courses $13.95–$21.95. AE, DC, MC, V.
   Open: Lunch Mon–Fri 11am–2:30pm; dinner Mon–Thurs 5pm–10pm, Fri–Sat 5pm–11pm. **Closed:** Sunday.

Located in historic Galtier Plaza, this handsome restaurant is at once spacious and intimate. Here you'll find traditional American cuisine with a contemporary touch, from great northern bean soup to white chocolate custard with raspberry sauce. Enjoy!

THE SAINT PAUL GRILL, 350 Market St., St. Paul. Tel. 292-9292.
   Cuisine: AMERICAN. **Reservations:** Recommended.
$ Prices: Appetizers $4.95–$8.75; main courses $9.50–$24; lunch $3.50–$6.95; Sun brunch $7.50–$11.50. AE, DC, DISC, MC, V.
   Open: Lunch Mon–Sat 11:30am–2pm; dinner Tues–Sat 5:30–11pm, Sun–Mon 5:30–10pm; Sun brunch 11am–2pm. Late-night menu until midnight daily.

Located on the ground floor of the distinguished Saint Paul Hotel, the Saint Paul Grill overlooks tiny, picturesque Rice Park, which is flanked by three other famous buildings as well—the St. Paul Central Library, the Ordway Music Theatre, and the Landmark Center. Popular with business, professional, and political figures at lunchtime, the Saint Paul Grill is the natural choice for dinner at any time, but particularly when something exciting is happening across the park at the Ordway Theatre. In those instances, manager Patricia Lovegreen advises reservations as early as two weeks in advance. The decor is similar to what you might have found in Chicago and New York grills during the 1920s and 1930s. Opaque ribbed glass set upon mahogany panels separates the booths, giving diners a nice amount of privacy. Whether at a booth or a table, though, what matters most is that you can be assured of the highest quality of fare and service.

Signature items include the sourdough bread and the red flannel roast beef hash, made with prime rib, beets, potato, and topped with an egg. Three specials are offered each week, with a daily change of potato and soup, a different vegetable each day, and a different fresh grill item. The superlative desserts change, too, thanks to pastry chef Lisa Steinhauer.

NORTHERN SUBURB

KOZLAK'S ROYAL OAK RESTAURANT, 4785 Hodgson Rd., Shoreview. Tel. 484-8484.
Cuisine: AMERICAN. **Reservations:** Recommended.
$ Prices: Appetizers $4.50–$8.95; main courses $13.95–$25.95; lunch $6–$9. AE, CB, DC, DISC, V.
Open: Lunch Mon–Sat 11am–2:30pm; dinner Mon–Thurs 4–9:30pm, Fri–Sat 4–10:30pm; Sun brunch 10am–1:30pm.

Whether you're seated indoors in one of the handsome dining rooms overlooking the outdoor gardens or outside on the veranda, you'll be pleased by the attentive service and reliable cuisine that has distinguished this restaurant for decades.

Four-course jazz brunches are particularly popular here, where your tab will depend on the dish you select. The main courses range from eggs Benedict to veal and fettuccine to "brunch steak." The meal is modeled on the jazz brunches offered at Brennan's in New Orleans. Main courses are complemented by a trip to the salad bar or, if you choose, a house salad or a cup of the Boston clam chowder.

MODERATE

DOWNTOWN

CAFE MINNESOTA BY BON APPETIT, Minnesota History Center, 345 W. Kellogg Blvd., St. Paul. Tel. 297-4097.
Cuisine: ECLECTIC. **Reservations:** Not accepted.
$ Prices: Soups $2.75; salads $4.75; sandwiches $3.95. Grill $4.25; main courses $4.95–$5.25.
Open: Continental breakfast Mon–Fri 8am–10am; lunch Mon–Fri 11:30am–2pm; desserts 2–3pm; brunch Sun 11:30am–3pm.
Closed: Dec 24, Christmas, New Year's Day.

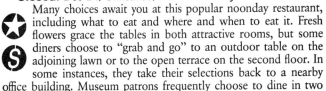

Many choices await you at this popular noonday restaurant, including what to eat and where and when to eat it. Fresh flowers grace the tables in both attractive rooms, but some diners choose to "grab and go" to an outdoor table on the adjoining lawn or to the open terrace on the second floor. In some instances, they take their selections back to a nearby office building. Museum patrons frequently choose to dine in two stages, delaying dessert until after they've visited the exhibits on the upper floors of this handsome historical center which is itself a work of art. As you enter the Heffelfinger Room at the front of Cafe Minnesota, you'll see a display of selections of the day—soups, salads, and sandwiches along with items from the grill and the carvery. Trio salads are a great favorite here, providing three sample-size choices among the half dozen or so salads of the day—everything from tuna niçoise to marinated mushroom salad with roasted tomatoes to curried rice with coconut, shrimp, and yogurt dressing. A perennial favorite at the Chef's Carvery is slow-roasted turkey breast with soufflé potatoes. The menu changes weekly, so there's always some element of adventure involved.

CAROUSEL, Radisson Hotel, 11 E. Kellogg Blvd., St. Paul. Tel. 292-1900.
   Cuisine: AMERICAN. **Reservations:** Recommended.
$ **Prices:** Appetizers $2.95–$5.50, main courses $6.50–$18.95. AE, CB, DC, DISC, MC, V.
   Open: Breakfast Mon–Fri 6:30–11am, Sat 7–11am, Sun 7am–noon; lunch Mon–Sat 11am–5pm, Sun noon–5pm; dinner Mon–Thurs 5–10:30pm, Fri–Sat 5–11pm; Sun jazz brunch 10am–2pm.

There's a lot to enjoy at the Carousel, located on the 22nd floor of the Radisson Hotel St. Paul. You'll find the most spectacular view of downtown St. Paul and the Mississippi River. Moreover, the central portion of this handsome dining room revolves almost imperceptibly so that from your table you'll be able to view the complete circle within a 45-minute period. But restaurants must be judged primarily on their cuisine, and the important news here is that despite a change in name and menu on March 1, 1994, longtime executive chef Ronald Bohnert remains at the helm of a restaurant which now serves breakfast, lunch, and dinner 365 days a year. Working witn Bohnert to forge a lighter ambience and a lighter assortment of foods has been general manager Eric Aune.

The opportunity to have breakfast in such sumptuous surroundings has attracted hotel guests and locals alike, many of whom sing the praises of a menu item called "Chef Ron's Famous French Toast"—thick slices of French bread dipped in egg batter and then grilled. It's served with a unique syrup containing raisins, apples, walnuts, and other goodies. At lunchtime and at dinner, you can enjoy one of the most popular specialties of this house, pecan walleye, a filet dipped in egg-and-pecan flour and served with toasted maple pecan butter and wild rice. While this item and a few others appear on both the luncheon and dinner menus, you'll have to come to the Carousel in the evening for their famous beef Wellington. Another reason to dine here in the evening, of course, is the spectacular dinnertime view.

Housed in a hotel that accommodates guests from all over the world, the Carousel routinely serves foreign visitors. Personnel also note with satisfaction that a large proportion of their guests first came here on prom night and have been returning for wedding anniversaries and other important milestones ever since. There's enough in the way of tradition to provide a sense of continuity, but there's also attention here to interesting innovation in methods of preparing and presenting foods. A number of interesting pasta dishes have been introduced along with delectable desserts like lemon raspberry roulade, one of my own personal favorites. Value, variety, and ambience don't combine more effectively anywhere than at this deservedly famous restaurant.

FOREPAUGH'S RESTAURANT, 276 S. Exchange St., St. Paul. Tel. 224-5606.

Cuisine: FRENCH. **Reservations:** Recommended.
$ Prices: Appetizers $3.50–$8.75; main courses $11.95–$17.75; lunch $5.95–$8.75; brunch $11.75. AE, MC, V.
Open: Lunch Mon–Fri 11:30am–2pm; dinner Mon–Sat 5:30–9:30pm, Sun 5–8:30pm; Sun brunch 10:30am–1:30pm.

One of the loveliest Victorian houses in the Twin Cities, Forepaugh's is also one of its finest French restaurants. Built in 1870 by businessman Joseph Lybrandt Forepaugh, this three-story mansion faces the home of Alexander Ramsey, first territorial governor of Minnesota. Now listed on the National Register of Historic Places, both houses are popular with visitors seeking fine examples of Victorian architecture and decor.

At Forepaugh's there are nine lovely dining rooms, each named for a past governor of Minnesota. From the Pillsbury Room you can enjoy a panoramic view of downtown St. Paul; in the Olson Room you can admire the richness of fine mahogany paneling; and in the Sibley Room you'll see historic photos of Victorian tea parties. The state fish takes on a delectably French aspect here in a dish called walleye à la meunière; New York sirloin, prepared to taste with a tangy green peppercorn sauce, is a favorite too. Main courses are served with salad, potato, and vegetable.

GALLIVAN'S, 354 Wabasha St., St. Paul. Tel. 227-6688.

Cuisine: AMERICAN. **Reservations:** Recommended.
$ Prices: Appetizers $4.50–$7.95; main courses $7.95–$35.95; lunch $4.95–$9.95. AE, DISC, MC, V.
Open: Mon–Sat 11am–1am.

This St. Paul landmark is comprised of three separate dining rooms with an adjoining bar and lounge. The spacious main dining room features dark woods and subdued lighting; the intimate library boasts bookshelves stocked with biographies, law books, and encyclopedias.

The loyal clientele here is composed largely of folks who work in the neighborhood—lawyers, judges, and civil servants from the nearby courthouse and city hall. The prices may prove a pleasant surprise to first timers. Main courses, which include a choice of soup or salad and a choice of potato, range from filet mignon to scaloppine of pork tenderloin. If you're a liver lover like me, you'll adore the broiled baby beef liver with bacon and onions; the broiled walleye pike is a favorite too. There's a long wine and liquor list.

MIDWAY AREA

DAKOTA BAR AND GRILL, 1021 E. Bandana Blvd., St. Paul. Tel. 642-1442.

Cuisine: AMERICAN. **Reservations:** Recommended.
$ **Prices:** Appetizers $4–$9; main courses $9–$18. AE, DC, DISC, V.
Open: Dinner Mon–Thurs 5:30–10:30pm, Fri–Sat 5:30–11:30pm, Sun 5:30–9:30pm; Sun brunch 10:30am–2:30pm.

The accent is all-American at the Dakota Bar and Grill, a gathering place that's won many local awards. The daily menu features a full complement of seafood, beef, chicken, lamb, and pork, along with tasty vegetarian dishes that have converted many a carnivore. Most dishes are made with ingredients from Minnesota and Wisconsin.

Executive chef Ken Goff's imaginative use of spices and garnishes excels in popular items like brie-and-apple soup. Another popular creation is fresh walleye in a toasted wild rice crust with cucumber-tarragon tartar sauce.

The fabulous desserts include a tart cherry rice pudding with almond crust and caramel and—if calories are no object—chocolate mousse with strawberry cream. For lunch, consider fresh salmon hash with wild rice, sweet peppers, and mint or grilled smoked ham with raspberry-rhubarb sauce. The Sunday brunch buffet features muffins, granola, coffee cakes, yogurt, and several hot dishes. Outdoor dining is popular here during spring, summer, and early fall, when flowering shrubs enhance the setting.

GRAND AVENUE

ACROPOL INN, 748 Grand Ave., St. Paul. Tel. 298-0151.
Cuisine: GREEK/AMERICAN. **Reservations:** Recommended.
$ **Prices:** Appetizers $4.95–$5.95; main courses $8.95–$12.95; lunch $5–$9. MC, V.
Open: Mon–Thurs 11am–9pm, Fri–Sat 11am–10pm. Closed Sunday.

For more than a decade, one of the most popular ethnic restaurants in the Twin Cities has been the Acropol Inn. Lamb is a favorite here; so are seafood, beef, and chicken dishes prepared American style. But mostly it's the authentic Greek dishes that keep people coming back again and again—everything from moussaka (ground meat, fried eggplant, and a special topping) to dolmas (ground meat and rice wrapped in grape leaves and topped with lemon sauce) to stefado (beef in wine sauce with potatoes and onions). The Greek salads, enhanced with imported feta cheese and olive oil, are delectable too. Dinner main courses include soup, salad, and homemade bread.

LEXINGTON, 1096 Grand Ave., St. Paul. Tel. 222-5878.
Cuisine: AMERICAN. **Reservations:** Recommended.
$ **Prices:** Appetizers $3.95–$7.95; main courses $7.95–$25.95; lunch $5.95–$8.95. AE, CB, DC, MC, V.
Open: Mon–Thurs 11am–10pm, Fri–Sat 11am–midnight; Sun brunch 10am–3pm; Sun dinner 4–9pm.

Located a few miles from downtown St. Paul, the Lexington is an institution in the Twin Cities; elegant and gracious, sprawling yet intimate, this restaurant has a reputation for fine food, beautiful surroundings, and reasonable prices. It started out decades ago as a one-room tavern serving steak sandwiches and hamburgers and has since evolved into a 360-seat restaurant with an extensive menu. You'll find traditional American fare like New York sirloin, spring lamb chops, fresh walleye almondine, and barbecued ribs. Main courses are served with a choice of potato and salad. There are five different desserts served each night, ranging from bread pudding with homemade caramel sauce to cheesecake.

The setting is as carefully designed as the menu: dark polished woods, crystal chandeliers, fine oil paintings, and a variety of rare artifacts. You won't find a lovelier setting, friendlier service, or finer food than that of the Lexington.

CATHEDRAL AREA

TULIPS, 452 Selby Ave., St. Paul. Tel. 221-1061.
  Cuisine: FRENCH. **Reservations:** Recommended.
$ Prices: Appetizers $3.95–$4.95; main courses $9.95–$18.95; lunch $3.95–$8.95. AE, DC, DISC, MC, V.
  Open: Lunch Mon–Fri 11:30am–3pm; dinner Mon–Sun 5–9pm.
In a small restaurant that's been voted "most romantic" by a local newspaper, Angela and Bob Piper offer a French cuisine that's hearty, nourishing, and tasty. Background music features the likes of Ella Fitzgerald at lunchtime and classical music in the evening. Table-cloths and the paintings of local artists brighten the three small dining rooms. Menu items include "heart healthy" dishes like chicken Minceur (chicken dusted with three peppers, garlic, and lemon wedges) for $8.95 and traditional French dishes like médaillons of tenderloin with beurre café de Paris (garlic, parsley, and pepper) for $14.95. Vegetarian dishes such as cheese ravioli with artichokes, olive oil, and butter for $9.95 also appear on every menu. All main courses are served with fresh vegetables. Desserts change regularly, though some, like flan with caramel sauce, make frequent appearances.

W. A. FROST AND COMPANY, 374 Selby Ave., St. Paul. Tel. 224-5715.
  Cuisine: AMERICAN. **Reservations:** Recommended.
$ Prices: Appetizers $6.95–$8; main courses $9.95–$18.95. AE, DC, DISC, MC, V.
  Open: Lunch Mon–Sat 11am–2pm; dinner daily 5–10:30pm; Sun brunch 10:30am–2pm; Sun dinner 5–10:30pm.
The ambience of bygone days dominates here, with tin Victorian ceilings, marble tables, Oriental rugs, and illuminated oil landscapes that date back to the turn of the century. There are also two functioning fireplaces, a popular feature during the winter months. As the seasons change, though, diners look forward to some of the Twin Cities' most picturesque outdoor dining, amid flowering bushes and trailing vines and under a living canopy of trees.

Favorite appetizers include the savory smoked salmon and cream-cheese torte and crispy Chinese chicken wings. A wide range of seafood is served here, everything from walleye to monkfish. And there's a variety of beef, chicken, and pasta dishes, all of which include potato and fresh vegetable. You'll also find one of the largest selections of imported beers and fine liquors in the area. At this fine restaurant people customarily come just as they are; don't be surprised to see casually clad diners.

MACALESTER/GROVELAND

KHYBER PASS CAFE, 1399 St. Clair Ave., St. Paul. Tel. 698-5403.
   Cuisine: AFGHANI. **Reservations:** Recommended for parties of five or more.
$ **Prices:** Appetizers $1.95–$2.95; main courses $5.25–$11.25; lunch $4.95–$7.25. No credit cards.
   Open: Lunch Tues–Sat 11am–2pm; dinner Tues–Sat 5–9pm.

Faculty members and students from nearby Macalester College and the University of St. Thomas make up more than half the regular diners here. Afghani articles decorate the white walls and Afghani music provides an exotic background in the comfortable dining room. Owner Masooda Amini Sherzad, who does all the cooking, explains that unlike other Middle Eastern or Indian cuisines, Afghani cooking uses fewer and milder spices and aims to enhance rather than overpower the food's natural perfume. Chicken, lamb, and vegetarian dishes are among the favorites here. One popular selection is the *kebob-e murgh,* chunks of boneless chicken cooked on a skewer and served with tomatoes, onions, and chutney; *korma-e sabzee* is a delicious spinach dish served with chunks of lamb; *korma-e dahl,* another popular item, features chunks of lamb with yellow lentils cooked in onions and garlic.

A full dinner, served with *basmati* rice, salad, chutney, and flat bread, runs from $6.75 to $11.25. Desserts are delicious. If you like puddings, you're bound to enjoy the *firni;* it's rich and creamy and flavored with a blend of cardamom, rosewater, and pistachios. Do try one of the special teas and, if you're a yogurt lover, try a glass of Dogh, plain yogurt diluted with water, mixed with cucumber, and garnished with mint. Finally, there's live traditional music every Friday night from 6 to 9pm (no cover charge).

RISTORANTE LUCI, 470 S. Cleveland Ave., St. Paul. Tel. 699-8258.
   Cuisine: ITALIAN. **Reservations:** Strongly recommended.
$ **Prices:** Appetizers $4.95–$6.95; pasta $5.95–$9.25; main courses $9.85–$13.95. MC, V.
   Open: Dinner Mon–Thurs 5–9:30pm, Fri–Sat 5–10:30pm, Sun 4:30–9pm.

The decor of this very popular restaurant is simple—white walls, black wrought-iron light fixtures, and white tablecloths. The menu, which changes four times a year, is divided into sections for antipasti, soup, salad, pasta, and meat or fish. There's also a four-course "taster's dinner," which includes the day's antipasti, pasta, and fish special with a choice of soup or salad, all in reduced portions. All flat pasta as well as desserts and bread are made on the premises; and all the mozzarella cheese is made in-house from fresh curd. Featured on the menu are antipasti like bruschetta con pecorino fresco (grilled home-baked bread with fresh goat cheese and dill), gazpacho

Neapolitan style, rigatoni alla bolognese (with ground veal, lamb, and beef simmered with tomatoes, red wine, and fresh herbs), and linguine alla puttanesca (fresh tomatoes, olive oil, garlic, Calamata olives, and capers). *Secondi* (meat and fish courses) include pollo piacere (sautéed chicken breast) prepared several ways. And then there are the sweets—Luci cheesecake, flourless chocolate torte (made daily with Belgian chocolate), and a variety of fruit tarts. There is an extensive wine list.

EASTERN SUBURB

LAKE ELMO INN, 3442 Lake Elmo Ave., Lake Elmo. Tel. 777-8495.
   Cuisine: AMERICAN. **Reservations:** Recommended.
$ Prices: Appetizers $3.75–$6.50; main courses $10.95–$22.95; Sun brunch $12.95 for adults, $6.95 for children. AE, DC, DISC, MC, V.
   Open: Lunch Mon–Sat 11am–2pm; dinner Mon–Sat 5–10pm, Sun 4:30–8:30pm; Sun brunch 10am–2pm.

Specialties here include a flavorful assortment of soups; my own favorite is the Minnesota wild rice and duck soup. Among the dinnertime dishes, there's a particularly attractive vegetarian plate featuring stuffed tomato with fresh spinach, wild rice, a medley of vegetables, stuffed mushrooms, asparagus, and linguine. Or try the salmon Wellington, a filet beautifully prepared with spinach and wrapped in puff pastry. The chicken Alfredo is a winning combination of *mostaccioli,* chicken, and parmesan cream sauce. Desserts here are spectacular, particularly during the Sunday "champagne brunch," when 20 or so are presented for your selection.

NORTHERN SUBURB

VENETIAN INN, 2814 Rice St., Little Canada. Tel. 484-7215.
   Cuisine: ITALIAN/AMERICAN. **Reservations:** Recommended.
$ Prices: Appetizers $3.25–$6.95; main courses $7.95–$21.95. AE, CB, DC, DISC, MC, V.
   Open: Lunch daily 11am–3pm; dinner Mon–Thurs 3–9pm, Fri–Sat 3–10pm.

About five miles north of downtown St. Paul, this restaurant is readily accessible to both of the Twin Cities. The location was largely rural when Congie and Joe Vitale first opened a vegetable stand on this site years ago. Today, after a succession of remodelings, the dining room seats 300 people, with room for 600 in the banquet halls. And nearly 200 more attend performances in the Venetian Playhouse.

You'll be offered a bib with your order of ribs or pasta, both of which rank high with the regulars. Seafood is a specialty, along with Italian dinners including veal scaloppine, eggplant parmigiana, and chicken cacciatore. Dinner includes an antipasto tray, tossed salad, and Italian bread; some dishes also include a side of spaghetti or baked potato. Main courses range from rigatoni with meatballs to a seafood platter that includes haddock, stuffed shrimp, whitefish, scallops, and lobster tail.

INEXPENSIVE

DOWNTOWN

WABASHA DELI & CAFE, 32 Filmore Ave. E., St. Paul. Tel. 291-8868.
Cuisine: DELI.
$ Prices: Breakfast $1.20–$2.70; lunch $1–$3.40. No credit cards.
Open: Mon–Thurs 6am–5:30pm, Fri 6am–2pm.

Whether you're interested in a ham-and-cheese omelet at breakfast time or a roast beef and Swiss croissant for lunch, the neat and friendly Wabasha Deli & Café is a very good bet. You'll be dining among state workers from nearby offices as well as neighborhood folks.

This is the only restaurant in town where you can find the full line of breads made by the nearby Baldinger Bakery, which supplies some of the finest restaurants in town. A rack in the dining room displays the loaves on hand; others—multigrain, caraway, you name it—are available in short order. You can also order take-out box lunches for less than $5 each, fruit and muffin trays for $4, and fruit baskets for $10 to $30 depending on the size.

GRAND AVENUE

CAFE LATTE, 850 Grand Ave., St. Paul. Tel. 224-5687.
Cuisine: SOUP/SANDWICHES/SALAD/DESSERTS. **Reservations:** Not accepted.
$ Prices: Salads $3.50–$4.75; sandwiches $3.75–$4.75; soups $2–$3.75. AE, V.
Open: Mon–Thurs 10am–11pm, Fri 10am–midnight, Sat 9am–midnight, Sun 9am–10pm.

You'll probably find a line at Café Latte, but don't hesitate to join the crowd. For the past eight years, this small restaurant has been providing the best in delicious and nutritious soups, sandwiches, and salads, along with some of the richest, most irresistible desserts in the entire Twin Cities area. Selections change each day, with the listing posted on a board near the doorway. Of the 100 varieties of bread baked on the premises here, four or five are offered every day. You'll have your choice as well among four different kinds of soup along with a stew and the ever-present chicken chili, which may be a bit hot for some palates. Make sure you leave room for dessert. In fact, after-theater crowds testify to the lure of Café Latte's cakes, tortes, fruit tarts, and espresso. You can buy a whole cake for $17 to $22 or settle for an individual serving for $2.25 to $2.95.

CHAPTER 7

WHAT TO SEE & DO IN THE TWIN CITIES

- **DID YOU KNOW . . . ?**
1. **THE TOP ATTRACTIONS**
2. **MORE ATTRACTIONS**
3. **COOL FOR KIDS**
4. **ORGANIZED TOURS**
5. **SPORTS & RECREATION**

The vitality of the Twin Cities is reflected in its ever-changing blend of the old and the new, not only in downtown areas but suburban ones as well. In St. Paul, a new, larger, and more comprehensive Children's Museum moved from Bandana Square to the very heart of the city. In suburban Bloomington, the Mall of America now occupies ground where tailgaters used to celebrate summertime in Minnesota before games at Metropolitan Stadium got underway.

Many of the Twin Cities proudest buildings, like the splendid mansions on St. Paul's Summit Avenue, have been listed on the National Register of Historic Places; other buildings, newer than tomorrow, will dazzle you with their soaring expanses of reflective glass. Don't miss Gaviidae Common, City Center, and Philip Johnson's award-winning IDS Tower in downtown Minneapolis. Be sure to visit the World Trade Center, not far from the state capitol in downtown St. Paul. The noted art collections in the Twin Cities are often housed in buildings that are themselves works of art.

The lakes of Minneapolis and St. Paul are legendary, not only for their beauty but for the many popular activities that take place there throughout the year.

SUGGESTED ITINERARIES

IF YOU HAVE ONE DAY From downtown Minneapolis, drive through South Minneapolis via Portland Avenue to Minnehaha Parkway, then drive east to Minnehaha Park for a view of the beautiful Minnehaha Falls and the statue of the young couple immortalized by Longfellow's famous poem. Visit the nearby historic Stevens House, then continue by going south on Hiawatha Avenue which will lead you to Highway 62. Look for signs for Fort Snelling. (En route you'll pass the huge U.S. Veterans Hospital.) Tour the restored Fort Snelling, at the confluence of the Minnesota and Mississippi rivers, taking time if possible to visit the museum on the site and to view the historical film.

?DID YOU KNOW . . . ?

- The first children's department in an American public library was established in Minneapolis in 1893; the first children's librarian arrived a year later.

- The University of Minnesota opened the country's first authorized university school of nursing in 1908.

- Minnesota issues more fishing licenses per capita than any other state.

- Cardiac pacemakers and supercomputers originated in Minnesota; so did 3M's "Post-it" notes and Scotch tape.

- The state bird is the loon, a sleek black-and-white waterfowl whose haunting cry can be heard on the lakes of northern Minnesota.

- The pink-and-white lady slipper, a large, lovely wildflower that flourishes in northern and eastern Minnesota, is the state flower. You mustn't pick one, though—it's against the law.

- Minnesota's official gemstone is the Lake Superior agate, a reddish stone with white stripes that's found in central and northern Minnesota.

After the Fort Snelling visit, take Highway 55, crossing the Mendota Bridge. Turn left on the Sibley Memorial Highway (Minnesota Highway 13) for a visit to old Mendota, site of one of the earliest fur trading posts. Tour the preserved Sibley House and Faribault House.

At this point, you may wish to return to the Mendota Bridge via Highway 13. Take Highway 55 across the bridge to Highway 5. Turn south on 5, proceed past the Minneapolis–St. Paul International Airport to I-494, then west to the Mall of America, the largest retail and entertainment complex in the United States.

You can finish the day's adventures here, taking time out for the kind of refueling you most enjoy.

IF YOU HAVE TWO DAYS A visit to the Twin Cities wouldn't be complete without at least a day dedicated to St. Paul. An excellent place to start is the new home of the Minnesota Historical Society located near the intersection of Kellogg Boulevard and John Ireland Boulevard. You'll find a wide variety of fascinating exhibits here describing the history of this "Land of 10,000 Lakes." Next door to the Historical Society is the impressive Cathedral of St. Paul, arguably the most magnificent structure overlooking the St. Paul skyline. Visit the nearby capitol, then drive downtown to a convenient parking spot near the World Trade Center and its adjacent shopping complex. Consider a stop for a bite here or across the street at Town Square, a major shopping complex that includes on its top level the world's largest indoor park. The carousel at Town Square Park will be of particular interest to the young members of your party. Before leaving St. Paul, take 4th Street one-way to Market Street for at least a look at Rice Park, which is bordered by four notable buildings: the Ordway Music Theatre, the St. Paul Central Library, the Saint Paul Hotel, and the Landmark Center.

IF YOU HAVE THREE DAYS If you're staying in Minneapolis, you may want to drive over the 3rd Avenue Bridge, where you can get a wonderful view of St. Anthony Falls and the Milling District that once distinguished Minneapolis as the flour capital of the world. After crossing the Mississippi River, turn right on University Avenue and proceed to and through the campus of the University of Minnesota. Continue on University Avenue into St. Paul, through the Midway District, then turn left on Lexington Avenue, which will lead you to Como Park, the Como Zoo, and the newly renovated Japanese garden. When you've completed your Como Park visit, return to University Avenue and proceed east toward downtown St. Paul to Rice Street, adjacent to the state capitol.

After you turn onto Rice Street, proceed to John Ireland Boulevard, where you'll turn right again to the St. Paul Cathedral. At this juncture, you'll come to Summit Avenue, perhaps the most impressive avenue of homes anywhere. Traveling west on Summit, you'll pass the governor's mansion, William Mitchell College of Law, Macalester College, and the University of St. Thomas. At the end of Summit, you'll come to the East Mississippi River Boulevard, upon which you can return to Minneapolis, taking time, if you like, for a relaxed meal at the Lexington Café on the corner of Lexington Avenue and Grand Avenue. Incidentally, Grand Avenue is a marvelous place to browse, since it is filled with quaint shops and popular restaurants.

IF YOU HAVE FOUR DAYS OR MORE   If time permits, include an overnight stay in Rochester, Minnesota, less than a 2-hour drive from the Twin Cities. This is, of course, the home of the famous Mayo Clinic. Free tours of the clinic are available to the public on weekdays, as are tours of Mayowood, the lovely home and grounds that were originally the home of the late Dr. Charles Mayo. The Mayo Medical Museum, also open to the public, offers a variety of interesting and informative films, videotapes, and exhibits.

1. THE TOP ATTRACTIONS

FORT SNELLING, Hwy. 5 at Hwy. 55, 1 mile east of Minneapolis–St. Paul International Airport. Tel. 725-2413 or 726-1171 for specifics on tours and special events.

One of the most popular sightseeing attractions in the Twin Cities isn't in either Minneapolis or St. Paul, but in between, at the confluence of the Mississippi and Minnesota rivers. This is the place where in 1819 Col. Josiah Snelling and his troops began construction of a fort to establish an official presence in the wilderness that had recently been won from Great Britain. President Thomas Jefferson had hoped this outpost would become a "center of civilization," and that's what occurred, as families arrived and built homes on the perimeter of land that had been ceded to the army by the Sioux. In 1837, after a treaty opened additional land for settlement, these families moved across the river to establish a community of their own, one that would later be known as St. Paul.

Fort Snelling played another important role in U.S. history. In 1837 Dred Scott, enslaved to an army surgeon, sued for his freedom on the basis of having lived for a time in the free state of Minnesota.

He lost the case, but the now-famous Dred Scott decision of the U.S. Supreme Court is often cited as a contributing factor to the start of the American Civil War. And in 1864 a young German military attaché named Count Zeppelin ascended 300 feet above the Old Round Tower in a large gas-filled canvas bag. Later, such vehicles, bearing the count's name, served as a common means of aerial transportation.

Since 1937 the Minnesota State Historical Society has maintained a living museum at Fort Snelling, where costumed guides re-create the activities and ceremonies of everyday army life during the 1820s. While you're here, don't overlook the interesting gift shop with its selection of authentic Native American handcrafted jewelry.

Admission: $3 adults, $1 children ages 6–15; children under 5, free.

Open: Mon–Sat 10am–5pm, Sun noon–5pm. **Directions:** From downtown Minneapolis, take I-35W to Hwy. 62, which leads into Hwy. 55. Follow signs about 1 mile to Fort Snelling. From St. Paul, take I-35E to I-494N; then proceed west to Hwy. 55, which will take you to Fort Snelling.

MINNESOTA HISTORY CENTER, 345 W. Kellogg Blvd., St. Paul. Tel. 296-9131.

This beautiful three-story museum houses an impressive array of artifacts and writings celebrating the history of Minnesota. A succession of exhibits brings everyone from researchers to schoolchildren to seniors back again and again to enjoy a visit to the past enlivened by contemporary technology. Videotapes and hands-on displays make visitors feel like participants in days and events gone by.

One particularly popular ongoing exhibit is called "Minnesota A to Z," in which each letter of the alphabet is paired with a feature of life hereabouts. Z, as you may have guessed, stands for "zero," a reference to our wintertime temperatures.

Do take time for lunch or dessert in Café Minnesota, located on the ground floor of the museum; or, if you prefer, take your selections outdoors for a picnic on the lawn or on the second-story terrace.

Open: Tues–Wed 10am–5pm, Thurs 10am–9pm, Fri–Sat 10am–5pm, Sun noon–5pm. **Directions:** East on I-35E to the Kellogg Blvd. exit. At the stoplight, turn left one-half block.

MINNESOTA ZOO, 13000 Zoo Blvd., Apple Valley. Tel. 432-9000.

The terrain at the Minnesota Zoo has been carefully created to resemble the authentic grasslands and woodlands of the wild animals that now make their home here. What may be the world's most remarkable cross-country skiing takes place in the Minnesota Zoo, where, for the price of admission, you glide within full view of camels, Siberian tigers, Asiatic wild horses, moose, snow monkeys, musk oxen, red pandas, and more.

Separate "trails" offer education so entertainingly that you won't even realize how much you've learned until you've left the 500-acre site, approximately half an hour from downtown Minneapolis and St. Paul.

The **Tropics Trail** is one of the most exotic areas of the zoo, an indoor oasis of plants and animals from faraway tropical areas. (Don't miss the Coral Reef exhibit with its lovely formations which provide the habitat for colorful tropical fish.)

The **Minnesota Trail** features animals indigenous to these parts; a beaver pond provides amazing evidence of the inborn engineering know-how of these industrious creatures. Other native Minnesotan animals in daytime and nocturnal settings include otters, lynx, weasels, and an assortment of creatures hailing from Minnesota's lakes, prairies, and forests.

The **Discovery Trail** will introduce you to some unlikely new friends. Visited with a tarantula lately? Or a sea star? You'll have the opportunity for close encounters with these and other unusual beings in the **Zoo Lab.** And you'll be able to watch an intriguing bird show, ride a camel or an elephant, pet a goat, and enjoy other hands-on experiences here.

On the **Northern Trail,** you'll be surrounded by tigers, Asian lions, coyotes, musk oxen, camels, wild horses, and moose. And you'll get to meet what may be your first-ever pronghorn, a graceful antelope look-alike.

The **Sky Trail** is an option you can enjoy for an additional $2 per person. This monorail weaves in and out of hills and lakelands as you view wild terrain and listen to "nature narratives" provided by knowledgeable guides.

Admission: $6 ages 13–64, $4 ages 65 and up, $2.50 children ages 3–12; children under 3, free. Parking is free.

Open: Mon–Sat 9am–4pm, Sun 9am–8pm. **Directions:** From downtown Minneapolis, take I-35W south to I-62 east to Cedar Ave. S. Zoo exit is marked on Hwy. 77 in Apple Valley.

MINNESOTA STATE CAPITOL, 700 Wabasha St., St. Paul. Tel. 296-2881.

The grandest of all Twin Cities sights is the Minnesota State Capitol, built in 1905 on a hill overlooking downtown St. Paul. Crowned by the world's largest unsupported marble dome, this magnificent structure was the design of Cass Gilbert, a young St. Paul architect whose later work included the Woolworth Building in New York City. At the base of the dome, modeled after the one Michelangelo created for St. Peter's in Rome, is a dramatic grouping of gilded figures titled *The Progress of the State.* Four prancing horses, symbolizing the power of Nature, are held in check by two women, representing Civilization. A charioteer, Prosperity, holds aloft a horn of plenty in one hand, while in the other he grasps a banner bearing the inscription "Minnesota."

The interior of the capitol building is equally impressive, with its marble stairways, chambers, and halls, and its fine oil paintings depicting important events in Minnesota history.

Tours: Free guided tours through the senate, house of representatives, and supreme court chambers offered Mon–Fri 9am–4pm, Sat 10am–3pm, Sun 1–3pm. **Directions:** From Minneapolis take I-94E; exit on Marion St.; turn left on John Ireland Blvd. From St. Paul, take I-94 or I-35E; exit at the capitol.

2. MORE ATTRACTIONS

ARCHITECTURAL HIGHLIGHTS

At the corner of Summit and Selby avenues, near the state capitol, stands one of St. Paul's proud architectural achievements, the 3,000-seat Renaissance-style **Cathedral of St. Paul,** constructed of Minnesota granite. John Ireland Boulevard, the street that extends just half a mile from the capitol to the cathedral, is named for the dynamic archbishop of St. Paul who served as a chaplain during the Civil War and later lent his energies toward raising the funds for this magnificent structure, which he dedicated to the people of St. Paul.

Beyond the cathedral, Summit Avenue, long the most prestigious of St. Paul's addresses, extends 4½ miles to the Mississippi River. On this distinguished street stands the country's longest span of intact **Victorian mansions,** and here, at 240 Summit Ave., you'll find one of the city's perennially popular tourist attractions, the mansion of "empire builder" James J. Hill, founder of the Great Northern Railroad. (For information about tours, phone 297-2555.) Among the more modest homes on this avenue is the one at 599 Summit, where F. Scott Fitzgerald lived in 1918 while finishing his first literary success, *This Side of Paradise.* And farther down toward the Mississippi, at 1006 Summit, you'll find the governor's stately residence.

Perhaps the most dramatic of St. Paul's restored structures is the **Landmark Center,** facing Rice Park at 75 W. 5th St. This massive early French Renaissance building with Gothic towers and pillars, turrets and gables, 20-foot ceilings and hand-carved mahogany and marble decoration, served for decades as the Federal Courts Building and Post Office. Eventually it fell into disrepair and was slated for demolition until a determined coalition of private citizens and public officials intervened. Returned to its former grandeur, today it houses all sorts of offices and is open to the public for free guided tours.

JAMES J. HILL HOUSE, 240 Summit Ave., St. Paul. Tel. 297-2555.

This handsome mansion was built for James J. Hill, who, during the late 19th century, founded the Great Northern Railroad, a major force in the settlement of newly opened lands extending from Chicago to the West Coast. The five-story home in which Hill lived with his family was by far the largest and most expensive home ever built in the upper Midwest, costing a total of more than $930,000. Luxurious touches included tile fireplaces, intricately carved woodwork, cut glass chandeliers, and stained-glass windows.

Admission: $3 adults, $1 children. Guided tours begin at 30-minute intervals. (Reservations are encouraged.)

Open: Wed–Sat 10am–3:30pm. **Directions:** From downtown St. Paul, take Kellogg Blvd. north to Summit Ave. by the Cathedral of St. Paul. Proceed west on Summit Ave. to the mansion. From downtown Minneapolis, take I-94 east to the Marion St. exit; proceed south to John Ireland Blvd., then west to Summit Ave.

ALEXANDER RAMSEY HOUSE, 265 S. Exchange St., St. Paul. Tel. 296-8760.

This beautiful Victorian home was built in 1872 for Minnesota's territorial governor, Alexander Ramsey. He later served as Minnesota's second governor, as a U.S. senator, and as secretary of war. A wooden carriage house on the property is now a gift shop and visitor's center. Reservations are recommended for the 1-hour guided tours conducted under the auspices of the Minnesota Historical Society.

Admission: $3 adults, $1 children ages 6–15; children under 5, free.

Open: Tues–Sat 10am–4pm. **Directions:** Coming from downtown Minneapolis, take I-94 to the Marion St. exit in St. Paul. Follow Marion St. to Kellogg Blvd. Go south on Kellogg Blvd. to W. 7th St. Proceed 2 blocks west on 7th St. Turn left and proceed 1 block to the mansion. From downtown St. Paul, take W. 7th St. and proceed west two blocks to Kellogg Blvd. Turn left and proceed 1 block to the mansion.

ART GALLERIES

Most galleries are open from 11am to 4pm Tuesday through Saturday, by appointment. Some are open Thursday evening until 8pm. Phone ahead to confirm hours.

DOLLY FITERMAN FINE ARTS, 100 University Ave. S.E., Minneapolis. Tel. 623-3300.

Located in a handsome building that formerly functioned as the Pillsbury Branch Public Library, this gallery offers a diversity of 20th-century American and European art, including painting by Milton Avery, bronze and marble sculpture by Richard Erdman, and works by Thornton Dial and A. R. Penck.

THOMAS BARRY FINE ARTS, 400 1st Ave. N., Suite 304, the Wyman Building, Minneapolis. Tel. 338-3656.

This gallery offers contemporary American work, including photography, prints, drawings, paintings, and sculpture. Artists include Don Gahr, Lynn Geesaman, Bruce Charlesworth, Ken Moylan, David Madzo, Scott Stack, and Steven Woodward.

FLANDERS CONTEMPORARY ART, 400 1st Ave. N., the Wyman Building, Minneapolis. Tel. 344-1700.

Flanders features museum-quality contemporary painting, drawing, and sculpture by nationally and internationally known American and European artists, among them Georgia O'Keefe, Albert Giacometti, Eric Fischl, Nancy Graves, and Tom Holland.

KRAMER GALLERY, 1012 Nicollet Mall, Minneapolis. Tel. 338-2911.

This distinguished gallery exhibits American and European artworks of the 19th and early 20th centuries; it also features Minnesota artists' work from this same period and specializes in Native American art and artifacts. For 20 years the gallery has provided professional restoration and appraisals for individuals, corporations, and museums.

McGALLERY, 400 1st Ave. N., Suite 332, the Wyman Building, Minneapolis. Tel. 339-1480.

McGallery is an avant-garde fine-art gallery offering works in a variety of forms—painting, sculpture, glass, ceramics, and others. Terri Hallman, Michael Padgette, Jean Gockley, Robert Johnson, Gary Welton, and Chris Hawthorne are among the artists represented here.

THOMSON GALLERY, 321 2nd Ave. N., Minneapolis. Tel. 338-7734.

Thomson Gallery offers contemporary drawings, paintings, prints, photography, and sculpture by such artists as Philip Larson, Lance Kiland, Steven Sorman, and Tom Rose. Much of the work shown here is of museum quality.

SUZANNE KOHN GALLERY, 1690 Grand Ave., St. Paul. Tel. 699-0477.

Regional painters are featured here, and if you don't see what you want on the walls of this small gallery, you're welcome to go downstairs for a look through the works stored there. Among the artists represented are the established midwestern artist Jerry Rudquist and regional artists like Tom Maakestad and Steven Carpenter. Suzanne Kohn also has a satellite gallery in Minneapolis at the International Design Center, 100 2nd Ave. N. (tel. 341-3441).

ART RESOURCES, 494 Jackson St., St. Paul. Tel. 222-8686.

Art Resources features the work of midwestern artists, with over 6,000 pieces of original art, ranging from abstract expressionism to classical realism.

RAYMOND AVENUE GALLERY, 761 Raymond Ave., St. Paul. Tel. 644-9200.

If you're interested in bringing top-quality crafts back from your visit to Minnesota, try this gallery, where you'll find baskets, jewelry, pottery, fabric, and other media.

LAKES

For information about Minneapolis's lakes, phone 348-2243. Three of the most popular lakes in Minneapolis form a chain that's believed to be part of the course followed by the Mississippi River some 25,000 years ago. Although the property close to **Lake of the Isles** is very expensive these days, you couldn't have given it away 100 years ago when it was a mess of swamps and marshes. The land was dredged in the late 1880s and by the turn of the century had become valuable real estate. Now a man-made lake, it's popular with fishermen because it's stocked with tasty sunfish and crappies. Lake of the Isles is popular with canoeists too for its irregular shoreline and varied landscape. During the winter a regulation hockey rink is set up, along with areas for general skating and a warming house. If you decide to walk around Lake of the Isles, remember that the path closest to the shore is for you; the other path is for bicyclists.

A channel connects Lake of the Isles to **Lake Calhoun,** so boaters can paddle from one to the other. No powerboats are permitted on city lakes, partly because of the noise and partly because the rapid churning of the water erodes the shoreline. Lake Calhoun is the largest of the chain of lakes, and at 90 to 100 feet, it's the deepest as well. Whatever the season, you're likely to see boats here—lots of one-man skimmers and sailboats in the summertime, iceboats (sailboats on blades) in the winter. This is perhaps the lake most popular with young adults.

The third link in the chain of lakes, **Lake Harriet,** may have the greatest appeal to families because of its delightful gardens and bird sanctuary. Lake Harriet Rose Gardens provides an annual display of glorious colors and scents for visitors. The Lake Harriet Rock Garden has been popular since 1929; it was refurbished in 1984. And the adjacent bird sanctuary features a wood-chip path for visitors who enjoy the solitude and serenity of an unspoiled woodland setting. If you're visiting the Twin Cities from late May until early September, join the crowds who arrive by boat, bike, or automobile to enjoy the nightly bandstand concerts at Lake Harriet. Along with Lake Calhoun and **Lake Nokomis,** Lake Harriet also features weekend sailboat races that draw throngs of participants and observers throughout the summer months.

MUSEUMS

AMERICAN SWEDISH INSTITUTE, 2600 Park Ave., Minneapolis. Tel. 871-4907.

The American Swedish Institute is a fairy-tale-like castle of pale limestone, with arches, turrets, a small balcony, and a tower. It's equally grand within, with decorative ceilings, intricately designed rugs of Swedish wool, and a glorious stained-glass window copied from a famous and historic Swedish painting.

This magnificent 33-room mansion was donated to the American Swedish Institute by Swan J. Turnblad, who came to this country in 1887 at the age of eight. By the time he was 27 Turnblad had become manager of the *Svenska Amerikanska Posten,* a Swedish-language weekly, and as its owner 10 years later he made it the largest Swedish-language newspaper in America. His general purpose for the institute, to "foster and preserve Swedish culture in America," has been admirably fulfilled. Artifacts in the mansion demonstrate over 150 years of the Swedish experience in the United States. On display are items Swedish immigrants brought with them from the old country and works of art by Swedish and Swedish-American artists. A film program is presented every Sunday at 2pm.

Admission: $3 adults, $2 seniors and students under 19.

Open: Tues, Thurs–Sat noon–4pm; Wed noon–8pm and Sun 1–5pm.

JAMES FORD BELL MUSEUM OF NATURAL HISTORY, University Ave. and 17th Ave. SE, Minneapolis. Tel. 624-7083.

The oldest museum in the state of Minnesota is still one of the most popular. Located on the Minneapolis campus of the University of Minnesota, it's famous for its three-dimensional scenes of Minnesota wildlife, which have proved fascinating to generations of visitors. Animals and birds in their natural habitats are painstakingly reproduced and displayed here; accompanying legends provide information in a concise and interesting way.

In the popular "Touch and See" room, children can examine for themselves the skins, bones, and skulls of a wide variety of animals, including mammoths and dinosaurs. Among the creatures on hand are stuffed wildlife specimens such as moose, elk, and caribou, as well as Lenny, a live Gila monster, which is sometimes kept company by visiting animals from the Como Park Zoo.

Admission: $3 ages 17–61; $2 ages 62 and older and children ages 3–16; children under 3, free. On Thurs all are free.

Open: Tues–Fri 9am–5pm, Sat 10am–5pm, Sun noon–5pm.

GIBBS FARM MUSEUM, Cleveland and Larpenteur Aves., Falcon Heights, St. Paul. Tel. 646-8629.

This popular museum re-creates life on a 7-acre farm at the turn of the century. Costumed guides are on hand to answer questions about the artifacts and activities on this homestead. You'll see how the Gibbs family's home grew from a one-room cabin to a large, comfortable farmhouse complete with parlor, sitting room, kitchen, bedrooms, and more. In a red barn you'll find farming, woodworking, and veterinary exhibits. Friendly animals await you behind the barn, and there's a one-room schoolhouse with wooden double desks, a pump organ, slate boards, and a school bell. A slide presentation explains what farming on the fringe of St. Paul was like in those days and a children's summer schoolhouse program is offered in July and August.

Information about individual programs, which vary from month to month, can be obtained from the Ramsey County Historical Society, 323 Landmark Center, 75 W. 5th St., St. Paul (tel. 222-0701).

Admission: $2.50 adults, $2 seniors, $1 children ages 2–18.

Open: May–Oct, Tues–Fri 10am–4pm, Sat–Sun noon–4pm.

MINNEAPOLIS INSTITUTE OF ART, 3rd Ave. S. at E. 24th St., Minneapolis. Tel. 870-3046.

Recognized internationally as one of America's great museums, the Minneapolis Institute of Art is located close to downtown Minneapolis. With a permanent collection of more than 80,000 objects of fine and decorative art representing more than 25,000 years of history, the museum contains treasures representing every age and cultural tradition.

Highlights include a 2,000-year-old mummy, **Doryphoros;** a 1st-century-B.C. Roman sculpture; Rembrandt's *Lucretia* (1666); Paul Revere's *Templeman Tea Service* (1792–93); and Monet's *Grainstack, Sun in the Mist* (1891). Other features include meticulously re-created period rooms; African, Oceanic, and New World galleries; fine examples of photography; a comprehensive collection of textiles; a justly famous collection of prints and drawings; and a restored example of the Prairie school of architecture—the Purcell-Cutts House.

Throughout the year, there is a varied schedule of family days, films, lectures, classes, and other special activities for people of all ages. There is no charge for entrance to the museum. A small admission is charged for occasional special exhibitions.

Open: Tues–Wed, Fri–Sat 10am–5pm; Thurs 10am–9pm and Sun noon–5pm. **Directions:** From downtown Minneapolis, go south on 3rd Ave. to 2400 3rd Ave. S. From downtown St. Paul, take I-94 to the 11th St. exit; at second stoplight, turn left onto 3rd Ave. and proceed to 2400 3rd Ave. S.

MINNEAPOLIS PLANETARIUM, in Minneapolis Public Library, 300 Nicollet Mall, Minneapolis. Tel. 372-6644.

The public is invited to attend the educational and entertaining shows that are presented every day at the downtown Minneapolis Public Library. Sharing the comfortable auditorium with you may be one or more student groups ranging from early elementary grades to college and university classes. Among the most popular of the 15 public programs offered here is "Skywatch," which combines film with a "guided tour" of the night sky that's been projected overhead on the 40-foot domed ceiling.

Open: You'd do well to phone ahead to find out the scheduled time for a program you'd like to attend.

MINNESOTA MUSEUM OF AMERICAN ART, in Landmark Center, 5th St. at Market St., St. Paul. Tel. 292-4355.

Founded in 1927, this museum presents exhibitions and a full range of art classes designed for young people and adults. With a collection including more than 10,000 objects, the Minnesota Museum of American Art is dedicated to expressing through art "the unfolding value of the American multicultural experience." The museum's galleries are located on the second floor of Landmark Center. The art school is on the fifth floor.

Admission: Free, but a $2 donation is encouraged.

Open: Tues–Sat 11am–4pm, Sun 1–5pm. **Closed:** Mon, major holidays, and between exhibitions.

SCIENCE MUSEUM OF MINNESOTA, 30 E. 10th St., St. Paul. Tel. 221-9454.

At the entrance of this immensely popular two-building complex you'll be greeted by Iggy, a 40-foot steel iguana that was sculpted by a 16-year-old St. Paul schoolboy. Boys and girls of all ages have an entertaining and educational time at this massive museum, which offers hands-on exhibits dealing with natural history, science, and technology. Members of an acting troupe turn up here and there to bring to life some of the figures who have played a part in the development of this area.

The East Building holds "Our Minnesota," a permanent exhibit featuring a 12-by-14-foot map of the state that permits visitors to walk or crawl across forests marked in green, croplands marked in gold, mines represented by taconite pellets, and lakes depicted by an expanse of blue plastic. The Hall of Paleontology features the dinosaur lab, in which visitors can watch fossils being cleaned, identified, and assembled. The West Building contains the Hall of Anthropology, the Physics and Technology Gallery, and the Collections Exhibit (miscellaneous artifacts from the collection), as well as a succession of traveling exhibits.

And then there's the Omnitheater, whose screen is a tilted dome, 76 feet in diameter, that puts viewers right into the center of adventures dealing with every time and every place.

Hours for the exhibit halls and the Omnitheater differ according to season; call 221-9454 for information. Call 221-9400 for information about prices for the Omnitheater and for Omnitheater-Museum combination tickets.

Admission: Exhibit hall $4.50 adults, $3.50 seniors and children under 12.

Open: Mon–Fri 9:30am–9pm, Sat 9am–9pm, Sun 10am–9pm.

WALKER ART CENTER AND MINNEAPOLIS SCULPTURE GARDENS, 725 Vineland Place, Minneapolis. Tel. 375-7577 or 375-7622.

To reach this attraction from downtown St. Paul, take 94W to the Hennepin-Lyndale exit. From the left lane, turn right. Just before the second set of lights, turn left. The Walker will be at your left. From downtown Minneapolis, follow 1st Avenue North to 11th Street. Turn left on 11th and go one block to Hennepin Avenue. Turn right, pass St. Mary's Cathedral; go under the bridge, then turn left and, after one block, turn right. The Walker will be at your left.

The Walker Art Center, adjoining the Tyrone Guthrie Theater and facing the Sculpture Garden, is famous for its permanent collection of contemporary art. In addition, some of the most prestigious exhibitions that tour the country make stops at the Walker. In February 1980, "Picasso: From the Musée Picasso, Paris" brought Picasso's work to the United States for the first time; these works were later incorporated into the Picasso retrospective at the New York Museum of Modern Art. The Walker is also known for the popular presentations it offers through its Department of Film and Video, its Department of Performing Arts, and its Department of Education.

Across Vineland Place, the Minneapolis Sculpture Garden, whose display of artworks and educational activities are managed by the Walker Art Center, has been attracting wide attention since it was dedicated in September 1988. The most extensive garden of its kind in the United States, it's been called the country's finest new outdoor space for displaying sculpture.

Probably the most readily recognizable work here is *Spoonbridge and Cherry* by Claes Oldenburg and Coosje van Bruggen—a 52-foot-long spoon bearing a cherry that measures 9½ feet in diameter, with a 12-foot stem. This sculptural fountain and reflecting pool stand in honor of William and Mary Weisman, parents of Minneapolis-born philanthropist and art collector Frederick R. Weisman.

The wide variety of 20th-century sculpture on display here includes work by artists Henry Moore, Isamu Noguchi, George Segal, and Jackie Ferrara. California architect Frank Gehry is represented by the dramatic *Standing Glass Fish* in the conservatory, which features horticultural displays throughout the year. To the surprise of many observers, the Sculpture Garden has become a year-round attraction, so come and see it for yourself, whatever the weather.

Admission: Art Center $3 adults, $2 students. Free on Thurs.
Open: Tues–Sat 10am–8pm, Sun 11am–5pm.

**FREDERICK R. WEISMAN ART MUSEUM, at University of
Minnesota, 333 E. River Rd., Minneapolis. Tel. 625-
9494.**

The Weisman Art Museum is the most immediately recognizable building on the Minneapolis campus of the University of
Minnesota. It may also be the most controversial. Even before
this unconventional building opened in November 1993, it had
aroused fervor among admirers and detractors alike. (The fact that
not one penny of taxpayers' money was spent on the structure helped
to temper the acrimony a bit.)

By now the Frederick R. Weisman Art Museum has become part
of the landscape, but many are still astonished to find this immense
work of "usable sculpture" standing high on a bluff overlooking the
Mississippi River and the downtown Minneapolis landscape. Irregu-
larly shaped, with part of its facade made of brushed steel and part of
terra-cotta brick, it aims to reflect respectively the industrial structures of metal or steel docks on the Mississippi, which it overlooks,
and the brick of the university's buildings nearby. Regardless of
whether you love it or hate it, you'll almost surely find it worth
mentioning after you've returned home. There's been virtually
unanimous praise for the galleries within. One major art critic cited
the Weisman for "five of the most gorgeous galleries on earth."

Actually a bit of poetic justice is at work here. For nearly 60 years,
the University Art Museum languished in cramped quarters at
Northrop Auditorium, then the University's home of performing arts;
many of the museum's works had, in fact, remained stored for years
because there was no room to display them. A stated goal for the new
museum was that it create "increased awareness" of the resources of
the museum's permanent collection. Awareness of the new building
has certainly increased awareness of the collection within. There's
something here to please and displease everybody, and you're bound
to consider a visit to the Weisman a memorable experience in every
sense.

Admission: Free.
Open: Mon–Fri 10am–6pm, Sat–Sun noon–5pm. **Closed:** All
major holidays as well as a number of university holidays.

PARKS & GARDENS

**COMO PARK, N. Lexington and Como Aves., St. Paul. Tel.
466-7291,** zoo 488-5571, conservatory 489-1740.

Nearly 100 years after being established in 1897, Como Park
remains one of the busiest, most versatile, and most beautiful parks in
the Twin Cities. There's literally something for everybody here, where
yesterday's children are now bringing children of their own. The
Como Zoo remains one of the biggest boons to Twin Citians; not as
cutting edge as the much newer Minnesota Zoo in Apple Valley,
Como nonetheless offers much in the way of entertainment and
education with no cost to grown-ups except perhaps for a treat or a
souvenir. (The gift shop is generally filled with attractive items at great
prices.)

Still on hand to perform for his many admirers is Sparky, the trained seal—or at least a descendent of the one with which today's 40-something folks grew up. Como Park is famous too for its flower conservatory, which has served as the setting for many a local wedding. It's truly a picture-perfect spot for so happy an occasion.

There's a formal Japanese garden here as well, along with an 18-hole golf course, cross-country ski trails, and walking paths. You'll also find paddleboats, canoes, bikes, and even roller blades for rent.

Directions: From downtown Minneapolis, take I-94 east to the Lexington Ave. exit; turn north on Lexington and follow signs to the zoo. From St. Paul take I-94 west to the Lexington Ave. exit; turn north on Lexington and follow signs to the zoo.

LAKE HARRIET PARK, Queen Ave. S. at W. 42nd St., Minneapolis.

This is one of the most popular parks in the city of Minneapolis. Many's the family that's attended concerts at the award-winning band shell on the shore of Lake Harriet. There's canoeing and sailing here and, a block away, a streetcar stop where volunteers oversee transportation for the benefit primarily of children who might otherwise never have the chance to experience this mode of travel. Riders can board either at the Lake Harriet stop at Queen Avenue South and West 42nd Street or at the Linden Hills stop at East Lake Calhoun Parkway just south of West 36th Street.

Admission: Trolley 75 cents per person. No charge for children under the age of 4. **Directions:** From downtown Minneapolis, take I-35W south to the 46th St. exit. Turn west on 46th St. and proceed to Lake Harriet. From downtown St. Paul, take I-94 to I-35W. Proceed south to the 46th St. exit. Turn west on 46th St. and proceed to Lake Harriet.

MINNEHAHA PARK.

One of Minnesota's most beautiful waterfalls and one of the state's most beloved statues stand just a few yards away from each other in Minnehaha Park. The Falls of Minnehaha and the bronze likeness of Minnehaha and Hiawatha both serve to memorialize the young lovers immortalized by Henry Wadsworth Longfellow in his famous poem, *The Song of Hiawatha*. Pennies contributed by the schoolchildren of Minnesota bought this statue back in 1893. Money well spent!

Minnehaha Park is the setting each summer for a succession of ethnic festivals; it's also popular for its hiking trails and picnic areas.

Directions: Take I-35W south to the 46th St. exit, then turn east on 46th St. and proceed to Portland Ave. Turn south on to Minnehaha Pkwy., then go east to Minnehaha Park.

NORMANDALE JAPANESE GARDEN, 9700 France Ave. S., Bloomington. Tel. 832-6000.

This lovely sanctuary, located on the campus of Normandale Community College, contains the essential elements of a Japanese strolling garden. Features include a traditional entrance gate, a waterfall, two small islands, bridges, a stream, and other authentic objects, none more meaningful than the Bentendo, a beautiful structure donated through the efforts of graduates of the U.S. Army Military Intelligence Language School veterans. During World War II, these Americans of Japanese descent were stationed in Minnesota at Camp Savage and Fort Snelling, where they studied the Japanese language and later served as members of the Military Intelligence Service. The passage of time has not diminished their gratitude for the kindness they encountered here in the Twin Cities, and the Bentendo in the Normandale Japanese Garden symbolizes that memory.

PHALEN PARK, Wheelock Pkwy. at Arcade St., St. Paul. Tel. 266-6400.
Named for an early St. Paul settler, this is the city's largest park. Open year-round, it offers a wide variety of activities, everything from golf to downhill and cross-country skiing. There are beaches and picnic areas, fishing, swimming, and boating opportunities and an amphitheater.
Directions: From downtown St. Paul, take I-35E north to the Wheelock Pkwy. exit; go east on Wheelock Pkwy. to Arcade St. From downtown Minneapolis, take I-94 to I-35E; go north on I-35E to the Wheelock Pkwy. exit; then go east on Wheelock Pkwy. to Arcade St.

SCULPTURE

There are two statues in St. Paul that rank high on any list of sight-seeing attractions. In the St. Paul City Hall/Ramsey County Courthouse, at Fourth and Wabasha avenues, Carl Milles's ✪ majestic 36-foot-tall onyx figure, *The Indian God of Peace,* stands in regal splendor. This 60-ton statue rotates very, very slowly. It can be seen Tuesday through Friday from 8am to 5pm, Sunday from 1 to 5pm.
On the slope between the capitol and the cathedral there's an often-overlooked symbolic tribute to a history-making Minnesotan—Charles Lindbergh. Lindbergh, who grew up in Little Falls, Minnesota, became in 1927 the first pilot ever to make a nonstop solo flight across the Atlantic Ocean. Sculptor Paul Granlund has honored him by creating two bronze figures, Lindbergh as a young man and as a small boy.

3. COOL FOR KIDS

The Twin Cities are a mecca for family fun. For those of you with restless youngsters on your hands, this section will head off any threat of boredom.

CHILDREN'S THEATRE, 2400 3rd Ave. S., Minneapolis. Tel. 874-0400.
Known throughout the world for its imaginative productions for youngsters, the Children's Theatre Company has developed classic

stories including *The Wizard of Oz, Cinderella, The Jungle Book* and *The 500 Hats of Bartholomew Cubbins* for presentation on the main stage. The theater auditorium seats 746; its sight lines are excellent.

Prices: Tickets $13.50–$23 adults, children under 17 and senior citizens 62 and over $9.25–$17.45.

MINNESOTA CHILDREN'S MUSEUM, 1217 Bandana Blvd., St. Paul. Tel. 644-3818.

At this hands-on interactive museum, children get to do all sorts of grown-up things. A combination of fun and learning awaits children six months to eight years old. Popular features include a high-action maze, a historic train, and an outdoor garden. The museum also features weekend programming, summer camps, and special group programs. Here, in a two-story reconverted blacksmith's shop, children can operate Morse code devices which signal simultaneously with a clicker and with blue lights so deaf children can receive messages of their own. Another top draw here is the crane-and-train exhibit, where children can use an electromagnetic crane to pick up and deposit metal disks. There are two floors of fun here, and parents seem as intrigued as youngsters.

Admission: $3.50 ages 3–64; children under 3 and seniors $2.
Open: Mon (summers only) and Tues 9am–5pm, Wed–Sat 9am–8pm, Sun noon–5pm.

OMNITHEATER, in the Science Museum of Minnesota, 30 E. 10th St., St. Paul. Tel. 221-9400.

The huge curved screen and the world's largest film projector literally propel you out into space, down to the ocean's floor, or to places in between. You can go to the Omnitheater early and wait in line, or phone 221-9456 and pay an extra 50¢ per ticket for advance reservations.

Prices: Tickets $5.50 adults, $4.50 senior citizens and children 12 and under.

SCIENCE MUSEUM OF MINNESOTA, 30 E. 10th St., St. Paul. Tel. 221-9454.

Children are encouraged to try their hand at everything from grinding grain to operating a computer. Exhibits here cover a wide range of times and places, so one visit may well lead to another.

Admission: $4.50 adults, $3.50 children 4–12, children under 4, free. If you attend the Omnitheater on the second floor, your admission to the rest of the Science Museum will be only $1.
Open: Oct–Mar, Tues–Sat 9:30am–9pm, Sun 10am–9pm; Apr–Oct, Mon–Sat 9:30am–9pm, Sun 10am–9pm.

TOWN SQUARE PARK, 445 Minnesota St., St. Paul. Tel. 227-3307.

On the top levels of the Town Square shopping, dining, and office complex is the world's largest indoor park. There's a small playground for children, lots of cozy seating for adults, and a picturesque setting of shrubs, trees, and waterfalls.

TWIN CITIES MODEL RAILROAD CLUB, Bandana Sq., 1021 Bandana Blvd. E., St. Paul. Tel. 647-9628.

Here children and their elders have the chance to see a remarkable exhibit in the making. Club members are still assembling historic tracks and artifacts that trace the history of railroading in this area during the past 50 years.
Open: Mon–Fri noon–9pm, Sat 10am–6pm, Sun 1–5pm.

COMO PARK ZOO, Midwest Pkwy. and Kaufman Dr., St. Paul. Tel. 488-5571.
Sparky, the performing seal, is everybody's favorite here, but there are lots of other animals to meet in the Primate and Aquatic buildings and in Wolf Woods. Sparky performs Tuesday through Friday at 11am, 2pm, and 4pm and on weekends at 11am, 2pm, 4pm, and 5pm.
Admission: Free.
Open: Daily 10am–6pm.

GIBB'S FARM, 2097 W. Larpenteur Ave., Falcon Heights. Tel. 646-8629.
In this turn-of-the-century farm, children can experience the surroundings of girls and boys who lived long ago. In addition to the farmhouse, the 7-acre site contains a red barn with old-fashioned tools and another barn with domestic animals.
Admission: $2.50 adults, $2 seniors, $1 children ages 2–18.
Open: May and Sept–Oct, Tues–Fri 10am–4pm, Sun noon–4pm; June–Aug, Tues–Fri 10am–4pm, Sat–Sun noon–4pm.

HISTORIC FORT SNELLING, Hwy. 5 at Hwy. 55, 1 mile east of the Minneapolis–St. Paul International Airport. Tel. 725-2413.
This restoration of the military post that brought the first settlers to these parts is now one of the most popular of all Twin Cities tourist attractions. Costumed guides encourage visitors to take part in the activities that kept soldiers and their families busy during those early days. Children particularly seem to enjoy the Round Tower, which provided a lookout up and down the Minnesota and Mississippi rivers. The schoolhouse, the blacksmith shop, and the hospital are just some of the fascinating and educational exhibits here.
Admission: $3 adults, $1 children ages 6–15; children under 5, free.
Open: Mon–Sat 10am–5pm, Sun noon–5pm. **Closed:** Nov–Apr.

JONATHON PADELFORD STERNWHEELER, Harriet Island, St. Paul. Tel. 227-1100.
Passengers board this authentic 19th-century riverboat on Harriet Island, located on the edge of downtown St. Paul, and sail the Mississippi for a 1½-hour round-trip. A taped narration points out special places, including Fort Snelling, and offers interesting facts. There are three sailings each day from June through August, and one sailing on Saturday, Sunday, and holidays during May and September. Phone for specific details.
Prices: Tickets $8 adults, $5.50 children under 12.

LAKE HARRIET TROLLEY, 42nd St. and Queen Ave. S.,

Minneapolis. Tel. 228-0263 (information), 291-7588 (charters).

Many older Twin Citians can remember riding old-fashioned streetcars, but most children have never had the experience—so they have a great time on the mile-long ride between Lake Harriet and Lake Calhoun. Just as in the old days, children buy tokens for the ride and a conductor collects them. This line is staffed by volunteers, hence the abbreviated hours.

Fares: 75¢ per person; children 4 and under, free.

Open: Memorial Day weekend to Labor Day, Mon–Fri 6:30pm–dusk, Sat 1pm–dusk, Sun and weekends 12:30pm–dusk. Sept after Labor Day, Sat 1pm–dusk, Sun 12:30pm–dusk; Oct, Sat 1–5pm, Sun 12:30–5pm.

MINNEHAHA FALLS/STATUE OF HIAWATHA AND MINNEHAHA, in Minnehaha Park, near the Mississippi River.

It was reportedly a description of Minnehaha Falls that inspired Henry Wadsworth Longfellow to write his famous poem about Hiawatha and Minnehaha. The two are reunited here in a graceful statue near the falls that bear her name. This whole area is a popular picnicking place for families. It's also the site of many large ethnic picnics, so you may run into costumed Scandinavians of all ages if you get here at the right time.

Directions: From Minneapolis, take Hwy. 55 for about 5 miles; turn left on Minnehaha Pkwy. and enter the parking lot on the right. From St. Paul, take Hwy. 94 west and get off at the Cretin-Vandalia exit; at the stop sign, turn left and proceed about 3 miles, turning right onto the Ford Pkwy., which becomes a bridge that crosses the Mississippi River; 1 block beyond the Ford Bridge, turn left on 46th St., proceed 1 block to Godfrey Ave., turn right on Godfrey, drive about a block, and turn left into the parking lot.

FAMILY FUNWAYS, 2100 N. Frontage Rd., Burnsville. Tel. 894-9782.

You'll have a choice among 40 rides and activities in this delightful family amusement park next to a Sam's Club. Go-carting is a great crowd pleaser, with three separate tracks: "kiddie" for ages 4 to 7, "family" for ages 7 to 80 or 90 or so; and "Slick" for the thoroughly reckless. Another favorite is minigolf unlike any you've encountered before. Here large animal figures represent the hazards. (Hitting the ball between the giraffe's legs will net you a better score than going around him.) There's really something for all ages here, including a petting zoo, batting cages, and large carnival rides.

Admission: No charge to enter amusement park. Prices, advertised as the lowest in the Twin Cities, vary according to the particular ride or activity you select.

Open: Mon–Sun 10:30am–10:30pm.

MURPHY'S LANDING, Hwy. 101 near Shakopee. Tel. 445-6900.

Unlike other living-history restorations in the area, Murphy's

Landing doesn't confine itself to one point in time. Instead, fifty years of Minnesota Valley history unfolds before visitors as they proceed from the 1840s fur trader's cabin to the 1850 timber farm and ultimately to a village of the 1890s. The costumes of the guides in each of the settings are consistent with the time period they represent. City children in particular enjoy seeing the farm animals roaming through the lanes; they also enjoy watching the churning, spinning, weaving, and other chores being carried on much as they were in the 19th century. Murphy's Landing is located about 11 miles west of the intersection of I-35W and Highway 13, about one mile west of Valleyfair.

Admission: $7 adults, $6 seniors and students 6–18; children under 5, free. Admission includes horse-drawn trolley shuttle and tours of the village.

Open: Tues–Thurs 11am–4pm; Fri–Sun noon–5pm. **Closed:** Nov–Apr.

VALLEYFAIR, Hwy. 101 near Shakopee. Tel. 445-7600.
If you're bringing children to the Twin Cities, you might want to spend a day at Valleyfair, an enormously popular theme park that occupies 60 acres and offers attractions for children and grown-ups alike. This is one of the most popular amusement parks in the entire Midwest. Valleyfair is located about nine miles west of the intersection of I-35W and Highway 13, about one mile from Murphy's Landing.

Admission: $17.50 regular admission, $9.95 children 4 years old to 48 inches tall, $9.95 seniors 62 and older; children under 3, free. Parking $3.50.

Open: May to early Sept daily 10am–8pm; closing time is occasionally later, call for latest hours. **Closed:** Oct to early May; weekdays after first week of Sept.

4. ORGANIZED TOURS

One of the best ways to get your bearings in the Twin Cities is to take a narrated tour. Here are three good options, depending on your preference and pocketbook.

IMPRESSIONS

The Falls of Minnehaha
Flash and gleam amoung the oaktrees
Laugh and leap into the valley . . .
From the waterfall he named her
Minnehaha Laughing Water.
—HENRY WADSWORTH LONGFELLOW, *THE SONG OF HIAWATHA*
(1855)

SCHEDULED TOURS

City tours are offered by **Gray Lines,** and last about four hours and take passengers through both Minneapolis and St. Paul, with time out at Minnehaha Falls and the Cathedral of St. Paul (if no service is underway). Prices are $15 for adults, $13 for seniors, and $7 for children 7 to 14 (children under 7 can ride free as long as they don't take a seat that could go to a fare-paying passenger). Tours run Wednesday through Sunday during June, July, and August. In May and September, tour buses run only on Saturdays and Sundays. Call 469-5020, or ask your concierge or front-desk personnel for further information.

Metro Connections offers scheduled tours seven days a week during June and August. Morning tours, approximately four hours long, include a visit to the new Minnesota History Center every day but Monday. Monday tours will provide an extra hour on the Nicollet Mall in downtown Minneapolis in place of the history center. Morning tours take three hours and do not include the stop at the history center or the Nicollet Mall.

These scheduled tours are offered Wednesday through Sunday during September, and Friday, Saturday, and Sunday during October. Pickups are made at the Mall of America, the Minnesota History Center, and at a number of hotels in Minneapolis and St. Paul.

Rates are $16 for adults, $14 for seniors 55 and older, $9 for children (two children rates per adult). No charge for children 5 and under when they do not occupy a paid seat. Reservations are required. Call 333-8687 for further information.

BY BOAT

For a change of pace, consider a tape-narrated, round-trip boat trip on an old-fashioned riverboat from Harriet Island in St. Paul to Fort Snelling. You'll experience a bit of local history as you travel the Mississippi on the *Jonathon Padelford* or the *Josiah Snelling,* authentic stern-wheelers belonging to the Padelford Packet Boat Company (tel. 227-1100). The company also operates in Minneapolis at the Boom Island landing, where you can board the *Anson Northrop* and the *Betsey Northrop* for a ride downriver past Nicollet Island and through the locks at Upper St. Anthony Falls.

CUSTOMIZED TOURS

Minnesota Travel Connections provides tours fashioned to fit the schedule and special interests of individuals and groups. Itineraries are designed by Dorothy Anderson who for 20 years has worked in conjunction with local corporations and convention bureaus to familiarize visitors with the Twin Cities and with Minnesota at large. You might enjoy one of her "Hidden Treasures Tours," such as "The Railroad Barons," a visit to sites associated with the life and career of James J. Hill and his son Louis; "Indian Heritage," which follows historic tribal paths through museum exhibits, or "From Oxcarts to

Precious Collectibles," which visits a mid-19th-century inn built for traveling fur traders and the military, a turn-of-the-century living-history farm, and a shop specializing in antique dolls and other collectibles. These customized tours vary in price according to the number of destinations and the size of the group. Call 291-2993 or toll-free 800/334-7608 for further details.

5. SPORTS & RECREATION

SPECTATOR SPORTS

Minneapolis and St. Paul have three major-league professional sports teams—the **Minnesota Vikings** NFL football team, the **Minnesota Twins** AL baseball team, and the **Minnesota Timberwolves** NBA basketball team. (**Note:** There have been attempts to sell the Timberwolves franchise, so the team may no longer play in the Twin Cities when you visit.) Tickets to Viking games are $25 for any seat and can be obtained by writing to 500 11th Ave. S., Minneapolis (tel. 333-8828). Twins tickets range in price from $4 to $17; write to 501 Chicago Ave. S., Minneapolis (tel. 33-TWINS). For Timberwolves information call 337-3865 or write to 600 1st Ave. N, Minneapolis.

RECREATION

Minneapolis and St. Paul abound with recreational activities. For information on recreation in Minneapolis, call 348-2143; for St. Paul, call 266-6400.

CANOEING

If you want to go canoeing, you can literally paddle your way through the neighborhoods of the Twin Cities. Canoeists can start out in Minnetonka, then follow Minnehaha Creek from Gray's Bay through suburban Hopkins, St. Louis Park, and Edina and then go on to a spot not far from the Mississippi River in Minneapolis. **AARCEE Recreational Rental**, 2910 Lyndale Ave. S., Minneapolis (tel. 827-5746), rents 15-foot Coleman canoes for $26 a day, $38 for up to three days, and 17-foot aluminum canoes for $32 a day, $45 for up to three days, including life jackets, paddles, and car-top carriers. Some hardy folks make the round-trip in one outing; others arrange for a car to be waiting for them when they reach the end of the route.

Shorter outings are popular at **Cedar Lake** in Minneapolis, and canoes and rowboats can be rented at **Lake Calhoun** for $4.50 an hour (cash only). A particularly popular course here leads canoeists through the chain of lakes that extends from Lake Calhoun to Lake of the Isles and then to Cedar Lake. In St. Paul, you can canoe or row on **Lake Phalen** for $4.50 per hour with a $25 deposit and photo ID.

FISHING

Want something to show for your day on the water? For fishing, try the lagoon in St. Paul's ever-popular Lake Phalen. You'll pay $5 to rent a fishing boat for the first hour, plus $2.50 for each additional hour (there's a $25 deposit on all boats, and you'll need a photo ID). Call 771-7507 for more information.

GOLF

There are more par-3 courses in the Twin Cities than in any other metropolitan area in the country. If golf is your game, here are a few courses for you to consider.

The **Majestic Oaks Golf Course,** 701 Bunker Lake Blvd., Ham Lake (tel. 755-2142), is privately owned but open to the public; it was rated among the top 50 American public golf courses by *Golf Digest.* There are two courses here. At the Platinum Course you'll pay $18 for 18 holes weekdays, $22 on weekends. The cost of playing the Gold Course, which opened in 1991, is $10 for 9 holes, $16 for 18 holes on weekdays. Carts are available for $10 at the 9-hole course, $20 at the 18-hole courses, and clubs can be rented for $5 (9 holes) or $8 (18 holes).

The **Braemar Golf Course,** 6364 Dewey Hill Rd., Edina (tel. 941-2072), offering a 27-hole regulation course and a 9-hole executive course, has hosted many national tournaments. Rates are $19 for 18 holes, $11 for 9 holes. There's also a driving range; rates are $5 for a large bucket of balls, $3.25 for a small. Rental carts cost $12 for 9 holes, $21 for 18 holes. Club rental is $7.

The **Francis A. Gross Golf Course,** 2201 St. Anthony Blvd., Minneapolis (tel. 789-2542), charges $11.50 for 9 holes and $16.50 for 18 holes. Carts are available at $12 for 9 holes, $20 for 18 holes, and clubs can be rented at $7 for 9 or 18 holes.

At the **Meadowbrook Golf Course,** 300 Meadowbrook Rd., Hopkins (tel. 929-2077), rates are $11.50 for 9 holes and $16.50 for 18 holes. Rental carts are available at $12 for 9 holes, $20 for 18 holes, and clubs can be rented for $7.

The **Hiawatha Golf Course,** 4553 Longfellow Ave. S., Minneapolis (tel. 724-7715), charges $11.50 for 9 holes and $16.50 for 18 holes. Carts are rented at $12 for 9 holes, $20 for 18 holes, and clubs are available for $7 (18 holes), $3.50 (9 holes).

In addition, the 18-hole and 9-hole public courses in St. Paul's **Como Park** remain among the best around. Rates are $17 for 18 holes until 4pm; $12 from 4 to 6:15pm; $8.50 after 6:15pm. Cost for playing the 9-hole course is $11.50. Call 292-7400 for further information.

At **Edinburgh USA** golf course in Brooklyn Park, 8600 Edinbrook Crossing (tel. 424-7060), green fees are $29 for 18 holes.

HEALTH CLUB

If you're looking for a health club facility during your stay, consider the **Arena Health Club,** located in downtown Minneapolis at 1st Avenue North between 6th and 7th streets (tel. 673-1200). It offers racquetball, squash, and full-size basketball courts as well as a

75-foot-long swimming pool and a running/walking track. There are three aerobics studios here as well.

The 13 branches of the **Northwest Racquet, Swim & Health Clubs** are among the more prominent athletic clubs in the Twin Cities. Beginning with a major focus on sports and exercise, the clubs have continued to lead the industry by expanding their menu of health, fitness, exercise, and sports programs. The $15 daily admission fee entitles guests to full use of the facilities, including 18 different types of aerobics classes, racquetball, squash, running tracks, swimming, weight equipment, and pick-up basketball. For an additional fee guests can reserve tennis courts, train with professional exercise instructors, indulge in a therapeutic massage, relax in a suntan bed, and lunch at the snack bars.

Out-of-towners are most likely to visit the comprehensive health facilities at the **Arena Club** in Target Center at 600 1st Ave. N., Minneapolis (tel. 673-1200); the **Burnsville Club** at 14600 Burnhaven Dr., Burnsville (tel. 435-7125); the **Crosstown Club** at 6233 Baker Rd., Eden Prairie (tel. 934-4137); the **Hiway 100 Club** at 4001 Lake Breeze Ave., Brooklyn Center (tel. 535-3571); the **Moore Lake Club** at 1200 E. Moore Lake Dr., Fridley (tel. 571-3080); the **98th St. Club** at 1001 W. 98th St., Bloomington (tel. 884-1612); the **Normandale Club** at 6701 W. 78th St., Bloomington (tel. 944-2434); and the **Northwest Club** at 5525 Cedar Lake Rd., St. Louis Park (tel. 546-5474).

SAILING

Colorful sailboats are a familiar part of the summertime scenery in Minneapolis and St. Paul, where the next best thing to sailing is watching the graceful boats gliding through local lakes. Sailboat races are a weekend event each summer at **Lake Nokomis,** at Cedar Avenue and 50th Street in South Minneapolis, but more leisurely boaters are welcome to enjoy the facilities as well. This is one of three Minneapolis lakes designated for sailing; the other two are **Lake Harriet,** at Lake Harriet Parkway and William Berry Road, and **Lake Calhoun,** at 3000 E. Calhoun Parkway, off Lake Street.

If you'd like to try your own hand at sailing, or even wind-surfing, head for **Lake Phalen.** You'll reach the lake from an entrance at Wheelock Parkway and Arcade Street (Highway 61) or Maryland Avenue and Johnson Parkway. Sailboats and wind-surfing boards at the boathouse there rent for $9.50 for the first hour and $6 for every hour thereafter. (A deposit and a photo ID are required for rentals.) Hours are 10am to sundown. Call 771-7507 for more information.

SWIMMING

In St. Paul, **Phalen Park** offers a lovely sandy beach which is adjacent to walking and jogging paths and other park facilities. In Minneapolis, try the beach at **Cedar Lake. Thomas Beach,** at the south end of Lake Calhoun, is a favorite with Twin Cities visitors too. In suburban Eden Prairie, you'll find the popular **Round Lake Park** north of Highway 5 and west of Highway 4. And in northwest Bloomington, you'll enjoy **Bush Lake;** exit onto Bush Lake Road from I-494, proceed south for about 1½ miles, and there you are.

TENNIS

Several local clubs offer guest rates to visitors and offer discounts to those affiliated with the International Racquet Sports Association of America (IRSA). Among these are the following:

Eagan Athletic Club, 3330 Pilot Knob Rd., Eagan (tel. 454-8790), offers indoor tennis for $10 per hour. Tennis-ball machines are available at $2 per hour. The club is open Monday through Thursday from 6am to 11pm, Friday from 6am to 10pm, and Saturday and Sunday from 7am to 10pm.

Nicollet Tennis Center, 4005 Nicollet Ave., Minneapolis (tel. 825-6844), charges $13 an hour for a court. The center, open daily from 7am to 11pm, is located in Martin Luther King Park. These well-maintained courts are among the most popular in the area.

With more than 100 free public tennis courts located throughout the city of St. Paul, it would be impossible to list them here, but at **Phalen Park** you'll find popular courts at Johnson Parkway and Maryland Avenue, in a particularly attractive location adjacent to Lake Phalen. Tennis is on a first-come, first-served basis. Other beautifully located courts are those in Minneapolis's **Kenwood Park,** at the north end of Lake of the Isles. The most centrally located Minneapolis courts may be the ones in **Loring Park,** at Hennepin Avenue and Harmon Place. On the edge of downtown Minneapolis, these courts have a view of Loring Lake. For information about municipal courts, call the Park Board (tel. 348-2226 for courts in Minneapolis, 292-7400 for courts in St. Paul).

WINTER SPORTS

For serious **skiing,** experienced downhill skiers often head north to **Duluth's Spirit Mountain** during the winter (see Chapter 11), but for cross-country and beginning downhill skiers there's a lot of fun to be had right in town. At **Como Park** in St. Paul there's downhill skiing, with a ski lift and a chalet featuring light food service. In **Wirth Park,** snow machines are ready to help nature along whenever necessary. At **Crosby Farm Park,** with an entrance off Shepherd Road and Mississippi River Boulevard, cross-country skiers can imagine they're off somewhere in the remote wilderness as they traverse the idyllic trails under a canopy of trees.

One of the big surprises of the past couple winters was the popularity of **snowtubing** at Wirth Park, where "Winter at Wirth," a comprehensive program of snow-related activities, has attracted people from throughout the Twin Cities. Adults pay $3 daily, children $1, for an innertube that will whirl round and round while one is sliding down the snowy hill.

You'll see **ice-skating** on virtually all city and suburban lakes; most have warming houses which provide a welcome and considerate touch.

CHAPTER 8

STROLLING AROUND THE TWIN CITIES

1. HISTORIC ST. PAUL
2. HISTORIC MINNEAPOLIS
3. THE NEW MINNEAPOLIS

Since the Twin Cities boast lots of historic buildings and cultural centers, I've provided you with walking tours that highlight their individual and common heritage. I also want you to see the more recent additions to the skyline in downtown Minneapolis.

WALKING TOUR 1 — HISTORIC ST. PAUL

Start: Rice Park, 5th Street at Market Street.
Finish: Minnesota History Center, 345 W. Kellogg Blvd.
Time: About 2¾ hours, including brief visits to some of the buildings along the way.

Begin your tour of historic St. Paul at:

1. **Rice Park.** Read the historic marker here explaining how this "urban oasis," which fills a complete city block with its trees, lawns, flowers, and fountain, has served as the site of circuses, celebrations, and concerts for almost 150 years. The park was named for U.S. Senator Henry M. Rice, who came to Fort Snelling from Vermont in 1839, became a fur trader, and later served as an intermediary in treaty negotiations with Sioux and Chippewa tribes.

   On the east side of the park, you'll find the distinguished:

2. **Saint Paul Hotel,** 350 Market St. Since 1910, this has been one of the finest luxury hotels in the Twin Cities, the destination of choice for businesspersons and tourists. The hotel was extensively renovated in the mid-1980s.

   On the south side of the square, at 90 W. 4th St., you'll find the handsome building that houses two important resources for Twin Citians, the:

3. **St. Paul Public Library** and the **James Jerome Hill Reference Library,** both housed in the same structure, an Italian Renaissance–style building erected in 1916. The exterior is Tennessee marble.

   Continue to the west side of Rice Park and enter the:

4. **Ordway Music Theatre,** 345 Washington St., which is well worth a visit whether or not you're attending a performance. A beautiful marble staircase will take you to the second floor, where huge windows provide a magnificent view of the city.

   On the north side of the park is the:

5. **Landmark Center,** 75 W. 5th St., which looks like a castle but is actually a restored Federal Court Building where you can visit courtrooms in which some of this country's most notorious gangsters came to trial. Despite its upstanding reputation, St. Paul was a refuge in earlier decades for several infamous characters, including John Dillinger and Ma Barker. Designed in a neo-Romanesque style, the building was erected in 1902. It now houses several arts organizations, including the Minnesota Museum of American Art.

   Across Washington Street from the Landmark Center you'll see the newly constructed world headquarters of the:

6. **St. Paul Companies.** A block away you'll find the:

7. **World Trade Center,** 7th and Wabash streets, an imposing office complex opened in fall 1987 for the purpose of encouraging and expediting international trade. The adjacent retail area includes a spectacular 52-foot indoor fountain as well as a diversity of shops and restaurants. The second-story skyway leads to:

8. **Town Square,** where you'll have a beautiful view of the Minnesota State Capitol, as well as a busy complex of offices and shops.

REFUELING STOP   Take the escalator down to the **Food Court** on the lowest level, where you'll find a variety of fast-food stands selling hamburgers, hot dogs, ice cream, yogurt, and ethnic fare. Gather some goodies for a picnic, then take the glass elevator up to:

---

9. **Town Square Park,** the world's largest indoor park. Here you'll find dining areas nestled in among the trees, bushes, and fountains. If you're so inclined, conclude your stay with a ride on the carousel.

   When you're ready to continue your tour, take the escalator or elevator down to the second floor skyway level and retrace your steps to the World Trade Center; then take the Wabasha Street exit and continue on Wabasha to the:

10. **World Theater,** 10 E. Exchange St. This is where Garrison Keillor, after a hiatus in New York City, has returned to broadcast local performances of his famous radio show. Pass, or enter if time permits, the:

11. **Science Museum of Minnesota,** 30 E. 10th St. Exhibits here range from the anthropological to the technological. Be

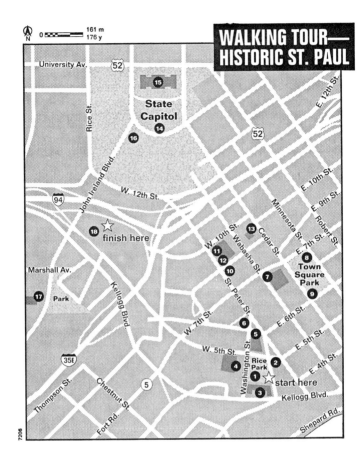

1 Rice Park
2 Saint Paul Hotel
3 St. Paul Public Library
4 Ordway Music Theatre
5 Landmark Center
6 St. Paul Companies
7 World Trade Center
8 Town Square
9 Town Square Park
10 World Theater
11 Science Museum of Minnesota
12 Omnitheater
13 Arts and Science Center
14 Capitol Mall
15 Minnesota State Capitol
16 Charles Lindbergh statue
17 Cathedral of St. Paul
18 Minnesota History Center

sure to notice Iggy, the giant steel iguana, who lolls in front of the main entrance serving as a bench for youngsters and their elders. You may want to return at another time to see an exciting and educational film in the circular second story:

12. William L. McKnight–3M Omnitheater. The screen here is 76 feet in diameter.

As you leave the main entrance of the Science Museum,

you'll be at 10th and Cedar streets, where you'll turn left and then proceed up to the:

13. **Capitol Mall,** which is bordered by diverse state office buildings, the most prominent of which is the:

14. **Minnesota State Capitol,** at Cedar and Aurora streets, situated on a hill overlooking downtown St. Paul. Flanked by a succession of broad, gray-granite terraces and crowned by the world's largest unsupported marble dome, this magnificent building is the work of Cass Gilbert, who later designed the Woolworth Building in New York City. The interior of the capitol is impressive, with its marble stairways, chambers, and halls and its classic oil paintings depicting events and persons from Minnesota history.

After leaving the capitol, take John Ireland Boulevard past the lovely:

15. **Charles Lindbergh statue.** Created by noted Minnesota sculptor Paul Granlund, this statue depicts Lindbergh as a boy and a man. At the far end of John Ireland Boulevard, you'll come to the majestic:

16. **Cathedral of St. Paul,** 239 Selby Ave., which occupies the highest site in the city of St. Paul. Dedicated in 1915, it's modeled after St. Peter's Basilica in Rome. Now follow John Ireland Boulevard to the new home of the:

17. **Minnesota History Center,** 345 W. Kellogg Blvd., where you'll find an astounding assortment of historical documents, artifacts, books, photographs, maps, and manuscripts, as well as a gift shop with a great selection of Minnesota memorabilia at some of the best prices in town.

WALKING TOUR 2 — HISTORIC MINNEAPOLIS

Start: Nicollet Mall and Washington Avenue.
Finish: Former Milwaukee Depot.
Time: 2 hours.

Begin your tour of historic Minneapolis at the location of the first bridge to span the Mississippi River, now the site of newly constructed:

1. **Hennepin Avenue Suspension Bridge.** The bridge leads to:

2. **Nicollet Island,** where in the mid-19th century sawmills and lumber mills, powered by St. Anthony Falls, established the village of St. Anthony as a prosperous industrial center. Today the northern half of the island is residential, while much of the rest is industrial. Cross the footbridge to:

3. **Main Street,** once literally the main street of Minneapolis. Follow Main Street to East Hennepin Avenue and, after a block, turn right again. There you'll see:

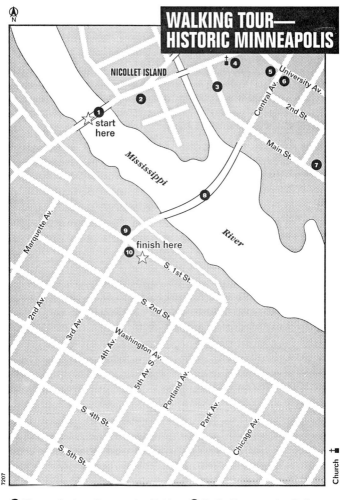

WALKING TOUR—
HISTORIC MINNEAPOLIS

N

NICOLLET ISLAND

start here

Mississippi

River

finish here

University Av.
Central Av.
2nd St.
Main St.
S. 1st St.
S. 2nd St.
Washington Av.
S. 4th St.
S. 5th St.
Marquette Av.
2nd Av.
3rd Av.
4th Av.
5th Av.
Portland Av.
Park Av.
Chicago Av.

Church

7207

1 Hennepin Ave. Suspension Bridge
2 Nicollet Island
3 Main Street
4 Our Lady of Lourdes Church
5 Ard Godfrey House
6 Dolly Fiterman Art Gallery
7 Pillsbury Company
8 Third Ave. Bridge
9 Minneapolis Post Office
10 Milwaukee Depot

4. Our Lady of Lourdes Church, the oldest continuously used church in Minneapolis. Opened in 1857 by the First Universalist Society, it was bought in 1877 by the French Canadian Roman Catholic community and designated a U.S. Historic Landmark in 1934.

A short distance east stands tiny Chute Park, which contains the:

5. **Ard Godfrey House,** University and Central avenues. Built in 1848, this is the earliest frame house still standing in Minneapolis. Ard Godfrey was a millwright from Maine who came here in 1847 to build a sawmill at St. Anthony Falls.

Across Central Avenue at University Avenue is the:

6. **Dolly Fiterman Art Gallery,** housed in a historic building which once served as a branch of the Minneapolis Public Library.

Follow University Avenue east for two blocks, then turn to the right and you'll see:

7. **Pillsbury Company,** one of the world's largest food manufacturers. From this site you can look across the river at other portions of the Mill District. Among them is the Washburn Crosby Mill, a predecessor of the now world-famous General Mills. (Minneapolis was long known as Mill City, the flour capital of the world.)

Back on Main Street, walk north to a:

REFUELING STOP   Pracna on Main, 117 Main St. SE, is a popular restaurant and bar, where outdoor dining flourishes during the summertime. Menu items include Reuben sandwiches, charbroiled chicken breast, and steak.

After your break continue north. You'll soon reach a circular staircase leading to the:

8. **Third Avenue Bridge,** which in turn will take you back to downtown Minneapolis. (If you'd rather avoid the stairs, take the 2nd Street exit from St. Anthony Main's upper level, then turn left to Central Avenue, which leads to the 3rd Avenue Bridge.) As you cross the bridge, look to the right and get a spectacular view of St. Anthony Falls and the Minneapolis skyline.

After crossing the bridge at the intersection of 3rd Avenue and 1st Street, see the:

9. **Minneapolis Post Office,** a huge sprawling complex that occupies two city blocks, replacing the original post office building on the same side of the street two blocks ahead. Across the street is the former:

10. **Milwaukee Depot,** 3rd Ave S., at Washington Ave. It's on the National Historic Registry. City officials and developers hope to transform this site into a retail and office complex.

WALKING TOUR 3 — THE NEW MINNEAPOLIS

Start: Northwestern National Life Insurance Company, 20 Washington Ave. S.
Finish: Hubert H. Humphrey Metrodome.
Time: 2 hours.

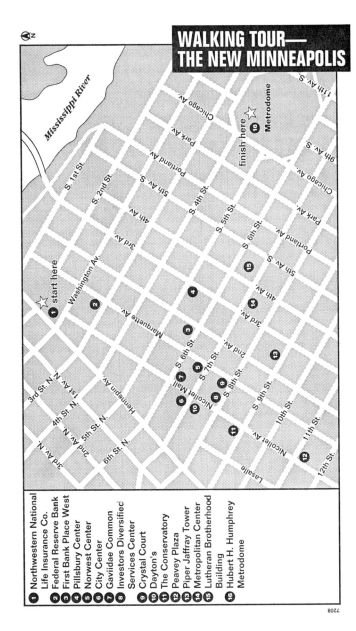

Mississippi River

☆ start here

N

finish here ☆

Metrodome

Washington Av.

S. 1st St.

S. 2nd St.

3rd Av.

4th Av.

Marquette Av.

S. 6th St.

S. 7th St.

Nicollet Mall

S. 8th St.

Hennepin Av.

3rd St. N.

1st Av. N.

4th St. N.

2nd Av. N.

5th St. N.

3rd Av. N.

6th St. N.

Nicollet Av.

Lasalle

Chicago Av.

Park Av.

Portland Av.

5th Av.

S. 4th St.

S. 5th St.

S. 6th St.

4th Av.

3rd Av.

2nd Av.

S. 9th St.

10th St.

11th St.

12th St.

Portland Av.

Park Av.

Chicago Av.

9th Av.

S. 11th Av. S.

1 Northwestern National Life Insurance Co.
2 Federal Reserve Bank
3 First Bank Place West
4 Pillsbury Center
5 Norwest Center
6 City Center
7 Gaviidae Common
8 Investors Diversified Services Center
9 Crystal Court
10 Dayton's
11 The Conservatory
12 Peavey Plaza
13 Piper Jaffray Tower
14 Metropolitan Center
15 Lutheran Brotherhood Building
16 Hubert H. Humphrey Metrodome

7208

During the past several decades, the skyline of Minneapolis has changed dramatically as a succession of sleek new buildings replaced their predecessors. One of the most acclaimed newcomers is located at 20 Washington Ave. S.:

1. Northwestern National Life Insurance Company. This is one of the loveliest and earliest landmarks of the new

Minneapolis. Modeled after the Parthenon, this magnificent marble structure with graceful Doric columns was pictured on the cover of *Time*.

Nearby, at 250 Marquette Ave., is the:

2. **Federal Reserve Bank Building,** reportedly the first American building designed on the cantilevered suspension system usually reserved for bridges.

Now walk to 120 6th St. S. to the:

3. **First Bank Place West,** a gleaming stainless steel building which is connected by skyway to the:

4. **Pillsbury Center** which contains a remarkable eight-story prismatic atrium. At 6th Street and Marquette Avenue, the 57-story:

5. **Norwest Center** lends an elegant tone to downtown Minneapolis. Constructed of a combination of buff-colored stone and white marble, it's considered one of the finest works of architect Cesar Pelli.

At the center of downtown, you'll find:

6. **City Center,** a 6-acre expanse which occupies the square block between 6th and 7th streets and Nicollet and Hennepin avenues. A newer addition to downtown faces City Center across Nicollet Mall:

7. **Gaviidae Common,** an elegant five-level shopping and entertainment complex anchored by two upscale department stores— Saks Fifth Avenue and Neiman Marcus. The tallest building in downtown Minneapolis stands across 7th Avenue from Gaviidae Common:

8. **Investors Diversified Services Center.** Known locally as the IDS Tower, it is considered one of the finest works of famed architect Philip Johnson. It stands 51 stories high and contains the:

9. **Crystal Court,** which serves as focal point of the city's skyway system.

On Nicollet Avenue, between 7th and 8th avenues, you'll find:

10. **Dayton's Department Store,** arguably the most popular family business in the Twin Cities. Dayton's is connected by skyway and subway to:

11. **The Conservatory,** a splendid glass-and-marble shopping center containing an upscale collection of shops and boutiques.

Farther up Nicollet Avenue at 11th Street:

12. **Peavey Plaza** adjoins Orchestra Hall and offers a picturesque outdoor setting for ice-skating during the winter and outdoor wining and dining during the festival, Sommerfest. On the way back toward the eastern edge of downtown, you'll pass some particularly handsome and interesting buildings.

At 222 S. 9th St. you'll come upon the:

13. **Piper Jaffray Tower,** a 42-story building that features innumerable panes of aqua-blue glass and provides a particularly dramatic addition to the skyline.

A few blocks away, at 333 S. 7th St., is:

14. **Metropolitan Center,** a gray granite building complemented with black, white, and green marble.

At the corner of 4th Avenue and S. 7th St. is the:

15. Lutheran Brotherhood Building, a marble and copper-colored glass structure.

And finally, five blocks away at 900 S. 5th St., there's the:

16. Hubert H. Humphrey Metrodome, maybe the most recognizable structure in downtown Minneapolis. Old-time Twin Citians still miss the fun and excitement of outdoor big-league play, but out-of-towners appreciate the certainty that the game they want to attend here won't be rained out.

CHAPTER 9

SAVVY SHOPPING

1. THE SHOPPING SCENE
2. SHOPPING A TO Z

In 1956, Southdale, the country's very first fully enclosed, climate-controlled shopping mall, opened its doors in the Twin Cities and changed American life forever. "Going to the mall" has become as American as apple pie, as thousands of communities followed the Twin Cities' lead.

Minneapolis and St. Paul have always been a mecca for shoppers. In addition to Southdale and the new Mall of America (see Chapter 11), there are well over 100 other shopping centers in the area; while it's impossible to tell you about all of them, what follows will give you an idea of the many and varied shopping experiences awaiting you in the Twin Cities.

1. THE SHOPPING SCENE

HOURS

Shopping hours are generally 9 or 10am to 8 or 9pm Monday through Friday, 9:30am to 6pm on Saturday, and noon to 5pm on Sunday. During holiday periods, shopping hours are usually extended.

GREAT SHOPPING AREAS

The specialty shopping along **Grand Avenue** in St. Paul has gained enormous popularity during recent years; even if you don't buy anything here, the browsing is bound to be memorable. There are two popular shopping malls on Grand Avenue: Victoria Crossing at 857 Grand Ave. and Milton Mall at Milton and Grand.

Downtown St. Paul has its own array of fine shops in two shopping malls which face each other across Cedar Street. At the World Trade Center, with its spectacular indoor fountain, you'll find apparel shops including **J. Riggings** and the **Limited,** while at Town Square, **Peck and Peck, Victoria's Secret,** and **Eddie Bauer,** among others, await you. A few blocks away at Carriage Hill Plaza, you'll find **Frank Murphy,** a longtime favorite among discriminating shoppers.

In **downtown Minneapolis** four giant department stores dominate Nicollet Mall: **Saks Fifth Avenue, Neiman Marcus, Montgomery Ward,** and **Dayton's.** There's one in the basement too—**Filene's.** The Conservatory shopping center is another standout in the Nicollet Mall. Other nearby shops in this area can be found in the City Center (tel. 372-1234) and the IDS Crystal Court (tel. 372-1660).

2. SHOPPING A TO Z

ANTIQUES

ANTIQUES MINNESOTA [MINNEAPOLIS], 1516 E. Lake St., Minneapolis. Tel. 722-6000.
This is the oldest, largest antiques mall in the Twin Cities, with four floors of items offered by 120 dealers. There's also a repair service. Open Monday.

ANTIQUES MINNESOTA [ST. PAUL], 1197 University Ave., St. Paul. Tel. 646-0037.
You'll find collectibles here as well as antiques and a repair service for vintage radios as well as clocks.

NAKASHIAN-O'NEIL, INC. 23 W. 6th St., St. Paul. Tel. 224-5465.
This may be the oldest establishment of its kind in the Twin Cities, dating back to 1906 and selling lovely works of porcelain, jade, and silver among other treasures. In addition to the antiques, there's a well-stocked gift boutique here as well.

WESTCOTT STATION ANTIQUES, 226 W. 7th St., St. Paul. Tel. 227-2469.
You'll find here thousands of antiques including glassware, furniture, toys, and more.

BOOKS

No Twin Cities shopping chapter would be complete without mentioning the abundance of bookstores. We have the distinction of being home to the first-ever B. Dalton Bookseller, which opened in suburban Edina back in 1966. There are now nearly two dozen B. Dalton Booksellers in this area. Add to that some six Barnes and Noble bookstores, about seven Waldenbooks, and a variety of independent and specialty stores, and you'll see that people hereabouts do a lot of reading. Here's a partial listing of the bookstores you'll find in the Twin Cities.

THE HUNGRY MIND, 1648 Grand Ave., St. Paul. Tel. 699-0587.
The Hungry Mind boasts an extraordinary selection of books—fiction, biographies, cookbooks, poetry, children's books, and more. The relaxed ambience here is enhanced by easy chairs and couches. Table of Contents, a recently opened café, shares the premises, so there's more than food for thought to be found here. And here's a tip: The store has a 30% off sale every June. The Hungry Mind offers a free story hour for children at 11am each Saturday. Also, there are free author events about three times a week; call for a schedule.

ODEGARD BOOKS, Victoria Crossing, 857 Grand Ave., St. Paul. Tel. 222-2711.

There are actually three separate Odegard bookstores here, one with a general stock, one devoted primarily to books on travel, and one which offers remainders and other deeply discounted books.

ORR BOOKS, 3043 Hennepin Ave., Minneapolis. Tel. 823-2408.

This busy independent store in Minneapolis's uptown area carries fiction; small-press literature; books on psychology, spirituality, Native Americans, and women; and general-interest books. The store discounts all new hardcover books and carries paperbacks as well.

RED BALLOON, 891 Grand Ave., St. Paul. Tel. 224-8320.

You'll find all sorts of children's and young adult books at Red Balloon, which claims to have the widest selection of picture books in the Midwest. Besides selling 20,000 titles, the Red Balloon also carries audio- and videotapes, as well as games and toys. The store offers free story hours for children at 10:30am each Wednesday and Saturday and also provides frequent author/illustrator visits and other special events.

CRAFTS

HEARTLEAF, 170 Cobblestone Lane, Burnsville. Tel. 892-0123.

As you explore Heartleaf, you will turn one corner after another to discover new delights, including handmade prints, painting, crafts, and pottery. Everything from floral displays to kitchenware, jewelry, Christmas items, toys, and Minnesota souvenirs awaits you here. Certain sections are arranged by the color of the products. Even if you don't buy a thing, you'll have a great time just looking around.

DISCOUNT SHOPPING

BANK'S, 615 1st Ave. NE, Minneapolis. Tel. 379-4321 (sales updates), 379-2803 (customer service). 1441 E. Magnolia St., St. Paul. Tel. 771-9175.

Some of the biggest bargains in town can be found at Bank's, but examine your selection carefully before buying. This is a clearinghouse for insurance companies whose clients have suffered reverses due to fire, flood, and other calamities. (Some shoppers routinely sniff for traces of smoke.) With a little care, though, you can save very big bucks here on name brand and designer clothes, with discounts ranging from 30 to 75% off regular prices.

BURLINGTON COAT FACTORY, St. Louis Park. Tel. 929-6850.

Burlington offers a lot more than coats. You'll find a wide variety of clothing for the whole family here, with periodic arrivals of ultrasuede apparel at very good prices.

LAST CALL ON FOUR NEIMAN MARCUS, 505 Nicollet Mall, Minneapolis. Tel. 339-2600.

On sale are women's garments and accessories from Neiman Marcus stores throughout the country. You'll save 50% to 75% off the original retail price.

LOEHMANN'S, at 98th St. and Normandale Blvd., Bloomington. Tel. 835-2510.

Loehmann's in suburban Bloomington offers discount designer fashions including Donna Karan. Among the items sold here are evening dresses, jackets, blouses, casual clothing, jewelry, purses, and umbrellas.

OPITZ OUTLET, 4320 Excelsior Blvd., St. Louis Park. Tel. 922-9088.

There are some great bargains in this discount store, which is only open from Friday through Sunday each week. (When the store is closed, it's being completely restocked.) You'll probably see a newspaper ad for Opitz sometime during your stay, but be aware you may have to read between the lines concerning the week's offerings. For example, if you see the words, "We've got a secret," you can be pretty sure it's Victoria's (meaning the well-known lingerie).

DOLLS

MARY D'S DOLLS & BEARS AND SUCH, 8409 W. Broadway, Commons Mall, Brooklyn Park. Tel. 424-4375.

Collectors of dolls will find a great assortment here along with a lot of expertise on the part of Mary D, who'll advise you about pitfalls to avoid when you're selecting collectible dolls. Madame Alexander and Barbie are among the beauties you'll encounter here.

FISHING SPECIALTIES

THORNE BROTHERS FISHING SPECIALTY STORE, 7500 University Ave. NE, Fridley. Tel. 572-3782.

If you're in the market for lures made exclusively for muskies, this is the place for you. The largest muskie wall in the country awaits you here. You'll also find equipment for making your own custom rod.

FOOD

BYERLY'S, 3777 Park Center Blvd., St. Louis Park. Tel. 929-2100.

You won't want to leave the Twin Cities without a visit to Byerly's, one of the world's most unusual supermarkets, as well as a self-contained shopping center par excellence. Retailers from throughout the world travel to the Twin Cities regularly to tour this flagship store of Don Byerly's chain. What's all the fuss about? In contrast to the usual supermarket, which carries 15,000 to 18,000 items, Byerly's carries over 25,000. And that includes everything from catsup for 25¢ to mustard for $25 (a French Dijon packaged in a ceramic jar). Besides food, there is a Gift Gallery here selling collectibles at prices ranging from $10 for small hand-carved wooden animals to $75,000 for a gold-plated 6-foot-tall bird cage. Laliques and Hummels are sold here too, as are imported women's accessories by Judith Leiber, whose snakeskin belts go for $50 to $300.

Services as well as goods are available at Byerly's. Particularly popular is the on-site cooking school, with classes in everything from ethnic to microwave to couples' cooking. News of these and other classes are published in the in-house publication, *Byerly's Bag.*

Other nice touches here are the wide carpeted aisles, on-site restaurants, delicatessens, salad bars, and the 24-hour service.

MALLS & SHOPPING CENTERS

For a detailed description of Mall of America, see Chapter 11.

THE CONSERVATORY, 808 Nicollet Mall, Minneapolis. Tel. 332-4649.

This remarkable shopping center opened in downtown Minneapolis in the fall of 1987, and chances are you've never seen anything quite like it. Designed as a "20th-century public square," the block-long Conservatory boasts two dramatic four-story glass atriums, two gracefully winding staircases, an abundance of decorative trees, and a ground-floor dining court.

Connected by skyway and by underground "serpentine" to **Dayton's,** one of the city's premier department stores, the Conservatory offers enticing wares of its own. Among the upscale retailers located here are the **Sharper Image,** a shop filled with wondrous electronic gadgetry, and the **Nature Company,** with unique gifts for those you left at home. A local firm that chose to locate at the Conservatory is **Frost and Bud,** a specialty gift shop. What souvenirs you'll discover here! Want to take home a set of boccie balls, a sundial, or a personalized birdhouse? The Conservatory can offer you these—and a whole lot more.

GAVIIDAE COMMON, 6th St. on the Mall, Minneapolis. Tel. 372-1222.

Directly across Nicollet Mall is this elegant downtown shopping complex whose list of tenants reads like a retailing "Who's Who": **Burberry's, Talbots, Laurel, Joan Vass, Lillie Rubin, Brentano's, Westminster Lace, Eddie Bauer, Anne Klein, Neiman Marcus,** and **Saks Fifth Avenue.** Their presence here indicates a real commitment to the Twin Cities and, in fact, to Minnesota as a whole. In fact, the name "Gaviidae"—Latin for loon—pays tribute to the state bird of Minnesota (a 20-foot wood and metal loon emerging from a pool of water is the focal point for the magnificent five-level atrium here).

CALHOUN SQUARE, at the corner of Hennepin Ave. and Lake St., Minneapolis. Tel. 824-1240.

In the trendy uptown section of Minneapolis (also known as "Yuptown"), you'll find Calhoun Square, a bustling two-story mall offering great shopping, dining, and people watching. Shops here include Al John's Beach Shop, Bay Street Shoes, Kitchen Window, and Toy Boat.

There are also three galleries featuring works of local artists, and more than 70 other shops and restaurants.

GALLERIA, 69th St. and France Ave., a block south of Southdale, Edina. Tel. 925-4321.

A fashionable upscale center with 60 shops and restaurants, Galleria has a picturesque setting, with lush greenery, soft lighting, and cobblestone walkways. You'll find stores specializing in hand-bags, books, swimwear, furs, cookware, dolls, gourmet foods, pottery, and a great deal more. When Galleria advertises a sale, run do not walk. At other times, be advised that prices—and quality—tend to be high.

RIDGEDALE, on I-394 (Wayzata Blvd.), 1 mile east of I-494, Minnetonka. Tel. 541-4864.

Ridgedale, which opened in 1974, is now a favorite for thousands of shoppers. A graceful fountain stands among palm trees in the skylit center court. Four sections extend in a pinwheel pattern and contain more than 140 specialty shops representing national and local retailers, including four major department stores—**Dayton's, Carson Pirie Scott, J C Penney,** and **Sears.** In addition, there are more than 20 merchants who offer unique specialty retail on the Minnetonka Market pushcarts. Open Monday to Friday from 10am to 9:30pm; Saturday from 10am to 8pm; Sunday from noon to 6pm.

SOUTHDALE, 66th St. and France Ave. S., Edina. Tel. 925-7885.

There were lots of unanswered questions when Southdale opened its doors for the first time. Would there really be enough business in the quiet community of Edina (just southwest of Minneapolis) to support two of the area's largest department stores, as well as 64 specialty shops, under one roof? Well, today more than 30 years after that grand opening, **Dayton's** and **Carson Pirie Scott** face each other across Southdale's busy courtyard, while a third department store, **J C Penney,** has been doing a brisk business as well. And nearly 200 specialty shops thrive elsewhere in the mall.

A splendid new four-story Dayton's opened right next door to the original store in 1990. The greatly enlarged new space made a variety of welcome innovations possible, including a full-service **Estée Lauder Spa,** complimentary coat checking, and a drive-through parcel-pick-up area accommodating six cars at one time. Serving as a backdrop to the dramatic display of top-quality merchandise throughout the elegant Southdale Dayton's are striking works of art, including three lovely murals.

In addition to the three big-name department stores, Southdale houses nationally known shops like **Crate and Barrel, J. Crew, Banana Republic, Talbots Kids, The Disney Store, Lerner's, B. Dalton, Nature Company, Museum Store,** and **Rand McNally.** But what may interest you more are the dozens of specialty shops with less-familiar names that feature fine apparel, jewelry, mementos, and more. You'll also find a full-service postal substation here, along with a Northwest Airlines ticket office, and two 1-hour photo processing shops.

MUSICAL INSTRUMENTS

HOMESTEAD PICKIN' PARLOR, 6625 Penn Ave. S., Richfield. Tel. 861-3308.

If you'd like to take a special harmonica back home with you, this is the place to find it. The Pickin' Parlor is a folk-music shop with a wide selection of instruments, CD's, LP's, and tapes.

CHAPTER 10

TWIN CITIES NIGHTS

1. THE PERFORMING ARTS
- **MAJOR CONCERT & PERFORMANCE HALLS**
2. THE CLUB & MUSIC SCENE
3. THE BAR SCENE

You'll be surprised by the diversity of entertainment awaiting you when the sun sets in the Twin Cities. The concert halls and theaters compare favorably with those elsewhere in the country, and so does the quality of entertainment. Some of the country's most popular entertainers perform in Twin Cities nightclubs, and some local entertainers have gone on to international stardom—the popular musician Prince being one. (The relatively low cost of an evening out will be a pleasant surprise too.)

Upcoming events are listed every Friday in the *St. Paul Pioneer Press* and the *Star Tribune*. There are, in addition, a number of widely available weekly and monthly periodicals, many of them free, that provide useful information.

1. THE PERFORMING ARTS

PERFORMING ARTS COMPANIES
OPERA & CLASSICAL MUSIC

THE MINNESOTA ORCHESTRA, Orchestra Hall, 1111 Nicollet Mall, Minneapolis. Tel. 371-5656.

The Minnesota Orchestra (formerly known as the Minneapolis Symphony) was founded in 1903, the eighth major orchestra to be established in the United States. In 1923 it was heard on crystal radio sets; one year later it became the second major American orchestra to make recordings of its performances. Under the leadership of Eugene Ormandy from 1931 to 1936, the orchestra gained international recognition through recordings and its concerts abroad.

Dmitri Mitropoulos served as conductor from 1937 to 1949. In 1957, under conductor Antal Dorati, the orchestra made a 34,000-mile tour of the Middle East sponsored by the U.S. State Department. During the 19-year tenure of Stanislaw Skrowaczewski, the group increased in size to 95 musicians and took up residence in its new home at Orchestra Hall. The Minnesota Orchestra also performs at St. Paul's Ordway Music Theatre (tel. 224-4222) and makes guest appearances throughout the nation and the world. Since September 1986 the orchestra has been led by the distinguished conductor Edo de Waart.

Prices: Tickets $10–$37.

ST. PAUL CHAMBER ORCHESTRA, 75 W. 5th St., St. Paul. Tel. 291-1144.

The St. Paul Chamber Orchestra, the nation's only full-time professional chamber orchestra, may be performing at the Ordway Music Theatre while you're here, or you may find them in one of the shopping centers, churches, or school auditoriums that used to welcome them during their homeless years when they were identified as "Music on the Move." The group originated in 1959 when a group of St. Paulites decided to find a conductor to head a group of freelance professional musicians who performed educational programs. They eventually established a 10-concert season, went on tour, and gained enough backing to incorporate under the name St. Paul Chamber Orchestra.

By the late 1970s the group had undertaken a number of important tours—to 140 American cities and to Western and Eastern Europe and the old Soviet Union. During this time it also gained a reputation for regularly combining established classical works and world premieres on the same program.

From 1980 to 1987, under the leadership of Pinchas Zukerman, the chamber orchestra hosted such music greats as Isaac Stern and Misha Dichter. Under Zukerman's leadership the local season expanded to 80 concerts and the St. Paul Chamber Orchestra gained fame as one of the country's best musical groups, with frequent guest appearances at Carnegie Hall, Avery Fisher Hall, and the Kennedy Center.

The orchestra now performs 150 concerts during a 40-week season that extends from September to June. In addition to performing at the Ordway, it makes music at seven other locations around the Twin Cities.

Prices: Tickets $9–$31.50.

THE SCHUBERT CLUB, 301 Landmark Center, 75 W. 5th St., St. Paul. Tel. 292-3267.

Vladimir Horowitz, Isaac Stern, Robert Casadesus, and Beverly Sills are among the renowned artists who've been brought to St. Paul several times by the Schubert Club, founded in 1882 and now one of

---

MAJOR CONCERT & PERFORMANCE HALLS

The Guthrie Theater, 725 Vineland Place, Minneapolis. Tel. 377-2224.

Northrup Auditorium, 84 Church St. S.E., University of Minnesota. Tel. 624-2345.

Orchestra Hall, 1111 Nicollet Mall, Minneapolis. Tel. 371-5656.

Ordway Music Theatre, 345 Washington St., St. Paul. Tel. 224-4222.

University Theatre, 120 Rarig Center, University of Minnesota West Bank Campus. Tel. 625-4001.

the oldest musical organizations in the United States. If you're a music lover, you might want to inquire about whether one of the 50 or so recitals they offer each year will be at the Ordway Music Theatre during your stay.

In addition to bringing celebrated artists from throughout the world to perform in the Twin Cities, the Schubert Club regularly commissions work from selected composers. One of these works, "From the Diary of Virginia Woolf" by Dominick Argento, won the Pulitzer Prize in music in 1975. This work was sung by Dame Janet Baker both here in St. Paul and at Carnegie Hall in New York City.

Among the club's other projects has been the establishment and maintenance of a musical museum containing over 75 keyboard instruments dating back to the mid-16th century.

Prices: Tickets $12–$25.

DANCE COMPANIES

No cities except New York and Washington, D.C., offer a more active professional dance scene than the one you'll find in Minneapolis and St. Paul. Whatever the season, there's likely to be at least one major performance during your stay. Calendars of local and touring dance programs are published weekly in local newspapers and magazines, and the **Minnesota Dance Alliance** (tel. 340-1900) will provide specific information about current and upcoming presentations.

You'll find the price of tickets to dance performances is remarkably low in the Twin Cities. Prices for touring dance productions range from $8 to $23; for local companies, $5 to $15.

The **O'Shaughnessey Dance Series,** a 6-week program offered during the spring of each year, is the only one of its kind in the country. Committed to spotlighting local professional dance companies, it undertakes a major selection process, then presents its annual series in the beautiful 1,800-seat O'Shaughnessey Auditorium, 2004 Randolph Ave., St. Paul (tel. 690-6700), on the campus of the College of Saint Catherine. Among the local troupes that have appeared in the O'Shaughnessey series have been the dynamic **Zorongo Flamenco Dance Theatre,** one of only five professional Spanish Gypsy dance troupes in the country, as well as **Danny Buraczeski Jazzdance, Zenon Dance Company,** and **James Sewell Dance.**

Summerdance, a 2-week series sponsored by the Minnesota Dance Alliance in June, also showcases the work of selected local companies and choreographers. In 1987 this festival took place in the intimate McKnight Playhouse at the Ordway Music Theatre (see above). The Children's Theatre Company (see below) and the Hennepin Center for the Arts, 528 Hennepin Ave. (tel. 332-4478), also play host to these programs from time to time.

ETHNIC DANCE THEATRE, 1940 Hennepin Ave., Minneapolis. Tel. 872-0024.

The Ethnic Dance Theatre is a performing arts ensemble of 45 dancers, vocalists, and instrumentalists dedicated to celebrating and preserving the dynamic traditions of ethnic dance and the music of diverse cultures of the world. Since 1974, EDT has brought its performances, lecture/demonstrations, and workshops to communities throughout the Midwest. Subjects are diverse, ranging from the vibrant Chinese Dance of the Red Silk Ribbons to a comical cowboy dance from Mexico's Norteno region.

Prices: Tickets $12–$16.

THEATER COMPANIES

Although Twin Cities theater didn't gain international prominence until the establishment in 1964 of the Tyrone Guthrie Theater, first-rate productions had been attracting theatergoers for a long time before that. The Old Log, one of the country's oldest stock companies, began staging professional productions in 1941. Theater in the Round, one of the country's longest-lived community theaters, staged its first performance in 1952. The Brave New Workshop, the country's oldest satirical revue, was founded in 1958, five years before Chicago's Second City company.

What's best about today's Twin Cities theater is that it's a year-round activity for audiences of widely different tastes. There's mainstream theater and avant-garde theater, dinner theater and coffeehouse theater, theater in the park and theater in the round, children's theater, historical theater, showboat theater, and a lot more.

In the Twin Cities theater is not primarily a business but an art; it's supported in large part by contributions from individuals and corporations. Ticket prices are relatively low in Minneapolis and St. Paul; a good seat will seldom cost more than $15 to $20, and student, senior citizen, and standby rates are lower still. Also, transportation poses few problems here: even outlying theaters are easy to reach by highway and freeway, and parking is either free or inexpensive.

What follows is a listing of some of the theatrical companies that await you in Minneapolis and St. Paul.

DUDLEY RIGGS' BRAVE NEW WORKSHOP, 2605 Hennepin Ave., Minneapolis. Tel. 377-6620.

For 35 years, Dudley Riggs's Brave New Workshop has been fulfilling its self-proclaimed role as "loyal opposition to all parties." It's the oldest continuing satiric theater company in America. Company members write their own material and, after each evening's series of sketches and songs, they create "instant theater" based on audience suggestions. Past productions, which have toured New York, Boston, Miami, and San Francisco, include *I Compute, Therefore IBM; The Vice Man Cometh;* and *Censorship of Fools or Jesse at the Helm.* Performances are 7pm Wednesday and Thursday, 8pm Friday, 8pm and 10:30pm Saturday, and 2pm and 7pm Sunday.

Prices: Tickets $10–$15.

CHANHASSEN DINNER THEATRE, 501 W. 78th St., Chanhassen. Tel. 934-1525 or toll free 800/362-3515.

With four distinctly different playhouses under one roof, Chanhassen Dinner Theatre, located some 20 miles southwest of downtown Minneapolis, has been offering a wide variety of productions for more than 25 years. The Chanhassen has earned consistently high marks for the quality and diversity of its productions, from

Equus, Loot, and *On Golden Pond* to *A Little Night Music, West Side Story,* and *Fiddler on the Roof.* In the last-named, a very young and very dark-haired Minnesotan named Loni Anderson acted and sang the role of Tevye's daughter, Tsietel.

The first thing visitors notice as they enter the enormous but somehow intimate theater complex is the oversize fireplace in the long lobby that leads to the various theaters, bars, alcoves, lounges, and other gathering places. There's a selection of entertainment here that includes show-only and show-with-dinner, supper, or brunch packages.

Chanhassen is easily reached at the junction of highways 5 and 501, near I-494, about 30 minutes from downtown St. Paul or Minneapolis.

Prices: Tickets about $30–$49.

CHILDREN'S THEATRE COMPANY, 2400 3rd Ave. S., Minneapolis. Tel. 874-0400.

In the large and stately building that houses the Minneapolis Institute of Arts, the Children's Theatre Company presents productions geared to children of all ages in its 746-seat auditorium. Based primarily on familiar classic and contemporary stories, the plays are lavishly produced and skillfully acted by a company of child and adult players.

Authors are often invited to participate in the staging of their plays; the late Dr. Seuss (Theodore Geiss) worked with the company on its production of *The 500 Hats of Bartholomew Cubbins,* and Astrid Lindgren gave advice on the play based on her book *Pippi Longstocking.*

Prices: Tickets $13.50–$23 adults, $9.25–$17.45 children under 17 and senior citizens 62 and over.

CRICKET THEATRE, 821 Marquette Ave., Suite 229, Foshay Tower, Minneapolis. Tel. 337-0747.

Cricket Theatre is a fully professional, nonprofit organization, which, for the past 24 years, has been dedicated to the development and production of breakthrough works by living playwrights. From the works of Sam Shepard in the 1970s to off-Broadway productions in the 80s and 90s, the Cricket has been at the cutting edge of new American drama. Performances are at 7:30pm on Thursday, 8pm Friday, 5 and 8:30pm Saturday, 7:30pm Sunday.

Prices: Tickets $14.75–$16.75. Student and senior discounts are available.

FRANK THEATRE, no permanent performance space at press time. Tel. 377-0501.

Founded in 1989 by two determined women, director Wendy Knox and actor Bernadette Sullivan, Frank Theatre is in search of a permanent home. The company stages interesting and provocative productions, including adaptations of *Closed Tottering House* by Finnish author Maria Koskiluoma and *Description of a Picture, Explosion of a Memory* by German playwright Heiner Muller.

GREAT AMERICAN HISTORY THEATER, 30 E. 10th St., St. Paul. Tel. 292-4323.

The Great American Theater commissions, produces, and tours plays that dramatize the history, folklore, and social issues of the American Midwest. Many works are originals.

Prices: Tickets Thurs and Sun, $12; Fri and Sat, $14. $2 discount for seniors and students.

THE GUTHRIE THEATER, 725 Vineland Place, Minneapolis. Tel. 377-2224.

Whatever your taste in theater, you'll surely want to include a Guthrie performance in your Twin Cities agenda. In 1964 the Tyrone Guthrie Theater gained worldwide fame as the home of a new classical repertory company, selected by the distinguished director for whom it was named. Lately there has been a succession of record-breaking presentations, among them the 1992 production of a cycle of Greek tragedies by Euripides, Aeschylus, and Sophocles.

There are several reasons to arrive early for a Guthrie performance: you'll want to see one of the country's largest public sculpture gardens just across the street and to explore the theater itself. Before you enter the auditorium, you'll be surrounded by a tempting array of dining, drinking, and shopping choices. The Guthrie shares an entry lobby with the adjacent Walker Art Center and is just steps away from the Walker's extensive, and often expensive, selection of gifts and souvenirs. The Guthrie's own smaller gift shop carries a variety of gifts and theater-related items.

Performances begin at 7:30pm Tuesday through Thursday, 8pm Friday and Saturday, and 7pm on Sunday (the theater is closed on Monday). Matinees are usually presented at 1pm on Wednesday and Saturday with an occasional matinee on Sunday, but call to confirm specific days and times.

Prices: Tickets $8–$42.

HEART OF THE BEAST PUPPET AND MASK THEATRE, 1500 E. Lake St., Minneapolis. Tel. 721-2535.

The success of the Heart of the Beast Puppet and Mask Theatre is a perfect example of one good turn begetting another. Established in 1973 with the stated purpose of serving a racially mixed community in one of the oldest business areas in the Twin Cities, this company of artists performed at outdoor sites and in rented theater spaces for nearly 15 years before being asked by the community to move into a former x-rated movie house. Now, with a 300-seat playhouse to call their own, Heart of the Beast Puppet and Mask Theatre has increased its audience more than 700% with family-oriented shows like *La Befana,* based on an Italian folk story, and *Invisible Child,* inspired by a traditional Swedish tale. Among its adult productions is *The Reapers Tale,* which provides a history of Columbus's arrival in the New World from the Native Americans' point of view. The company also produces an annual festival on the first Sunday of each May (participants numbered about 21,000 in 1990).

Prices: Tickets for all seats $5; free for children under 3. Those willing to usher are admitted free.

ILLUSION THEATRE, 528 Hennepin Ave., Minneapolis. Tel. 339-4944.

Headquartered at the Hennepin Center for the Arts, this company has pioneered a new form of theater: in 1977 the group became the first in the country to use drama as a means of preventing sexual abuse and interpersonal violence. *Touch,* an original play for children, has been performed throughout the country in schools and churches. So have two other works, *No Easy Answers,* written for adolescents, and *For Adults Only,* designed for grown-up audiences. Most recently, three new plays have been added to the repertoire: *Family,* dealing with relationships among family members, as well as *Amazing Grace* and *The Alphabet of Aids,* both of which deal with HIV/AIDS. A recent popular and critical success by Illusion Theatre was *Let Gospel Ring,* created by local playwright Kim Hines and directed by Richard D. Thompson. This humorous review traced the history of gospel music from its roots in slavery to current times.

In addition to the touring productions of these plays, the theater performs in the Twin Cities from February to July. All performances are at 8pm, except on Sunday when they begin at 7pm.

Prices: Tickets $10 Thurs and Sun, $15 Fri and Sat.

JUNGLE THEATRE, 709 Lake St., Minneapolis. Tel. 822-7063.

Since its first performance in 1991, this storefront playhouse has presented an astonishingly diverse number of first-rate productions. Actors from the Guthrie and other local theaters regularly perform here in plays that run the gamut from the comedy *Only You* to serious drama like *Who's Afraid of Virginia Woolf?, The Miracle Worker,* and *The Diary of Anne Frank.* There's absolutely no way of predicting what type of play will be on the boards while you're in town, but if past experience is a guide, you can't go wrong attending a production at Jungle Theatre.

LAKESHORE PLAYERS, 4280 Stewart Ave., White Bear Lake. Tel. 429-5674.

Lakeshore Players, one of the oldest community theaters in the area, has provided musicals, comedies, and other family-oriented entertainment to suburbanites and city folk alike for over 40 years. Recent hits include *A View from the Bridge* and *Cabaret.* Six productions are staged here each year.

Prices: Tickets $8–$10, with discounts for children and seniors.

MIXED BLOOD THEATRE COMPANY, 1501 4th St. S., Minneapolis. Tel. 338-6131.

This professional theater was founded in 1976 to produce works with an ethnically diverse cast. Mixed Blood has by now received numerous local awards for productions like *The Boys Next Door, A My Name Is Alice,* and *For Colored Girls Who Have Considered Suicide When a Rainbow Is Enuf.* Founder Jack Reuler has also received national awards for his theater's commitment to color-blind casting and cultural diversity.

Mixed Blood productions are presented in a 100-year-old firehouse with a large, flexible space and various settings. Show time is 8pm on Thursday and Friday; on Saturday there are two performances at 7 and 9:30pm; Sundays at 3 and 7pm.

Prices: Tickets $7.50 Thurs, $12.50 Fri, $15 Sat, and $10 Sun.

OLD LOG THEATER, 5175 Meadville St., Excelsior. Tel. 474-5951.

This popular playhouse on the shores of Lake Minnetonka is a family affair where Don Stolz has been staging Equity productions since 1941. In fact, the Old Log is the Twin Cities' oldest theater company. The small original theater, now used as a scenery shop, was replaced in 1960 by the present Old Log, which is closer to the water's edge and, with 655 seats, one of the largest theaters in the Twin Cities area.

Comedies are the specialty of this house, and eldest son Tom Stolz has developed through the years into an adept comic actor, notable for his droll deadpan delivery in productions as diverse as *Brighton Beach Memoirs* and *Bedfull of Foreigners*. Other family members make their own contributions behind the scenes and at the front of the house.

From time to time more serious work has been presented at the Old Log, including admirable productions of *Look Homeward, Angel* and *84 Charing Cross*. If you're in the Twin Cities during the Easter season, you might want to phone the theater for word on Tom Stolz's annual tour-de-force performance in *The Gospel According to Saint Mark*.

Shows are at 8:30pm Wednesday through Saturday and at 7:30pm on Sunday.

Prices: $14 Sat, $12.50 all other performances.

PARK SQUARE THEATRE, Minnesota Museum of Art, 305 St. Peter St., St. Paul. Tel. 291-7005.

Park Square Theatre offers two distinctly different seasons, the main Classic Season, January through June, consisting of five productions from the repertory of Western theater classics, and Summer on Seventh Place, July and August, which features light family entertainment such as mysteries and period comedies.

PENUMBRA THEATRE, 270 N. Kent St., St. Paul. Tel. 224-4601.

At Penumbra Theatre you'll find Minnesota's only black professional theater company. Penumbra has another claim to fame as well; at this writing, it's the only Twin Cities professional troupe to have staged the plays of August Wilson. Its production of the renowned St. Paul playwright's *Fences*, starring Penumbra founder Lou Bellamy, won high praise in 1990. (Wilson's *Fences* is the only play in American theatrical history to have won the Pulitzer Prize, the Tony Award, the New York Theater Critics Award, the Outer Critics Circle Award, and the American Theater Critics Association Award.) Call for information about current productions—you won't be disappointed.

Prices: Tickets $12–$16.

PLYMOUTH PLAYHOUSE, the Kelly Inn, 2705 Annapolis Lane, Plymouth. Tel. 553-1600 or 989-5151.

At this intimate theater you'll have an evening of first-rate entertainment if past history is any guide. Previous hits here have included long runs of *Nunsense, Pump Boys and Dinettes,* and *Ain't Misbehavin',* the Tony Award–winning musical about Fats

Waller. Productions at Plymouth Playhouse are presented by Troupe America, a nationally known entertainment company, founded in the Twin Cities by producer-director Curt Wollan, whose touring productions have entertained audiences coast to coast.

Prices: Tickets $14–$16.

RED EYE COLLABORATION, 126 N. Washington Ave., Minneapolis. Tel. 870-0309.

The only resident experimental theater company in the Twin Cities, Red Eye Collaboration performs in a 70-seat studio theater in the downtown Minneapolis Warehouse District. You'll know you've found the theater when you see a warehouse with a large neon sign featuring a blue fish. Four mixed-media productions are staged each year by the Red Eye Collaboration, along with one work-in-progress series. All performances are at 8pm.

Prices: Tickets vary per production.

THEATRE DE LA JEUNE LUNE, 105 1st St. N., Minneapolis. Tel. 333-6200.

This company began in 1978 when a fledgling international theater group was founded by four students, two Twin Citians and two Parisians, who met while studying at the École Jacques-Lecoq in Paris. Productions by this constantly interesting group tend to be highly physical and visually exciting, reflecting elements of clowning, farce, mime, and vaudeville. Recent hits include *Children of Paradise* and *The Green Bird*.

Prices: Tickets $8–$17.

THEATRE IN THE ROUND PLAYERS, 245 Cedar Ave., Minneapolis. Tel. 333-3010.

Since 1952 talented Twin Citians have participated in the productions of Theater in the Round, or TRP as it's known locally. More than half a million theatergoers have attended this community theater housed in a one-story brick building in the west-bank theater district. Some of the Twin Cities' top directors have worked here with aspiring actors and technicians who have gone on to professional careers in theater, TV, and film.

Play selection here is eclectic: The biggest hits to date have been *Equus, Of Thee I Sing, The Mousetrap, Mrs. Warren's Profession,* and *Cyrano de Bergerac*. Plays by aspiring authors are produced as well. Performances are held at 8pm Friday and Saturday and at 7pm on Sunday.

Prices: Tickets $9.50.

UNIVERSITY THEATRE, 120 Rarig Center, University of Minnesota West Bank Campus, 330 21st Ave. S., Minneapolis. Tel. 625-4001.

The University of Minnesota Theatre Department's four separate stages at the handsome Rarig Center consistently present a wide variety of enjoyable entertainment. You'll also enjoy the perennially popular Showboat production.

Prices: Tickets at Rarig Center $9; summertime Showboat $10 Tues–Sat, $8 Sun.

MAJOR CONCERT HALLS & ALL-PURPOSE AUDITORIUMS

NORTHROP AUDITORIUM, University of Minnesota's Main Campus, 84 Church St. SE, Minneapolis. Tel. 624-2345.

A stage for distinguished performances since 1929, the 4,800-seat Northrop presents some of the premier ballet companies in the world. It also welcomes superstars such as Mikhail Baryshnikov, contemporary dance headliners, and culturally diverse groups, including the American Indian Dance Theatre and Africa Oye! An annual holiday *Nutcracker* as well as a jazz series add to the variety.

Prices: Ticket prices vary. Call 624-2345 for information.

ORCHESTRA HALL, 1111 Nicollet Mall, Minneapolis. Tel. 371-5656.

As its name implies, Orchestra Hall was built as a home for the internationally acclaimed Minnesota Orchestra. Since it opened in 1974, this 2,400-seat hall has offered diverse programs featuring a range of famous artists, from Isaac Stern and Itzhak Perlman to Andy Williams and the late Pearl Bailey.

Since 1980 the annual Viennese Sommerfest featuring guest conductors has drawn very large audiences to Orchestra Hall for programs including everything from light classics to orchestral masterworks. David Zinman is the festival's artistic director.

Prices: Tickets $2–$45.

ORDWAY MUSIC THEATRE, 345 Washington St., St. Paul. Tel. 224-4222.

After St. Paul's only major downtown performing arts building was closed in 1980 because of structural deterioration, the family of Lucius Ordway offered to donate $10 million toward a new music hall if public and private interests in the Twin Cities would match that commitment and that contribution.

Since its triumphant opening on January 1, 1985, the Ordway Music Theatre has been praised not only for the programs it presents, but for the beauty it imparts to the historic Rice Park area of St. Paul. The Ordway's design combines the new and the old, with its glass walls set into a facade of brick and copper and its state-of-the-art acoustics. Doormen await theatergoers at the entrance to the handsome lobby; a magnificent spiral stairway leads to the Grand Foyer and upper Promenade, both of which offer spectacular views of the city. The spacious lobby provides upholstered couches and window-wall mahogany benches just right for conversation, refreshments, and people watching.

The 1,800-seat Main Hall and the 315-seat McKnight Theatre have hosted distinguished musicians from the Twin Cities as well as famous acts like Leontyne Price, Mel Tormé, and the Ballet Folklórico Nacional de Mexico.

A series of touring Broadway shows appears at the Ordway each year. Past productions have included *Les Miserables, The Phantom of the Opera,* and *Guys and Dolls.*

Prices: Ticket prices vary according to event. Students can get discounts prior to some performances; call for more information.

2. THE CLUB & MUSIC SCENE

COMEDY CLUBS

Twin Cities comedy clubs have become something of a one-man show thanks to Scott Hanson, a local impresario and comic whose own credits include local performances at the Guthrie Theater and at Riverfest. On the national scene, he's opened for Jay Leno, Roseanne Barr, and Rodney Dangerfield.

More recently, though, Hanson has developed two comedy "galleries"—in Minneapolis at St. Anthony Main, 219 SE Main St. and in St. Paul at 175 E. 5th St. Performances in Minneapolis are Tuesday, Wednesday, Thursday at 8pm; Friday, Saturday at 8pm and 10:30pm. In St. Paul, performances are Wednesday, Thursday, Sunday at 8pm; Friday 8:30pm; Saturday 8pm and 10:30pm.

Admission: Fri and Sat $9.95; weekday nights $7.95. The phone number for both locations is 331-JOKE.

ROCK

FIRST AVENUE CLUB, 701 1st Ave. N., Minneapolis. Tel. 338-8388.

A cavernous former bus depot serves as the site of one of Minneapolis's largest, busiest, and most famous nightspots. The 1,200-seat First Avenue Club is familiar to moviegoers around the world as the setting for Prince's movie *Purple Rain*.

There's recorded music for dancing four times each week at First Avenue, where hi-tech sounds and lights provide a noisy and exciting atmosphere. Live acts are presented here too, in styles ranging from country to pop to jazz.

Admission: Prices vary on concert nights. Tickets Fri–Sat $1 8–9pm, $3 9–10pm, $5 10pm to 1am, 1am to closing; Sun $5; Tues two-for-one night, call for details.

GLAM SLAM, 110 N. 5th St., Minneapolis. Tel. 338-3383.

Since its September 1990 opening, Glam Slam has been the only Twin Cities nightclub offering in-person performances by Prince and other celebrated Paisley Park recording artists. And, thanks to another exclusive Glam Slam agreement, this is the only place you'll hear unreleased material produced at Paisley Park, Prince's widely admired state-of-the-art recording complex.

The second-floor private area at Glam Slam is reserved for members only, but don't fret. There's plenty to enjoy on the main floor of this 20,000-square-foot nightclub, where nationally known artists perform rock, country, hip-hop, and jazz. Located in Minneapolis's Warehouse District, Glam Slam, which is open five nights a week, Tuesday through Saturday, boasts the area's most advanced sight, sound, and lights.

Admission: Ticket prices vary; call for specific information.

7TH STREET ENTRY, 701 1st Ave. N., Minneapolis. Tel. 338-8388.

While some promising unknowns play First Avenue from time to time, the usual launching pad for new talent is the adjoining 7th Street Entry, which is open daily and features at least three live bands each night. Formerly a storage area, this room has become the club in which publicists try to book their young clients, hoping to catch the eye of scouts who've made this a regular stop in their search for new talent.

You'll find drinks of all kinds here, and the small kitchen serves nachos and pizza. Phone 332-1775 for daily recorded information about performances. If you'd rather speak to a real person, call the number listed above Monday through Friday from noon to 5pm.

Admission: Prices vary; call for specific information.

JAZZ

If you want specific information about the jazz entertainment being offered during your stay in the Twin Cities, call **Jazzline** (tel. 633-0329), a service of the Twin Cities Jazz Society. They provide a lengthy rundown on the artists appearing throughout the Twin Cities at clubs, bars, restaurants, hotels, parks, plazas, and even on local radio. During the summer months, much of the jazz hereabouts is performed outdoors.

DAKOTA BAR AND GRILL, at Bandana Sq., 1021 E. Bandana Blvd., St. Paul. Tel. 642-1442.

The Dakota Bar and Grill, which offers live jazz seven nights a week, has developed into one of the top jazz venues in America, featuring artists like Harry Connick, Jr., Wynton Marsalis, Max Roach, Betty Carter, Carmen McCrae, and Joe Williams. The Twin Cities' finest local jazz musicians appear here regularly as well.

See Chapter 6 for a description of the fine restaurant here.

Admission: Prices vary; call for specific information.

MIXED BAG

FINE LINE MUSIC CAFE, 318 1st Ave. N., Minneapolis. Tel. 338-8100.

Unlike thematic nightclubs that limit themselves to one musical niche or another—jazz, rock and roll, or blues, for example—this is a "showcase room," which according to owner Joel Conner means the Fine Line is free to put any kind of music onstage, so long as it's of a high quality.

Groups performing here have included Bonedaddies, a Cajun group from New Orleans; Zvuki Mu, rock and rollers from the Soviet Union; and bellAmitri, a group from Scotland.

Situated in the Warehouse District of downtown Minneapolis, the Fine Line somehow manages an aura of intimacy while accommodating some 460 patrons at small tables on two levels.

The eclectic dinner menu, with prices ranging from $6 to $14, includes a lot of fish, pasta, and chicken, along with a wide variety of appetizers and drinks.

It's a good idea to call before coming to see whether the fare being offered will suit your taste. And keep this place in mind for its Sunday brunch, a long-standing tradition. Evening hours at the Fine Line are

Monday through Friday 5pm until 1am and Saturday and Sunday 6pm until 1am.

Admission: Menu items $6.95–$14.95 plus an additional cover charge that varies according to the artist. Call for specific information.

NEW RIVERSIDE CAFE, 329 Cedar Ave. S., Minneapolis. Tel. 333-4814.

At the New Riverside Cafe you'll hear a variety of music by Twin Cities bands and vocalists. In this 20-year-old collective, where the owners also serve as managers and maintenance staff, the often first-rate musicians are paid by tips from patrons and a meal from the café. You'll find the work of local artists mounted on the wall here as well. "The Riv" is a vegetarian, alcohol-free restaurant with a reputation for tasty food in a wholesome environment. Check it out. Music entertainment begins at 7:30pm Tuesday through Thursday and at 9pm Friday and Saturday and lasts until 11pm on weekdays, until midnight on Saturday.

Admission: Free.

O'GARA'S BAR AND GRILL, 164 N. Snelling, St. Paul. Tel. 644-3333.

At O'Gara's you'll find a complex that's far outgrown the pub founded in March 1941 by James Freeman O'Gara of County Sligo. The pub originally served food and liquor to locals who manufactured World War II munitions. Nowadays you can enjoy music in O'Gara's piano bar and listen to a variety of bands in the Garage on Friday and Saturday from 7:30pm to 1am. Food and drink are served in the expanded dining and drinking areas. Students, professors, and white-collar types mix affably with the blue-collar regulars.

Admission: Prices vary; call for specific information.

DANCE CLUBS/DISCOS

CATTLE COMPANY, 4470 W. 78th St. Circle. Tel. 835-1225.

On the strip in Bloomington, this nightspot has DJs on hand seven nights a week from 8pm to 1am (Sunday until midnight). A wide mix of dance music, from the fifties and sixties to the current Top 40, is featured here.

Admission: $3 cover on Sunday only.

3. THE BAR SCENE

CHAMPPS SPORTS BAR AND GOURMET HAMBURGER GRILL, 2431 W. 7th St., at Sibley Plaza in St. Paul. Tel. 698-5050.

People of all ages, sizes, backgrounds, and temperaments mix merrily here amid large TV screens showing, of course, sports events. When visiting the Twin Cities, sports celebrities from out of town head for Champps, and local sports figures congregate here as well. The atmosphere is jovial, and food and drink prices are moderate.

Known as "one of the top six sports bars in the nation," Champps is always busy.

There are six other Champps Sports Bars in the Twin Cities—in Richfield at 66th and Lyndale Ave. S. (tel. 861-3333); in Minnetonka at 1641 Plymouth Rd. (tel. 546-3333); in New Brighton at 2397 Palmer Dr. (tel. 639-0339); in Maplewood at 1734 Adolphus St. (tel. 487-5050); in Burnsville at 1200 W. County Rd. 42 (tel. 898-5050); and in Minneapolis at 100 N. 6th St. (tel. 335-5050).

J. COUSINEAU'S, 13540 Grove Dr., Maple Grove. Tel. 420-8355.

Conveniently located near the junction of I-694 and I-94, this popular pub has a full menu and choice of beverage servings. Cousineau's is famous for its enormous half-yard and full-yard ale glasses, reproductions of the glasses used in England during the 17th and 18th centuries. After quaffing your selections, feel free to purchase the 1-foot glass at $29.95, half-yard glass at $35.75, or the full-yard glass at $59.95. (Less hearty or less thirsty souls can imbibe from smaller vessels.)

A second J. Cousineau's is located at 2501 Coon Rapids Blvd. in Coon Rapids, to the north (tel. 757-5555).

SWEENEY'S SALOON, 96 N. Dale St., St. Paul. Tel. 221-9157.

At Sweeney's Saloon you'll find a boisterous place with a large selection of beers, to say nothing of daily food specials that really are special. Thirteen tap beers, including a few brewed in New Ulm, Minnesota, are also available. The saloon is open Monday through Friday from 11am to 1am and Saturday and Sunday from 9am to 1am.

CHAPTER 11

EASY EXCURSION TO MALL OF AMERICA

1. ENTERTAINMENT
2. SHOPPING
3. NEARBY PLACES TO STAY
4. WHERE TO DINE

What can you do at Mall of America in nearby Bloomington? Well, in the country's largest shopping-and-entertainment complex, you can certainly expect to shop and be entertained. But you can do a surprising variety of other things here as well.

You can, for example, marry at Mall of America. **The Chapel of Love,** with seating for 75, will gladly provide any requested element of the wedding, including the bridal couple's garb, the flowers, and even the clergyman or judge.

You can go to school at Mall of America, attending classes under the auspices of the **Metropolitan Learning Alliance,** a consortium of five local school districts and the distinguished University of St. Thomas. With four classrooms, a computer lab, and a faculty of professional educators, the Alliance offers transferable high-school and adult-education classes as well as training seminars for Mall of America employees.

You can have an X-ray or a surgical procedure at the Mall of America at a clinic staffed by members of **Family Physicans P.A.,** a medical group of general practitioners and specialists that has practiced in the Twin Cities for more than 50 years. (A staff member reports that a vasectomy was performed at this clinic recently because the patient wanted to be able to say he got it at the Mall.)

If your teeth need cleaning or repairing or pulling, that can be done at the Mall as well. **Mall of America Dental Center** shares the waiting room and telephone service of Family Physicians P.A.

What else can you do at the Mall of America? Well, perhaps you ought to walk around to familiarize yourself first with the three landscaped levels of shopping and dining as well as the fourth level devoted primarily to clubs, movies, and other forms of entertainment. One way to learn your way about without wasting valuable shopping time would be to arrive at 7am, when the Mall's central doors open to admit the daily walkers. At 10am stores open for business.

You'll soon notice as you look around the Mall the four distinctively designed thoroughfares that surround Camp Snoopy, home of the two-story-high inflated beagle who welcomes all comers with an upraised paw. Each of the Mall's avenues has its own centerpiece.

On upscale **South Avenue,** anchored by Macy's and Bloomingdale's, the centerpiece is LEGO Imagination Center.

There's a trendy, high-tech aspect to **East Broadway,** with Bloomingdale's at one end and Sears at the other. Serving as the centerpiece of East Broadway is the Rotunda, a large open space where major events and performances take place.

North Garden, which lies between Sears and Nordstrom, is the most changeable avenue. Skylights provide the natural illumination here, where the landscape changes according to the season. The centerpiece is Golf Mountain.

And finally, there's **West Market,** which has the aspect of a quaint European village with crisscrossing bridges and merchandise carts. The centerpiece here is Mall of America's cart marketplace of nearly 50 specialty carts.

The shopping at Mall of America must certainly be among the best in the world. That's the educated view of many visitors who travel here from abroad, primarily from the United Kingdom, Japan, Germany, and Canada. Many visitors have flown in with the cooperation of locally based Northwest Airlines, which has fashioned a number of attractive packages including airfare, accommodations, and even travel to other parts of the state in conjunction with a visit to the Mall. But there have been other kinds of NWA promotions too, including one that made national headlines. From mid-November 1993 to early January 1994, Northwest offered round-trip rates ranging from $39 to $78 for those interested in flying from selected American cities for a Saturday of shopping at the Mall of America. Participants typically left home at about 5am unencumbered by coats, but carrying empty suitcases of all sizes; they returned just before the midnight deadline. The promotion proved so successful that Northwest is considering similar programs for the future.

Visitors to Mall of America are usually already familiar with its four famous department-store anchors—**Macy's, Bloomingdale's, Nordstrom,** and **Sears.** (Only Sears had been represented previously on the local shopping scene.) But what makes this mall a shopper's paradise is the added adventure involved in checking out hundreds of carefully selected specialty shops and dozens of shopping carts and in-the-wall shops.

Shopping is, of course, only one of the myriad activities available to you here at this largest of American shopping and entertainment complexes. Entertainment comes in many forms throughout Mall of America, but especially on Level 4 where there are no fewer than 14 movie screens and 9 night clubs. Even children, whose entertainment usually begins and ends at Camp Snoopy, can find fun on Level 4, particularly at the Saturday Ranger Roundup, which takes place each Saturday at the **Gatlin Brothers' Music City Grill.** Children can get deputized here and receive the badge to prove it. They also receive a variety of perks, including line-dancing lessons, a face-painting session, games and prizes, and a buffet lunch of hot dogs, chili, and chips ($2.50).

At Bloomingdales' Children's Department, girls and boys can enjoy a unique play area which simulates a drive-in movie theater with kid-sized cars and video monitors plus assorted games and puzzles.

Meanwhile, children of absolutely all ages can play a round or two at **Golf Mountain** or suit up for the exciting interactive laser game called **Starbase Omega.** They can also sample a variety of sports at **Oshman's SuperSports USA,** where the choices vary with the seasons, as action on an ice rink makes way for practice on a baseball diamond.

For those whose favorite entertainment is hand-to-mouth, there is always an abundance of restaurants and food stands at the ready at sites throughout the mall. **Wolfgang Puck's Pizzeria,** for example, offers a variety of delectable choices in a small restaurant on the third floor at Macy's. The third-level Food Court houses a long line of varied fast-food counters and kitchens with comfortable seating provided for customers.

I started this introduction with a question concerning what to do at Mall of America and will now proceed to offer some specific recommendations. But answers to your own particular questions are as close as the nearest telephone. **One Call for the Mall** at 612/883-8800 will put you in touch with any of the Mall's tenants from 7am to 10pm Monday through Saturday and 9am to 7pm on Sunday. There are 12 operators on duty and they're well trained to deal with whatever queries may come their way.

GETTING TO MALL OF AMERICA   Mall of America is only a few minutes away from both Minneapolis and St. Paul as well as from Minneapolis–St. Paul International Airport. From downtown Minneapolis, drive south on I-35W to the intersection with I-494; then drive east on I-494 to the Highway 77 (Cedar Avenue) exit. Turn south and follow the directional signs. From downtown St. Paul drive south on I-35E to I-494; then drive west on I-494 to the exit at 24th Avenue and follow directional signs.

Bus transportation to and from Mall of America is available throughout the Twin Cities area. Express buses (marked Route 80) go to the Mall from downtown Minneapolis every 20 minutes Monday through Saturday and every 30 minutes on Sundays. Patrons can board these buses at several locations on Nicollet Mall. From downtown St. Paul, passengers can take buses marked Route 54, which provide service every 30 minutes throughout the week. The fare for all passengers in both cities is $1.50 during nonrush hours, $1.75 during the rush. During nonrush hours, people age 65 and older ride for 25¢.

All buses drop passengers at Mall of America Transit Station located on the east side of the complex, between Bloomingdale's and Sears. For further information concerning bus service to Mall of America, call 373-3333 and then press "1" for route and schedule information.

1. ENTERTAINMENT

Just walking around Mall of America, all four levels of it, is first-rate entertainment. A wide diversity of people come here from all over the world, and their presence adds to the sense of excitement and vitality.

MALL OF AMERICA

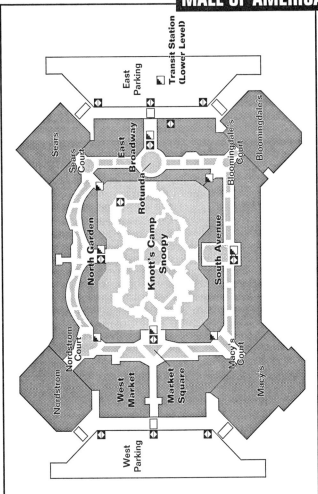

Transit Station
(Lower Level)

East Parking

Sears

Sears Court

East Broadway

Bloomingdale's Court

Bloomingdale's

North Garden

Rotunda

Knott's Camp Snoopy

South Avenue

Nordstrom Court

Macy's Court

Nordstrom

West Market

Market Square

Macy's

West Parking

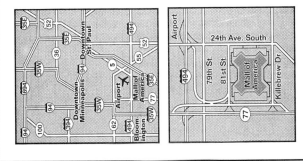

35E
52
52
35E
86
55
35W
5
694
94
Downtown Minneapolis
94
Downtown St. Paul
35E
Airport
Mall of America
77
100
394
62
494
Bloom- ington
35W

Airport
494
79th St.
81st St.
24th Ave. South
Mall of America
Killebrew Dr.
77

◆ Elevator   ◆ Escalator   ■

6602

KNOTT'S CAMP SNOOPY, 5000 Center Court, Mall of America. Tel. 883-8600.

First and foremost for entertainment at the Mall is **Camp Snoopy,** named for a cartoon character created by Minneapolis-born Charles M. Schulz. It's the largest indoor themed entertainment park in America. With seven acres of rides and attractions for visitors of all ages, there's something for everybody here. Particularly popular among the youngest visitors to the Mall is the **Snoopy Bounce,** which takes place within the capacious tummy of the world's most famous beagle. Then there are the **Linus Loop,** a junior Ferris wheel, and the **Americana Carousel,** a hand-painted replica of the bright, exciting merry-go-rounds of yesterday. For older visitors there are thrills aplenty on the **Log Chute,** a daunting ride in a hollowed-out log through a mountain where animated figures await. A 40-foot drop over a gushing waterfall also awaits you at the splashy conclusion of this ride. The **Screaming Yellow Eagle** features three attached rows of theater-style seats in which visitors are first locked, then rocked from side to side while rising higher and higher, and finally periodically dropped until they almost, but never quite, hit the ground. And of course there's the **Ripsaw Roller Coaster** whose screaming passengers constantly remind passersby that there's an exciting amusement park in their midst. It's important to know that in the interest of safety there are height restrictions on all rides Prices for rides range from about $1.50 to $3.

More entertainment awaits at Camp Snoopy's four separate theaters. **Ford Playhouse Theatre** offers live shows, 3-D films, and dinner-theater presentations. At **Wilderness Theatre** you can watch a delightful wildlife show featuring live animals from all over the world. The **Silver Stein Restaurant Stage** offers the fun of a year-round Oktoberfest with costumed performers singing and dancing in true Bavarian style. Finally there's the **Northwood Stage,** a rustic playhouse in which a variety of live-entertainment shows is offered. Of course the **Peanuts characters** are on hand throughout Camp Snoopy to meet, greet, and be photographed with visitors of all ages. The milieu is all very Minnesotan, not only because of the abundance of greenery but because staff members are so friendly, accommodating, and just plain nice.

LEGO IMAGINATION CENTER, 164 South Ave., Mall of America. Tel. 858-8949.

Located on the south side of Camp Snoopy is the first permanent LEGO Imagination Center to be opened in the United States. It features 60 large-scale LEGO models, including a space shuttle about 15 feet long and a dinosaur about 20 feet high. A number of other dinosaurs "live" here, plus some models with moving parts (circus performers, lions, tigers). There are, in addition, a number of very active construction workers, who assemble the sets of LEGO bricks and DUPLO blocks on sale in the store here. Prices range from $2.39 for simple trial-size kits to $200 for a kit designed to build an industrial-type robot capable of following directions.

But a fine time can be had at the LEGO Imagination Center without spending a penny. Six tables, each capable of accommodating six children or adults, are piled high with DUPLO blocks and LEGO bricks, which can be used on the premises for creations limited only by the imagination of the builders.

STARBASE OMEGA, 318 South Ave., Mall of America. Tel. 858-8015.

Interested in fulfilling a futuristic fantasy during the course of a 20-minute interplanetary experience? Thousands of visitors to Mall of America have found this opportunity irresistible since Starbase Omega, "the ultimate laser game," first arrived. Here's the deal: A shape-shifting alien race, determined to take over the galaxy, has declared war on the Galactic Council which, in turn, has established an earth station at Mall of America to recruit earthlings to help in the battle to save Starbase Omega, an orbiting space station which will serve as a base of operations. (Are you still with me?) Each recruit, at a cost of $8.50 for one experience, $12.75 for two, is taken to the Ready Room to be outfitted with a vibrating sensor shield containing a battery pack that attaches to a laser blaster. Next comes a briefing from the squad captain concerning the rules and the penalties for breaking them. Once the campaign begins, there's no running, jumping, or climbing permitted. You must keep both hands on your weapon at all times, and you must stay at least three feet away from others. Firing within that radius results in your score being scrambled! Despite this kind of stringent discipline, recruits keep coming back for more; in fact whole families have been known to enlist together. As the 20-minute experience draws to an end, recruits return to the Ready Room and then proceed to the Gift Shop, where their squad captain announces individual and team scores, bringing the experience to an end.

VICTORIAN PHOTOGRAPHER, 148 East Broadway, Mall of America. Tel. 854-1853.

Did you ever have the feeling that in a past life you were an aristocrat or a gunslinger or an Indian chief—or maybe a woman of elegance and wealth or a lady of ill repute? Here at Mall of America, prize-winning photographer Ralph Berlovits can present you with a photograph that shows exactly how you might have looked back then. With a degree in art history to his credit along with a 20-year career as a professional photographer, Berlovitz has perfected the art of portraiture as it was practiced 100 years ago, even as he's made use of contemporary products and methodology. Velcro plays a large part in the magic he weaves, enabling his subjects to cover their street clothes with period clothing, hats, and other accessories from his vast collection of costumes and props. Using a hand-painted scenic backdrop and the kinds of posing chairs used in Victorian studios, Berlovitz takes time to remind his subjects that in those days people didn't smile for the camera; then, after a 5-second exposure, he proceeds to process your photo, using a unique paper process that enables him to present the finished product to you just 61 minutes later. Whatever the milieu you select—the old West, the Civil War, the Victorian era, or the Roaring Twenties—you're likely to find Ralph Berlovitz's brown-toned photo a meaningful souvenir of your visit to Mall of America. Prices at this writing are $17 for a 5″ x 7″ portrait of one person, $22 for an 8″ x 10″, and an added $5 for each additional person.

EVENING ENTERTAINMENT

At night you'll find a lot of activity on the east end of Mall of America's fourth level, known as the **Upper East Side.** One cover charge will get you into all the nightclubs; the charge is $3 on Wednesday, Thursday, and Sunday and $5 on Friday and Saturday. There's no cover charge on Monday or Tuesday. If you're a student with an ID card, there's no charge for you on Thursday night either.

GATLIN BROTHERS MUSIC CITY AND GRILLE. Tel. 858-8000.

If you like country music, this is the place for you. There's a big stage where local and national artists perform, and a big dance floor where free line-dancing lessons are offered at 6pm each weekday evening and every hour on the hour from 3 to 8pm every Saturday. Barbecued ribs are a favorite here, served, of course, with the Gatlin Brothers' famous rib sauce.

AMERICA'S ORIGINAL SPORTS BAR. Tel. 858-5483.

There's an abundance of TV here on screens of all sizes, along with a basketball hoop, pool table, golf game, darts, and, for dancers, a boxing ring. Local sports figures often drop in.

FAT TUESDAY. Tel. 851-9032.

This is where those delicious daiquiris are, all 19 flavors of them. There's a wonderful view of Camp Snoopy and the rest of the Mall from up here, so get a good seat and sip slowly. These delectable drinks can sneak up on you.

2. SHOPPING

With hundreds of shopping opportunities, things can be a bit overwhelming for a newcomer. You'll find large directories posted at strategic places on every level and every thoroughfare. You'll also see newspaper stands piled high with copies of a free weekly periodical, "Best of the Mall," which will help to orient you in addition to offering you discount coupons as well as news about sales and other miscellaneous matters. The following are some of my favorite stores.

STORES

ARTS AND KIDS, 132 North Garden, Mall of America. Tel. 854-7096.

The purpose of this attractive store is to promote and enhance creativity among children. Most of the games, puzzles, books, and kits here are designed for children from 2 to 12, but many of them are challenging enough for teenagers and their elders. Even toddlers enjoy "The Hungry Caterpillar," a board game that calls upon players to match colors and shapes. Older boys and girls enjoy stencil kits and water soluble pencils and crayons that can be used both for drawing and painting. Some kits include looms that enable older boys and girls to weave with beads. And others, like the architectural kits, provide instruction in creating floor plans for buildings that are erected from pieces of clear acrylic. How-to books provide instruction in a miscellany of crafts including origami.

BAREBONES, 100 North Garden, Mall of America. Tel. 858-8652.

There seems always to be a crowd at BareBones, a store that seems ill-suited to its neighborhood at Mall of America. Located right next door to Nordstrom, arguably the Mall's most elegant department store, and across from FAO Schwarz, world famous for its extensive and expensive line of playthings and collectibles, BareBones is a relatively small, comfortably cluttered shop with silvery skeletons draped here and there on its exterior walls while leering human skulls occupy a variety of vantage points within. Some of the items for sale here take a decidedly lighthearted approach to the human condition—a "thinking cap" with anatomically correct brains printed all over the crown and a white bony hand whose hollow fingers hold brightly colored toothbrushes. But glance up at the walls and you'll find carefully detailed charts in full color that provide a meticulous rendering of various parts of the human body and the systems that keep it functioning. Other charts trace the course of pregnancy and birth, while still others provide step-by-step instruction for successful CPR. Now and again a voice on the loudspeaker issues a challenge and a reward—"How many bones are there in a human body?" "How many miles of blood vessels in a human body?" If you know the answer, (206 and 62,000, respectively), you're invited to report it to a sales associate who will then OK you for a 10% discount on your BareBones purchase. (The questions, broadcast every two hours, are changed every couple of months.)

Customers' questions concerning the charts, models, books, and other related merchandise on sale here are answered by staff members, often with a little help from a catalog published by the Illinois Anatomical Chart Company, which, for more than 20 years, has been creating charts, models, and other anatomical items for practitioners, hospitals, and medical schools. Somewhere along the way, a small gift catalog was developed featuring amusing novelties— key chains, earrings, and the like—associated with the decidedly serious work of the company. The gift catalog gradually grew larger and larger and ultimately turned into a retail outlet in Skokie, not far from where the Chart Company continues its educational work to this day. The stores at Skokie, Mall of America, and the one in Osaka, Japan, are the only BareBones shops presently in existence, but others are on the way. Meanwhile, here at the Mall or through the catalog, you'll find such items as "Mr. Superskeleton" ($640), who comes with a flexible spine, nerve endings, and indication of muscle origins, and "Petite Pete," who is 8 feet tall ($9.90) and was designed by Johns Hopkins School of Medicine and carries with him a teacher's guide and terminology printed on his base. Also popular, for the younger set, are life-size anatomically correct dolls with birth certificates, disposable diapers, and hospital ID bands on their wrists.

EUROPEAN GIFTS, 170 North Garden, Mall of America. Tel. 858-9855.

With its exterior strip of stained-glass paneling and its mass of merchandise within, European Gifts has the look of the kind of small shop you might encounter in any city in Europe. Here you'll find Lladro figures from Spain, Hummels from Germany, wool and cotton tapestries from Belgium, and crystal items by Matts Jonasson and Swarovski. And then there's the collection of German beer steins, ranging in height from 2 feet to 40 feet and in capacity from 1½ ounces to 8 gallons. Co-owners Tom and Maria Cornell offer the work of a few selected American artists here as well—the limited-edition Cairn Creations by North Carolina's Tom Clark and the solid porcelain dolls by Dollmaker in Tennessee.

Primarily, though, visitors to the Mall come in search of items imported from Europe and find that the cost of shipping their purchases home is far outweighed by the savings they realize because there's no sales tax on items shipped to any address outside the state of Minnesota.

FAO SCHWARZ, 134 West Market, Mall of America. Tel. 854-0755.

It was in 1870 that Frederick August Otto Schwarz, an immigrant from Westphalia, Germany, first opened his "Schwarz Toy Bazaar" on Broadway in New York City. Today, with 20 branches throughout the United States, the newest one occupies a prominent place at Mall of America. A wide selection of unique toys is available in all price ranges. You'll find pencils, stickers, and small rubber dinosaurs here for 50¢; you'll also find a gasoline powered Mercedes for $8,200. (Actually, in this market, the $6,000 Jeep has proved more popular.)

Among the toys from around the world displayed here are wooden Brio train sets from Sweden. Crafted from select beechwood that's free of knots and cracks, these trains are operated by magnets, by kid power, and reportedly by grandparents who remember them from their own childhoods. Prices range from $10 for a single car to $160 for a large set.

From Germany, FAO Schwarz imports a wide assortment of individually hand-sewn Steiff stuffed animals, made of unique fabrics and fibers. These toys are notable for being durable playthings even as they increase in value as they age. (Among the most famous Steiff stuffed animals of all time, of course, were the jointed mohair stuffed bears that were so admired by President Theodore Roosevelt that they were nicknamed "teddy bears.")

From France come Corolle dolls, winner of more than 2 dozen international awards for design and playability. Made to look and feel as real as possible, these dolls have realistically sculpted faces, and, in most cases, rooted hair that's designed to be washed and combed. In fact most Corolle dolls can be bathed by and with children.

You'll find the Mall's FAO Schwarz store a comfortable place to browse and to buy. Customer service is legendary here, with customers' names being kept until an item that's out of stock has finally been forwarded from any one of the 20 FAO Schwarz stores all around the country. Gift wrapping here is, of course, complimentary.

HOLOGRAM LAND, 284 East Broadway, Mall of America. Tel. 854-9344.

This fascinating store, which carries the largest selection of holographic merchandise in the upper Midwest, has become popular enough to prompt the opening of a cart elsewhere in the Mall. The knowledgeable staff here can answer your questions or find answers for any questions concerning the emerging science of holography. Prices range from less than $1 to more than $2,000. Co-owner Susan Rickert explains the shop's success this way: "What we're really selling here is wonder." Surely there's a lot to wonder about in the large variety of holographic pictures that line the walls, somehow capturing three-dimensional images in two-dimensional spaces. A small image of William Shakespeare looks back at you silently and then begins to move its lips. Another figure inexplicably changes from a man into a werewolf. A woman sips a glass of wine; a rosebud blooms. Wherever you look there's something to wonder at among the toys, jewelry, watches, T-shirts, and other items, all of which display action that changes before your eyes. The good news for visitors is that virtually everything here is easily packed and carried; other items can be shipped at nominal cost. Each purchase of a holographic three-dimensional picture is accompanied by an informative pamphlet that explains how the hologram is made and how available lighting will affect the viewing of the piece. (A unique light arm developed by Hologram Land can be used in spaces where proper illumination would otherwise be a problem.) For those living close enough to visit the Mall on a regular basis, there's a special bonus, the determination of the shop's co-owners to share their own love of learning with others, the younger the better. Consider, for example, the Hologram Land Kids Club, whose members, ages 4 to 14, are eligible not only for ID cards, discounts, and free gifts on their birthday, but also participation in the "B's or Better" campaign, which offers special rewards for academic achievement at the end of each school marking period.

LEARNING WORLD, 106 North Garden, Mall of America. Tel. 858-9578.

Here's a children's educational store with items on hand not just for boys and girls, but for their teachers as well. For more than 50 years classroom teachers and day-care providers have ordered posters, blackboard borders, flash cards, and charts of all kinds from the widely known Moyer's Catalogue. Eventually that catalog turned into a chain of retail stores, one of which opened at Mall of America and quickly became popular with local folks and visitors alike under the name "For the Love of Kids." In June 1994 this name was changed to the less ponderous "Learning World," but despite the name change, the purpose of this large cheery store remains the same—to provide a wide selection of materials for children primarily from infancy on up through the age of 12. Toddlers enjoy the large floor puzzles depicting everything from dinosaurs to Noah's Ark to endangered species, while older boys and girls enjoy activities designed to develop their own hand-to-eye coordination. Sand Art and jewelry-making sets are particularly popular with children in the 8-to-12 age group.

You'll find here a full line of CDs as well as audio- and videotapes offering performances by Raffi, Fred Penner, and the gang from Sesame Street among other children's favorites. For the youngsters you've brought along or those awaiting a souvenir upon your return home, you might look through the collection of traveling kits containing everything from magnetic checkers to stickers to games designed to be played by oneself or with a companion.

OSHMAN'S SUPER SPORTS USA, 340 West Market, Mall of America. Tel. 854-9444.

This sprawling sporting-goods store, second in size only to the Mall's four anchor department stores, needs lots of space for the multitude of activities that take place on these premises. The motto here is "Play before you pay," which means that you're likely to find yourself on a three-quarters-size racquetball court with glass-wall front, laminated wood floors, and automatic ball machine. The baseball batting cage has an automatic ball machine too. There's a hard-surface area designed for testing in-line skates and a 50-foot archery range equipped with simulated lighting to enable you to select the correct rifle scope or binocular for dawn, night, or poor lighting. Activities vary according to the season: At the right time of year expect to find a moving deck simulating ski conditions. There's a contoured practice putting green and a wildly popular Par T Golf simulator (a computerized video golf course programmed with seven of the world's top courses, including Pebble Beach, Spyglass Hill, Quinta do Lago, and The Belfry).

Other departments offer apparel and footwear for women, men, and children, not to mention sunglasses, sports bags, exercise equipment, and, of course, gifts. There's also a service-and-repair shop here where you can have a baseball glove relaced, a bowling ball drilled, a ski mounted and tuned up, a tennis racket strung, and a golf club repaired. Tents are for sale here; so are sleeping bags and fishing rods. And while you're making your way from department to department, you can see and hear live sporting events thanks to RV monitors and speakers throughout the store.

RYBICKI CHEESE, 382 West Market, Mall of America. Tel. 854-3330.

Chances are you'll see a man with a large wedge of Cheddar cheese on his head as you approach the sample table outside Rybicki's cheese store. The hat, which really does look good enough to eat, is actually made of foam rubber, and there are also a smaller cheesy baseball cap, cheesy tie, and cheesy earrings for sale here. But novelties aside, the chief reason for visiting this shop is the wide variety of fresh Wisconsin cheese, including dill, garlic, hot pepper, bacon, salami, smoked Swiss, smoked cheddar, and many others. Dick Rybicki, who was a Wisconsin cheese maker for 43 years before opening his own small retail store, stocks a few imported cheeses as well and reports that customers enjoy putting together their own varieties either to ship home to others or to carry home for themselves. Among the favorites here is 4-year-old Cheddar for those who like their cheese sharp. "The longer it ages, the sharper it gets," Rybicki explains. He and his wife and partner, Jan, are happy to provide samples of any cheese on the premises. Prices range from $2.89 per pound for mild Cheddar to $13.95 per pound for imported Roquefort.

SCIENTIFIC REVOLUTION, 160 West Market, Mall of America. Tel. 851-0901.

Gifts for all ages and tastes and degrees of sophistication are available at Scientific Revolution, a store whose stated purpose is to make science fun again. There's a large collection of rocketry equipment here, including starter kits, launchpads, and rockets of all sizes. State-of-the-art items like laser pointers and binary clocks are here as well, along with hard-to-find items such as laboratory quality microscopes. Prestigious universities have been known to call for chemical glassware and some schools buy their science textbooks here. There's a large Einstein section featuring books, videos, posters, shirts, and even a Thinker's Mug. Escher has a section of his own as well with T-shirts, books, puzzles, and other memorabilia. And then there's Galileo, represented at Scientific Revolution in the water section by the Galileo thermometer invented in 1495.

While many of the items for sale on these premises are of interest primarily to knowledgeable adults, some are geared to the interests and capabilities of scientifically inclined youngsters. Consider, for example, the environmental test kits that enable children nine and over to test carbon monoxide in the air and acidity in the rain.

CARTS & IN-THE-WALL SHOPS

Among the many delights here at Mall of America are the succession of merchandise carts and in-the-wall shops offering a remarkably wide diversity of items. While you'll find the greatest concentration at West Market, there are dozens of others located on all levels and all thoroughfares. What follows, in alphabetical order, is a necessarily brief introduction to a few of them.

EARTHWEAR, East Broadway, Mall of America. Tel. 851-9460.

Everything sold here is made of natural materials—wood, clay, bone, silver, amethyst, pink quartz, and the like. You can buy a marble for 25¢ or a harmony ball for $34.95. (A harmony ball contains chimes within, by the way.) Necklaces, earrings, and dream catchers (to ward off bad dreams) are all handmade.

COW A BUDDIES, West Market, Mall of America. Tel. 854-0764.

Cows and pigs are represented here in every form imaginable. Mugs, magnets, T-shirts, shopping bags, pencils, and key chains are among the items for sale here. While most can be described as inexpensive novelties, the large stuffed cow and pig go for $79.95 each—a hefty sum.

FRABJOUS, South Avenue, Mall of America. Tel. 858-8048.

The endearing title of this in-the-wall store comes, of course, from Lewis Carroll, who used it to describe something wonderful or superb. That's what shoppers think about the summertime crinkle-cotton outfits and wintertime sweatshirts sold here, all of them hand silk-screened and most of them decorated with floral designs.

GiGGLES, ETC., West Market, Mall of America. Tel. 858-9615.

Many of the items for sale here may, in fact, make you want to giggle. Don't suppress the urge. The whole point of what's offered here is to provide amusing gifts or souvenirs. One of the biggest sellers is the T-shirt that comes with three small oblong pockets in front and the caption, "Warning! Grandmother with photos." The photos, of course, fit into the plastic pockets, while the grandmother fits into the Hanes T-shirt, which can safely be machine washed and air dried. There's a similar shirt for pet owners with only one pocket, but it's a great deal larger. (Apparently more people have one dog than one child.) Other T-shirts proclaim other messages having to do with family relationships between the generations and between siblings. Among the types of items you won't find for sale here are T-shirts, sweatshirts, or other children's apparel with names printed on them. "We stopped selling those for safety reasons," says co-owner Phyllis Cohen. Instead her cart does a brisk business in personalized artistic name plaques for use in children's rooms. Customers can give the child's name, pick the pattern, and have the whole matted and framed and ready to ship or pack in just a few minutes.

LEFTORIUM, West Market, Mall of America. Tel. 858-9750.

"Since the right side of the brain controls the left side of the body, only left-handed people are in their right mind." That's one of the messages on mugs and T-shirts for sale here; it could also stand as the battle cry for that part of the population which has had to deal with everyday items made without them in mind. Rulers sold here go from left to right, 12 to 1, so the left-handed user won't have to hold it upside down to make it "work." The thumbpiece on the left-handed scissors is finally on the correct (left) side, making it possible to get an even cut. The left-handed watch has a stem on the left side so it can be more easily wound. Although most of the shoppers here are reportedly right-handers in search of a gift for a left-handed relative or friend, there's a certain poignancy to the proclamation on one of the more popular T-shirts: "It's a left-handed thing. You wouldn't understand."

THE MAP STORE, South Avenue, Mall of America. Tel. 858-9888.

You'll find helpful maps of Minneapolis and St. Paul at this in-the-wall shop, along with travel books and travel-related jewelry. The most popular item, though, is, of all things, a shower curtain decorated with a map of the world.

MINDWARE, South Avenue, Mall of America. Tel. 851-0014.

Articles for sale here will engage your creativity and powers of lateral thinking. Popular games include Escape from Alcatraz, a small hand-held puzzle which challenges the user to get a ball out of a cage without using force. Mind Trap is a bit like Trivial Pursuit, but with an emphasis on lateral thinking. While the more prevalent linear thinking prompts assumptions based on experience, lateral thinking requires a different approach. Example: "Q. Why are 1990 dollar bills worth more than 1989 dollar bills? A. Because there's one dollar more." Get it?

RECYKIDABLES, West Market, Mall of America. Tel. 858-9024.

As its name implies, this cart sells children's clothing made from recycled cloth. Surplus adult shirts, defective or overstocked, are reused for rompers, dresses, leggings, and other goods of apparel for infants and toddlers. Each item, hand sewn by one of 15 local stay-at-home mothers, is unique.

3. NEARBY PLACES TO STAY

For additional accommodations convenient to Mall of America, see Chapter 5.

EXPENSIVE

CROWN STERLING SUITES, 7901 34th Ave. S., Bloomington, MN 55425. Tel. 612/854-1000 or toll free 800/433-4600. Fax 612/854-6557. 311 suites. A/C MINIBAR TV TEL.
- **Directions:** I-494 to 34th Ave. S. exit; south one block.
- **$ Rates** (including full breakfast): $135 suite. AE, CB, DC, DISC, MC, V. **Parking:** Free.

Located just 1 mile from Mall of America, 2 miles from the airport, and 12 miles from downtown Minneapolis and St. Paul, this hotel has a lot to offer. There's a very special added attraction two blocks away—the lovely Minnesota Valley National Wildlife Refuge, with tranquil trails, intriguing exhibits, and a variety of presentations on ecological matters. Inquire about the hotel's special package of useful accessories—fanny pack, calculator, Crown Sterling T-shirt, and coupon book offering sizable discounts at Mall of America.

Facilities: Indoor pool, whirlpool, steam room, sauna.

MODERATE

COUNTRY INN & SUITES BY CARLSON, 2221 Killebrew Dr., Bloomington, MN 55425. Tel. 612/854-5555 or toll free 800/456-4000. Fax 612/854-5564. 140 units including 46 2-rm suites and 10 whirlpool suites. A/C TV TEL. **Directions:** I-494 to Cedar Ave. (Hwy. 77), then south on Hwy. 77 to Killebrew Dr.

$ Rates (including breakfast): Single, weekday $69, weekend $79 with $10 charge for each additional person; Single suite, weekday $105, weekend $115, with no charge for additional persons; Celebration suite, weekday $115, weekend $175 with no charge for additional persons. Children 18 and under stay free in parents' room or suite. 10% discount for seniors. AE, DC, DISC, MC, V. **Parking:** Free.

Situated across from Mall of America, this property serves as a Carlson showplace for guests from around the world, so a bit of finery is considered very much in order. Despite departures in architecture and decor, however, the more familiar features of the traditionally rustic Country Inn & Suites will greet you as you enter the cozy lobby with its lace curtains, parquet-wood floors, fireplace, oak staircase, dried-flower arrangements, stenciled wall coverings, and easy chairs. Accommodations here come in three forms. Deluxe guest rooms with two queen-size beds; deluxe suites with king-size bed, sofa sleeper, microwave, refrigerator, two TVs, two telephones and wet bar; and Celebration Suites with expanded living and bedroom areas and amenities along with a private whirlpool.

HOLIDAY INN INTERNATIONAL, 3 Appletree Sq., Bloomington, MN 55420. Tel. 612/854-9000 or toll free 800/ HOLIDAY. Fax 612/854-9000. 432 rms, 132 suites. TV TEL

$ Rates: $80 single; $90 double. Seniors $72 single; $82 double. AE, CB, DC, DISC, MC, V. **Parking:** Free.

This handsome 13-story building boasts a truly imposing lobby with a two-story atrium and furnishings done in peach and green. These same tones give an air of tranquility to the guest rooms as well.

Dining/Entertainment: Two appealing dining spots, the moderately priced Applebutter and the more elegant Pippins, are popular with local folks as well as with visitors. That's true of the Greenhouse Lounge as well.

Services: Free 24-hour airport shuttle service leaving every half hour; room service.

Facilities: Swimming pool, whirlpool, sauna, fitness center with Nautilus equipment and aerobics classes, suntan booth, hair salon.

MALL OF AMERICA GRAND HOTEL, 7901 24th Ave. S., Bloomington, MN 55425-1221. Tel. 612/854-2244 or toll free 800//222-8733. Fax 612/854-4737. 322 units. A/C TV TEL. **Directions:** I-494 east to 24th Ave. S. Drive to corner of 24th Ave. S. and 79th St.

$ Rates: Sun-Thurs $115, weekend $89 single or double. Concierge level $129 and up. AARP members $89 anytime. Children free of charge in parents' room.

Equidistant from downtown St. Paul and downtown Minneapolis, this Twin Cities landmark, known for 20 years as The Registry Hotel, has long been a destination for out-of-town visitors and local folks celebrating a special occasion. Now its location just four minutes from the Minneapolis–St. Paul International Airport and across from Mall of America has given the place a new lease on life and a new name after its official alliance with Mall of America in 1994. Following a $3.5-million renovation, the Grand Hotel offers impeccably decorated guest rooms with custom designed furnishings, original works of art, and classic artifacts.

The warm, welcoming atmosphere here becomes evident as you enter the Lobby Lounge where comfortably upholstered furnishings and an oversized fireplace provide a congenial place for personal and professional conversation. Another popular meeting spot is the tropical, centrally located Cabana Court, overlooked by 32 cabana rooms, each with its own patio or balcony. Also overlooking the Cabana Court is Café Gazebo, a cheery dining room serving breakfast, lunch, and dinner daily. Ravel's, a bustling nightspot, offers a complimentary buffet each day along with specialty drinks. Accommodations on the Concierge Floor offer terry-cloth robes, hair dryer, fresh flowers, and access to a private lounge providing continental breakfast plus hors d'oeuvres and cocktails each day. The indoor pool is popular and so is the health club, which is outfitted with a treadmill, stairmaster, stationary bikes, universal weights system, and other top-of-the-line equipment. Complimentary transportation is provided to and from the airport.

MINNEAPOLIS–ST. PAUL AIRPORT HILTON, 3200 E. 80th St., Minneapolis, MN 55425. Tel. 612/854-2100 or toll free 800/HILTONS. Fax 612/854-8002. 300 rms, 9 suites. A/C TV TEL **Directions:** Hwy. 494 to 34th Ave. Turn right and proceed to first stoplight at 80th St. Turn left and go one block to hotel.

$ Rates: Standard room $89–$115 single or double; suite $145 and up. Children stay free in parents' room. AE, CB, DC, DISC, MC, V. **Parking:** Free.

This Hilton is located just across the road from the National Wildlife Refuge, so guests enjoy the same no-fly-over provisions as the neighboring animals. Another popular retreat is in the handsome complex, whose two-story waterfall imparts a serenity of its own. If there's time, try the hotel's much honored Biscayne Bay Restaurant, a popular destination for area residents as well as visitors to these parts. Food and drink are also available at Café Carabella and Flamingo's nightclub, which offers live entertainment Monday through Saturday. And, of course, there are always Mall of America and Mystic Lake Casino, to which free transportation are provided. Children have a special indoor pool of their own. Babysitting can be arranged through the concierge.

SHERATON AIRPORT INN, 2525 E. 78th St., Bloomington, MN 55420. Tel. 612/854-1771 or toll free 800/325-3535. Fax 612/854-5898. 235 rms, 8 suites. A/C TV TEL

$ Rates: $95 single; $105 double; $115–$135 suite. AE, DC, DISC, MC, V. **Parking:** Free.

For nearly 20 years visitors to the Twin Cities have enjoyed staying at the Sheraton Airport Inn. Now, a new beautifully landscaped four-story structure has been built adjacent to the original two-story building. The huge lobby contains cozy nooks and crannies that businesspeople find useful for private conferences, plus an abundance of couches and coffee tables set amid plants and palm trees.

Dining/Entertainment: A full-service dining room, the Timbers, is popular. There's also a lounge with big-screen live TV coverage of major sporting events, as well as live music.

Services: Free 24-hour daily shuttle to and from the international airport (if you aren't picked up within 12 minutes of your initial call, your first night is free).

Facilities: Swimming pool, whirlpool, exercise room.

THE THUNDERBIRD MOTEL, 2201 E. 78th St., Blooming-ton, MN 55425. Tel. 612/854-3411 or toll free 800/328-1931. Fax 612/854-1183. 263 rms. A/C TV TEL

$ Rates: $71–$79 single; $77–$85 double. Seniors receive a 10% discount. AE, DC, DISC, V. **Parking:** Free.

You'll find a lot more than a comfortable and convenient place to stay at The Thunderbird Motel. Located less than three miles from Minneapolis–St. Paul airport, Thunderbird is one of dozens of motels on the Bloomington strip, but it has certain notable features. A towering statue of a Native American chief dominates the front lawn, and a graceful Apache rides his steed atop a granite pedestal near the main entrance.

The theme extends to the guest rooms, where paintings, draperies, and even the carpeting show a Native American motif. But there are 20th-century trappings at the Thunderbird too. This is the only hotel on the strip with both an indoor and outdoor swimming pool. You'll have the use of sun lamps, a whirlpool, a kiddie pool, and picnic tables in the vicinity of the spacious kidney-shaped indoor pool. And across the hall from these, a sauna and exercise room are available without extra charge to guests of the hotel.

The Totem Pole dining room is open from 11am to 10pm Monday through Friday, with weekend dinners served from 5 to 10:30pm and all-you-can-eat brunches from 10:30am to 2:30pm. There is also free shuttle service to and from the airport and Mall of America.

INEXPENSIVE

EXEL INN, 2701 E. 78th St., Bloomington, MN 55425. Tel. 612/854-7200 or toll free 800/356-8013. Fax 612/854-8652. 205 rms. A/C TV TEL

$ Rates: $43–$53 single or double. Seniors receive 10% discount. AE, DC, DISC, MC. **Parking:** Free.

Exel Inn is located just four miles from the Minneapolis–St. Paul International Airport. This brick complex of two two-story buildings offers attractive rooms at reasonable rates. The rooms, decorated in shades of blue and gray, are kept scrupulously clean. HBO is available in each room, at no additional cost.

4. WHERE TO DINE

MODERATE

MRS. KNOTT'S RESTAURANT, 5000 Center Court, Mall of America. Tel. 883-8776, reservations 883-8775.
   Cuisine: AMERICAN. **Reservations:** Not necessary.
$ Prices: Sandwiches $5.95–$6.95; burgers $5.95–$6.25; main courses $8.95–$12.95. AE, DISC, MC, V.
   Open: June–Aug Mon–Thurs 9am–9pm, Fri 9:30am–9:30pm, Sat 9am–10pm, Sun 9am–7pm. Call concerning hours Sept–May.

There's a country kind of feeling at Mrs. Knott's, where the atmosphere is reminiscent of the farming community in which Walter and Cordelia Knott opened a roadside stand back in 1920. Shortly thereafter the Knotts opened a small tearoom where, by 1927, people were making a special effort to buy Cordelia's biscuits and jam. Seven years later, Walter's first crop of boysenberries enjoyed instant popularity with diners, and at this point Cordelia decided it was time to serve real meals of southern fried chicken. This remains a favorite at Mrs. Knott's restaurants, now run by the children and grandchildren of Walter and Cordelia. Framed pictures of the family farm and of family members hang on the walls of this rustic restaurant where the green-and-mauve decor extends to the clothing worn by servers: green or mauve dresses for the women, mauve or green vests to go with the white shirts and black trousers and ties worn by the men. There's a comfortable atmosphere here and the food is reliably good and the service courteous.

NAPA VALLEY GRILLE, 220 West Market, Mall of America. Tel. 858-9934.
   Cuisine: CALIFORNIA ECLECTIC. **Reservations:** Recommended.
$ Prices: Appetizers $6.50–$9; salad $5–$6.50; pasta $9–$12; main courses $9–$12 lunch, $14–$23 dinner; Sun brunch $8–$11. Children's lunch, main dishes $4, dessert $2. AE, DC, DISC, MC, V.
   Open: Lunch Mon–Sun 11am–4pm; dinner Mon–Thurs 5–10pm, Fri–Sat 5–10:30pm; Sun brunch 11am–3:30pm.

Napa Valley Grille, one of the most elegant and expensive restaurants at Mall of America, may seem intimidating to passersby. There are, for example, those white linen tablecloths that lend an air of formality to lunchtime settings. But afternoon or evening, a growing number of diners has discovered here a warm, congenial atmosphere that combines the finest in dining with the most gracious surroundings. Guests arrive wearing business suits or jogging suits, carrying briefcases or shopping sacks, accompanied by colleagues or children. Constants are the attentive service, the fine quality of food ingredients, and the imaginative, artistic presentation of the delicious food.
   As its name implies, California's Napa Valley, with its bountiful

harvest of fresh food and famous grapes, serves as the inspiration for a cuisine that combines the best in local products with the finest wine of California. Executive chef Evan Steine selects pheasant, quail, and partridge from local game farms, lamb from nearby Spring Valley, and freshwater fish from Minnesota trout farms. Organically grown lettuce, baby spinach, tomatoes, and green beans are grown expressly for Napa Valley Grille by local farmers. A notably unpretentious wine steward is on hand to offer suggestions to sophisticates and neophytes alike.

The international reputation of Mall of America brings a great number of people here from overseas, and many of them express surprise and pleasure at their dining experience at Napa Valley Grille. French visitors, for example, are astonished at the texture and flavor of the goat cheese from Wisconsin and the feta cheese that's produced even closer to home.

Chef Steine, who graduated from the New England Culinary Institute in Montpelier, Vermont, and apprenticed with a French chef on Nantucket Island, delights in the availability of fine fresh seafood in this decidedly inland city. Located in the center of the country, just minutes away from a major airport, Napa Valley Grille receives daily shipments from the East Coast, the West Coast, Alaska, and Hawaii. Popular first courses here include Dungeness crab cakes with orange-ginger vinaigrette, watercress and crispy leeks, and smoked salmon with sun-dried tomato crostini, baby greens, capers, and mascarpone. Popular main courses are pesto-grilled shrimp and scallop brochette and roasted rack of lamb or pork. Desserts are outstanding, and so, of course, are the wines.

TUCCI BENUCCH, 114 West Market, Mall of America. Tel. 853-0200.

Cuisine: ITALIAN. **Reservations:** Recommended.

$ Prices: Antipasto $3.95–$5.95; pizza $7.50–$15.95; salad $3.25–$8.95; pasta $7.50–$9.95; main dishes $10.50–$13.95. Children's menu $4.50. AE, DC, DISC, MC, V.

Open: Mon–Thurs 11:15am–10pm, Fri–Sat 11:15am–11pm, Sun noon–9pm.

Closed: Christmas, Thanksgiving Day, Easter Day.

Everything about Tucci Benucch is Italian. Designed to resemble an Italian country home, this popular restaurant offers "outdoor" dining on a patio where vines hang from a trellis. As you proceed through a succession of inner rooms, you'll encounter the kind of old Italian dwelling in which family pictures decorate the walls and wooden chairs hang from the ceiling. Old wine bottles hang in the wine room, while in the kitchen, tea kettles, spices, and miscellaneous utensils wait to be used. In the barn, you'll see saddles, rakes, a hose, and lanterns. And in every room you'll find cheerful diners who've come for a variety of Italian favorites from minestrone and baked spaghetti to thin-crust pizza with a wide choice of toppings; the great salads include one featuring spinach and goat cheese. Popular main dishes include roasted garlic chicken and veal parmesan, but save room for a house specialty—*tiramisù*, a combination of lady fingers, marsca-pone cheese, Kahlúa, cocoa, and espresso. Different versions of this classic Italian dessert appear in different Twin Cities restaurants, a fact that doesn't surprise Tucci Benucch manager Dan McGowan. "There are as many *tiramisù* as there are Italian grandmothers," he explains. Children generally opt for the ice cream that's listed on their special menu along with a beverage and their choice of pizza, chicken fingers, buttered noodles, or spaghetti and meatballs.

INEXPENSIVE

DADDY'S DELI, 393 South Ave., Mall of America. Tel. 858-9760.
   Cuisine: DELI.
$ **Prices:** Breakfast $1.25–$3.25; soup $1.55–$3.50; sandwiches $1.75–$5.75; salad $1.95–$4.95; platters $4.50–$4.95.
   Open: Mon–Thurs 10am–9pm, Fri–Sat 10am–9:30pm, Sun 11am–7pm.

You're never too late for breakfast at Daddy's Deli where well-prepared omelets, pancakes, french toast, and muffins await you morning, afternoon, and evening. Bagels are a great favorite here, and sandwiches range from a hot dog to a Big Daddy's (a triple decker containing roast beef, corned beef, turkey breast, Swiss cheese, American cheese, lettuce, tomato, coleslaw, and Russian dressing).

Sharing the same address and phone number and proprietor in this third level Food Court is **Healthy Turkey,** where you'll find fresh roasted turkey breast in a variety of forms: gourmet sandwiches, gourmet salads, Caesar salads, and pasta salads.

HEALTHY EXPRESS, 126 South Ave., Mall of America. Tel. 854-1400.
   Cuisine: HEALTHFUL.
$ **Prices:** Salad $1.95–$3.15; sandwiches $2.65–$4; yogurt $1.55–$3.75. AE, DC, DISC, MC, V.
   Open: Breakfast 8–10am; regular menu 10am–9:30pm.

There's an irresistible selection of juices, yogurts, smoothies, sandwiches, pastas, muffins, cookies, and other good nutritious things awaiting you at the Healthy Express. Of course everything you find here will be 100% pure and natural, preservative free, and low in fat and sodium. The selection changes daily, but you can always count on flavorful salads and hearty soups, along with fresh juices, bagels galore, and, maybe best of all, delectable smoothies, a blend of fresh fruit, juice, and yogurt along with sometimes surprising additions like peanut butter. (You get to choose the ingredients.) It's nice to know that anything you buy here will be nutritious as well as delicious.

JOHNNY ROCKETS, 370 South Ave., Mall of America. Tel. 858-8158.
   Cuisine: AMERICAN.
$ **Prices:** Sandwiches $2.25–$4.55; malts $2.95. AE, DC, DISC, MC, V.
   Open: Mon–Sat 9am–9:30pm, Sun 9am–7pm.

This California-based 1950s grill is part of a network that extends throughout this country and well beyond. There's a Johnny Rockets in Mexico and one in Japan as well. But the one at Mall of America is very special because it's the first one to arrive in Minnesota, although others reportedly are on their way. If there's a Johnny Rockets in your neck of the woods, you already know about their nickel jukeboxes and dancing servers and hand-packed ice cream and, of course, their chili and their mammoth hamburgers, perhaps the biggest around. There's lots of good food and good fun to be found here, as many Minnesotans have already discovered.

PANDA EXPRESS, 374 South Ave., Mall of America. Tel. 858-8115.

Cuisine: MANDARIN.
$ Prices: Main dishes $3–$5 regular portions, $4.80–$8 large portions; combination plates $4.40–$5.40.

Come here for authentically prepared Mandarin food at remarkably low prices. Items include beef with broccoli, a combination of sliced marinated beef stir-fried with broccoli in an oyster-based soy sauce; orange-flavored chicken, lightly battered and fried; and vegetable chop suey, a stir-fry combination of zucchini, carrots, broccoli, mushroom, bamboo shoots, baby corn, and water chestnuts. Another Panda Express is on the opposite side of the Mall, at 350 North Garden (tel. 858-8116).

PLANET HOLLYWOOD, 402 South Ave., Mall of America. Tel. 854-7827.

Cuisine: AMERICAN. **Reservations:** Not accepted.
$ Prices: Appetizers $4.95–$8.50; salad $6.95–$10.95; sandwiches $6.50–$8.95; pasta $8.95–$10.50; grilled platters $10.95–$16.95. AE, DC, MC, V.
Open: 11am–1am daily.
Closed: Christmas.

It's not unusual for the owners to be present for the grand opening of a new restaurant, but the owners of Planet Hollywood have turned every opening into a star-studded spectacular. That was certainly the case at Mall of America in 1993, when Planet Hollywood shareholders Sylvester Stallone, Bruce Willis, and Demi Moore turned up along with Patrick Swayze, Melanie Griffith, Don Johnson, Whoopi Goldberg, Luke Perry, and Wesley Snipes, among many others. Almost as exciting to the 35,000 or so onlookers on hand for the occasion was the glamorous glitzy aura of the brand new restaurant where priceless movie memorabilia decorated the walls and hung from the ceiling. Among them were the carousel horse Dick Van Dyke rode in *Mary Poppins,* the costume Judy Garland wore in *Easter Parade,* and the backpack Dan Ackroyd used in *Ghostbusters.*

It's a pleasure to report that the food at Planet America is remarkably good. This is a family restaurant where there's no cover charge for all the entertainment that surrounds you. The menu, which remains the same from 11am to 1am each day, lists a wide assortment of soup and salad, pasta and pizza made right on the premises. Cheeseburgers are the biggest sellers, and turkey burgers and vegetable burgers are very popular too. In second place among favorite foods is Cajun chicken breast, seasoned with Cajun spices, grilled, and served on an onion turnover with mustard sauce, lettuce, tomato, and red onion. The most expensive—and some say the most delicious—item on the menu is the 14-ounce aged New York sirloin strip, grilled to order.

CHAPTER 12

OTHER EASY EXCURSIONS FROM THE TWIN CITIES

1. ST. CROIX VALLEY
2. MINNESOTA VALLEY
3. ROCHESTER
4. MANTORVILLE
5. MISSISSIPPI RIVER TOWNS
6. DULUTH

By now you know that the Twin Cities could easily keep you occupied throughout your entire stay. If time permits, though, you might want to visit some of the places that lure local folks out of town for weekend excursions. Stillwater is a popular destination with pleasant shops and restaurants. Rochester, home of the famous Mayo Clinic, is close enough for the 90-minute drive, a bit of sightseeing, and a return on the same day. For the river-town rambles or a visit to Duluth, you'll probably want to set aside at least one night, maybe more.

1. ST. CROIX VALLEY

The lovely St. Croix River forms the border between Minnesota and Wisconsin, to the east of the Twin Cities. The area is reached easily via I-94 or Minnesota Highway 36.

STILLWATER

This is where Minnesota began. It was on August 28, 1848, that 61 delegates gathered in Stillwater to draft a petition asking Congress and President James K. Polk for the "organization of the Territory of Minnesota." The following year, under the sponsorship of Sen. Stephen A. Douglas, the bill was passed.

Nestled in the picturesque St. Croix River Valley, Stillwater today is readily reached by boat or car, and during the summer pleasure craft from throughout Minnesota and nearby Wisconsin occupy the docks that are located a block or two from the city's main street.

Once you get to town, your first stop should be the **Stillwater Area Chamber of Commerce,** 423 S. Main St. (tel. 612/439-7700). You'll find maps here, along with brochures about minitours, lodgings, antiques, and other information of interest. For a more personalized introduction to the area, you can make a local phone call from the Twin Cities to **Valley Tours,** 101 W. Pine St., Stillwater, MN 55082 (tel. 612/439-6110), which offers 1-hour walking tours for individuals and groups seven days a week. Tours can also be arranged for those who prefer driving their own car rather than walking. Itineraries can be customized according to the special interests of the individual or group. Special arrangements are made for larger groups or groups arriving in buses. One-hour tours for 1 to 5 people cost $5 each, for 6 to 15 people, $3 each.

WHAT TO SEE & DO

As you approach Stillwater on Highway 36, you'll pass one of the area's most popular destinations. Turn left on Manning Avenue North (Highway 15) and you'll find **Aamodt's Apple Farm,** 6428 Manning Ave. N. (tel. 612/439-3127), a 180-acre orchard with its own processing plant, gift shops, bakery, and lunchroom. A large carving of Johnny Appleseed stands in the renovated 1800s barn, where visitors munch contentedly on apple goodies—apple-cheese soup, apple salad, and most popular of all, giant apple-oatmeal cookies. And of course they're washing it all down with tasty apple cider. At this writing, Aamodt's is open from August to March. If you're lucky enough to be here in spring, enjoy the visual and aromatic pleasure of apple-blossom time at Aamodt's.

There's a diversity of outdoor fun to be found at such Stillwater picnic sites as **Pioneer Park,** on a bluff at Second Street overlooking the scenic St. Croix River, and **Lowell Park,** two blocks east of Main Street, which borders downtown from north to south. In the large amphitheater at Pioneer Park, musical events are held all summer, and during the town's annual spectacular, **Lumberjack Days,** local talent shows are presented along with a variety of lumber-related activities, including log-rolling, tree-climbing, and cross-chop-sawing demonstrations by professional lumberjacks. Call the Chamber of Commerce (tel. 612/439-7700) for the particular July weekend on which it will be held during your stay. On Sunday the festivities end with a grand parade that features marching and musical groups from all over the state.

Among the most interesting public buildings in Stillwater is the **County Historic Court House,** 101 W. Pine. Built in 1867, this is the oldest standing courthouse in Minnesota. In addition to being a repository of historic artifacts and files, the building serves as a setting for groups like the Friday Courthouse Quilters. Civic, business, and professional groups meet in the spacious second floor. The front patio, with an expansive view of the St. Croix Valley, appears as background in many photographs of local weddings.

One of the newest buildings in this historic town is the replica of an old one, the depot for the **Minnesota Zephyr,** one of Stillwater's most popular dining and sightseeing attractions. Passengers board meticulously restored 1949 railroad dining cars for a trip that carries them through some of the most beautiful landscape in Minnesota. You'll pass the meandering St. Croix River on one side and picturesque limestone river bluffs on the other, then make your way through forests where maple, ash, oak, walnut, white birch, and other state trees abound. The entire journey proceeds at about five miles per hour and takes about 3¼ hours; a delightful four-course dinner is included. The cost of this visit to the past is $49.50 per guest, with one glass of wine included in the price of the meal; cocktails and gratuity are not included. On Thursdays through Saturdays, you'll board at 6:30pm, depart at 7:30pm, and return at 10:45pm. On Sundays, you'll board at 11:30am, depart at noon, and return at 3:15pm. For reservations and further information, call 612/430-3000, a local phone call from Minneapolis and St. Paul.

The *Minnesota Zephyr's* depot is also an attraction, with a railroad-and-logging museum and a gallery of historic photos of downtown Stillwater. There's a gift shop and snack bar as well.

Shopping is especially enjoyable in Stillwater because so many of the stores are located in historic structures. On Main Street you'll find a group of fine specialty shops in a complex called the **Grand Garage and Gallery,** 324 S. Main St. At the **Brick Alley Mall,** 423 S. Main St., two 19th-century structures separated by an old alley have been connected by an enclosed walkway. Elsewhere in town, **Tamarack Gallery,** 112 S. Main St. (tel. 612/439-9393), attracts art collectors from throughout the Midwest, while sweater and outerwear collectors have a fine time in another restored building where the **Winona Knitting Mills,** 215 S. Main St. (tel. 612/430-1711), offers a wide selection of apparel at prices about 30% to 50% lower than in department and specialty shops. But by far the largest number of items under one roof can be found at **The Mill Antiques,** 410 N. Main St. (tel. 612/430-1818). With 81 dealers displaying antiques on three levels in this 20,000-square-foot mall, it's hard to imagine you won't find something tempting enough to buy.

WHERE TO STAY

Expensive

LOWELL INN, 102 N. 2nd St., Stillwater, MN 55082. Tel. 612/439-1100. Fax 612/439-4686. 21 rms. TV TEL
$ Rates (including meals): Fri–Sat $209–$289 per couple; Sun–Thurs $109–$179 per couple. MC, V.

A beautiful three-story structure with large white columns, arched windows, and a comfortably furnished veranda, this inn first opened in 1930. Sumptuously furnished with a mixture of French provincial and Victorian reproductions and antiques, the romantic rooms are much in demand by couples who find this the perfect place for an anniversary celebration. In fact the demand is so great that you might have trouble getting a room here, so do call ahead for reservations. Rates depend on the room's size, location, and accoutrements. Four of the rooms have Jacuzzis (presumably these don't date back to the 18th century), one room has its own adjoining living room, and one boasts a shower-in-the-round, with fixtures imported from Italy.

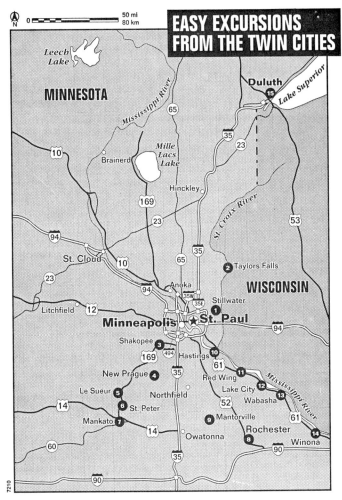

EASY EXCURSIONS FROM THE TWIN CITIES

Duluth **15**	Mantorville **9**	Shakopee **3**
Hastings **10**	New Prague **4**	Stillwater **1**
Lake City **12**	Red Wing **11**	Taylors Falls **2**
Le Sueur **5**	Rochester **8**	Wabasha **13**
Mankato **7**	St. Peter **6**	Winona **14**

Moderate

AFTON HOUSE, 3291 S. St. Croix Trail, Afton, MN 55001. Tel. 612/436-8883. Fax 612/436-6859. 15 rms. TV TEL
$ Rates (including continental breakfast): $60 basic double room; $120–$135 double room with river view and Jacuzzi. AE, DISC, MC, V.

Just minutes away from Stillwater, about four miles south of I-94, you'll find the delightful Afton House. On the banks of the St. Croix River, the inn's guest rooms have been furnished individually with antiques that include trundle beds, clipper chairs, and English armoires. Four of the rooms have small private balconies, with a larger one available to all guests.

ASA PARKER HOUSE, 17500 St. Croix Trail N., Marine on St. Croix, MN 55047. Tel. 612/433-5248. 5 rms.
$ Rates (including breakfast): $99–$135 double.
About 10 miles north of Stillwater, you'll find one of the best loved bed-and-breakfasts in the St. Croix Valley. Located in the National Historic District of Marine on St. Croix, this Greek Revival house was built in 1856 by a Vermont lumberman; it retains the Ionic columns, flat-roofed portico, and elegant balcony reminiscent of stately New England mansions. Some of the rooms have a wood-burning stove. The warmth in this home, though, emanates from innkeeper Marjorie Bush, who'll greet you on arrival with an irresistible display of home-baked sweets to accompany your wel-coming tea. You'll also enjoy a bountiful breakfast. You can enjoy looking around the tiny historic village with its 100-plus-year-old village hall and library, its neoclassical bank, its old-fashioned barbershop, and other reminders of days gone by. Marjorie's guests are welcome to use her well-stocked library, along with a private clay tennis court and screened gazebo.

WILLIAM SAUNTRY MANSION, 626 N. 4th St., Stillwater, MN 55082. Tel. 612/430-2653 or toll free 800/828-2653. 5 rms.
$ Rates (including breakfast): $89–$139 double.
Listed in the National Register of Historic Places, this elegant mansion now has five guest rooms, each named for a member of the William Sauntry family, for whom it was built in 1878. Parquet floors, stained-glass windows, a painted canvas ceiling, and cherry-and-oak woodwork reflect something of the luxurious life-style enjoyed by Sauntry, an Irish immigrant whose rags-to-riches story has by now become local folklore. Among the antiques brought here by innkeepers Martha and Duane Hubbs are an 1893 Chickering grand piano and an 1868 Mason and Hamlin pump organ. There are, they'll tell you proudly, no reproductions in this house. There's a large four-course breakfast.

WHERE TO DINE

Expensive

BAYPORT COOKERY, 328 5th Ave. N., Bayport. Tel. 612/430-1066.
    Cuisine: FRENCH/AMERICAN. **Reservations:** Required.
$ Prices: Prix-fixe dinner $24.95.
    Open: Wed–Thurs, Sun 6:30pm seatings. Fri–Sat 6pm, 7:30pm, 8:30pm seatings.
Twin Citians go out of their way to enjoy the culinary skill of Kirk

Bratrud, a young chef whose cuisine combines the best of French cooking with that of America's Napa Valley. This is a restaurant in which the dinner selection always comes as a surprise to diners. You won't know until you're handed the one-page hand-printed menu what that evening's fixed-price five-course fare will be. "They must trust us and be open to new experiences," Bratrud explains. The fact that so many return again and again indicates that their flexibility and sense of adventure have been well rewarded. Bayport Cookery seats only 35 at a time, and the atmosphere is restful and romantic. Bayport is just southeast of Stillwater.

While there's no such thing as a typical dinner at the Bayport cookery, a representative five-course meal might offer a first-course roulade filled with scallop mousseline, asparagus, and beets, followed by soup featuring caramelized corn and red bell pepper in corn milk garnished with tarragon. On to the third course—truffled pommes Anna served with corn lettuce and sliced truffles, dressed with shallot and champagne vinaigrette. The main course might be split roasted game hen served with grape, spinach, and peppercorn sauce and layered potato cake with King Bolete mushrooms. And for dessert your waiter might offer plums poached in spiced merlot wine, served with raspberry and marscapone ice cream.

LOWELL INN, 102 N. 2nd St. Tel. 612/439-1100.
Cuisine: AMERICAN. **Reservations:** Recommended.
$ Prices: Lunch $11.75–$20.75, dinner $20.95–$35.95. MC, V.
Open: Lunch noon–2:30pm; dinner in Matterhorn room Fri–Sat seatings at 6 and 9:30pm; Sun–Thurs 6–8:30pm.

The Lowell Inn attracts diners from throughout the state. You can dine in one of three rooms: The elegant George Washington Room with its sheffield silver, dresden china, and antique sideboards; the Matterhorn Room, notable for its acid-etched stained-glass windows and authentic Swiss carvings; and the Garden Room, which contains an indoor trout pool. The Matterhorn Room features a beef-and-shrimp fondue dinner with a European wine-tasting for $92 per couple; the George Washington Room and the Garden Room have the same varied American menu. Lunch and dinner hours vary from room to room, so phone ahead for specifics.

Moderate

AFTON HOUSE, 3291 S. St. Croix Trail, Afton. Tel. 612/436-8883.
Cuisine: AMERICAN. **Reservations:** Recommended.
$ Prices: Lunch $5.95–$13.95; dinner $12.95–$21.95; Sun brunch $10.95, holiday brunch $12.95; Sun cruise brunch, $21. AE, DISC, MC, V.
Open: Lunch Mon–Sat 11:30am–2:30pm; dinner Mon–Thurs 5:30–9pm, Fri–Sat 5–10pm, Sun 4:30–9pm; Sun brunch 10am–2pm.

Just minutes south of downtown Stillwater, Afton House is accessible by road and by river. Close enough to the Twin Cities to make it a special dinner destination, this beautiful inn, now on the National

Register of Historic Places, caters to a wide variety of patrons throughout the year. Skiers from nearby Afton Alps make this a mandatory stop during the winter months. And during the summer boaters tie up at the on-site dock.

In the elegant Wheel Room, dinner favorites include steak Diane garnished with fresh vegetables and poached salmon served with champagne sauce. The Catfish Salon features a variety of burgers, sandwiches, and soup selections. The Sunday cruise brunch includes a 2-hour cruise.

FREIGHT HOUSE RESTAURANT, 305 S. Water St. Tel. 612/439-5718.
   Cuisine: AMERICAN. **Reservations:** Not accepted.
$ **Prices:** Lunch $4.95–$8.50; dinner $6.95–$14.95. AE, CB, DC, DISC, MC, V.
   Open: Mon–Thurs 11am–9pm, Fri–Sat 11am–10pm, Sun 11am–9pm.
A block off Main Street, this restaurant overlooks the St. Croix River. The building it's housed in is listed on the National Register of Historic Places and was once occupied by an old railroad company. The large picture windows here provide diners with a panoramic view of the river. Prices are moderate, with a lunch of a salad, sandwich, or hamburger going for about $6. Barbecued ribs at $13 remain a longtime favorite for dinner.

VITTORIO'S, 402 S. Main St. Tel. 612/439-3588.
   Cuisine: ITALIAN. **Reservations:** Recommended for dinner.
$ **Prices:** Lunch $5.50–$8.75; dinner $11.75–$17.75. AE, MC, V.
   Open: Lunch Mon–Sun 11am–3pm; dinner Sun–Thurs 3–11pm, Fri–Sat 3pm–midnight.
Vittorio's features tasty northern Italian food in a large restaurant with four dining rooms and a lounge where a 19th-century brewery once stood. Popular dinner main courses, served here with antipasto salad and garlic toast, include ravioli carne (meat-filled pasta prepared with the house red sauce) and pollo alla cacciatora (chicken sautéed in wine and served with a portion of baked cannelloni rossi).

Inexpensive

BRINE'S, 219 S. Main St. Tel. 612/439-7556.
   Cuisine: AMERICAN. **Reservations:** Not accepted.
$ **Prices:** Sandwiches $2.95–$3.95; all-you-can-eat rib dinner $8.95. MC, V.
   Open: Sun–Thurs 8am–9pm, Fri–Sat 8am–10pm.
A general store back in the 1860s, Brine's offers informal dining on the second floor. Old-world delicatessen items, along with hamburgers and milk shakes, are the specialties of the house. The all-you-can-eat rib dinner starts at 5pm.

DOCK CAFE, 425 E. Nelson St. Tel. 612/430-3770.
The dining here is justifiably popular and the setting is second to none. The interior of this large but cozy restaurant is decorated with a

miscellany of interesting artifacts, some, including a graceful racing scull, suspended from the ceiling. And then there's the exquisite view of the St. Croix River and the bluffs of Wisconsin beyond. But the Dock's greatest claim to fame is seafood, including grilled salmon and blackened catfish. Also popular are tournedos of beef and chicken saltimbocca. Popular desserts include a cheesecake whose flavors vary from week to week and a chocolate raspberry truffle torte covered with fudge frosting. Dessert wines and specialty coffees round out your choices here. Main courses cost about $14 to $17; desserts run about $4.25.

Coffee Shop

ENO'S, 904 S. 4th St. Tel. 612/430-0656.
    Open: Mon–Fri 7:30am–6:30pm, Sat 7:30am–2:30pm, Sun 9am–2pm.
This small bakery and coffee shop is well known to residents of Stillwater, many of whom remember it as an adjunct of a sprawling wholesale bakery that serviced some of the area's most prestigious restaurants and supermarkets. Passersby, attracted by the aroma, would come in and ask to buy a loaf of bread, so a tray of cash was kept on a back counter to accommodate them. Carol Hamre, owner of the small bakery and coffee shop that evolved right across the street, recalls that some of the most ardent admirers of Eno's original wholesale bakery were "high school kids who'd drive into the parking lot during lunch hour to get carbohydrated." Now everybody can enjoy Eno's fresh-baked delights, including items like wild rice bread, toffee hazelnut scones, and chocolate chunk ginger cookies. For those who prefer to munch at once, there's a comfortable double rocker, some garden chairs, and small white tables on site. Others take their selections home to enjoy them later. Inexpensive.

COPAS

Just north of Marine on St. Croix, on the way to Taylors Falls, you'll come upon a truly unique two-room restaurant that offers a greater variety of food and activity than you'll encounter anywhere else in the St. Croix Valley.

CRABTREE'S KITCHEN, 19173 Quinnell Ave. N., Copas. Tel. 612/433-2455.
    Open: Tues–Sat 9am–8pm, Sun 9am–7pm. **Closed:** Monday.
This friendly family restaurant features old-fashioned American home-style cooking, and that, according to owner Terry Bennett, explains the Porsches and Corvettes that frequently pull into the driveway; driven by youngsters who've come for the meat loaf and Swedish meatballs. Other favorites include pork tenderloin, walleye pike, and, of course, burgers, sandwiches, salads, and homemade soups. Two bakers are on duty to prepare the bread, muffins, pies, and other baked goods. Family-style breakfast is brisk. Since this place functions as a local hangout, you'll find diners in both rooms pretty much anytime you arrive. Prices range to about $9. But Crabtree's

customers don't live on food alone. There's also the petting zoo featuring sheep, donkeys, goats, horses, and a llama. And there are winter-weekend sleigh rides featuring a team of Belgian horses who'll stop to let folks get off and on again as many times as they like. (Rides cost $3 for adults and $1 for children 12 and under. A bit more expensive are the $15 romantic rides for couples.) In warm weather a donkey-drawn wagon is a popular form of transportation; also popular are chuck-wagon cookouts guaranteed by owner Terry to be identical to those cowboys used to prepare.

OSCEOLA

Osceola, on the Wisconsin side of the St. Croix Valley north of Copas, has several tourist attractions. For train buffs, Osceola serves as one of three stops on the **St. Croix River Valley Passenger Railroad Line,** re-creating the railroading experience of the first half of the 20th century. At nearby **Trollhaugen,** a longtime favorite among ski enthusiasts, you'll find 22 of the best-groomed ski runs in the Midwest. Other fitness fans look to Osceola as to Mecca, for this is the home of **Horst's Aveda Spa,** which is described in detail at the end of this chapter.

If you'd like to spend a night or two in Osceola, you'll enjoy the **St. Croix River Inn Bed and Breakfast,** 305 River St., Osceola, WI 54020 (tel. 715/294-4248). Rates for two are $100 to $200 (Friday to Saturday) and $85 to $150 (Sunday to Thursday). Situated high on a bluff overlooking the picturesque St. Croix River, this meticulously restored 80-year-old limestone house provides a few amenities that the original structure lacked. Each of the seven rooms has, in addition to its Victorian decor, a private bath with Jacuzzi. To enhance the atmosphere, you'll also find a stereo cassette player and tapes in your room. A full breakfast will be brought to your door in the morning.

For lunch or dinner, try **Royal Christie's Restaurante,** at Trollhaugen (tel. 715/755-2955). This lovely rustic room has field-stone walls, a huge fireplace, a fine view of the slopes, and, during much of the winter season, a great view of skiers as well. You'll enjoy fine fare here at very reasonable prices. Appetizers range from $1.75 to $4, dinner main courses from $5.95 to $22.95. The Friday night fish fry with salad bar is one of the area's best buys at $6.50 and the same can be said for the Sunday buffet held at noon to 8pm for the low cost of $7.50.

TAYLORS FALLS

For a view of the St. Croix River Valley, follow Highway 95 from Stillwater. Drive past lush farmlands, magnificent bluffs, and dramatic waterways until you reach Taylors Falls, nestled on the northern end of 900-acre Interstate Park, which extends from one side of the St. Croix to the other and includes within its scope the towns of St. Croix Falls, Wis., and Taylors Falls, Minn. (This was the first interstate park ever established in the United States.)

Taylors Falls is famous for its **hiking, camping, boating,** and

swimming, as well as its good **fishing,** with plenty of catfish, smallmouth bass, northerns, and walleyes to be caught here. But this area's greatest claim to fame derives from **potholes** and **logjams.** You can see for yourself an enormous pothole more than 60 feet deep that was created out of volcanic rock during the meltdown of ancient glaciers. No remnants of the Taylors Falls logjam remain, but the legend endures: In 1886 when lack of rain prevented logging companies from floating their wood downriver, huge piles of logs accumulated on the riverbanks. When heavy rains did begin, there was a mad dash to get the wood on its way. Since the St. Croix River narrows and bends just below Taylors Falls, a logjam developed that eventually reached a height of 30 feet and a length of more than 2 miles. Another tie with the past is Taylors Falls' famous **historic residential area** where 19th-century homes and churches have been carefully preserved.

WHERE TO STAY

Moderate

THE OLD JAIL COMPANY, 102 Government Rd., Taylors Falls, MN 55084. Tel. 612/465-3112. 3 units.

$ Rates (with full breakfast): Jail Cottage, $100; Apartment, $110; Playhouse, $90.

The Old Jail Company, consisting of three small apartments, is the oldest bed-and-breakfast in Minnesota. It started life as the lockup for unruly locals and it still has bars on its windows. The Apartment and the Playhouse are in the Schottmuller Building, once an old saloon and boardinghouse. Both buildings are on the National Register of Historic Places. All three units have their own kitchen, bathroom, sitting room, bedroom, and private entrance. All are decorated with country antiques.

Inexpensive

SPRINGS INN, 1 block west of the junction of Hwys. 8 and 95, Taylors Falls. Mailing address: P.O. Box 11, Taylors Falls, MN 55084. Tel. 612/465-6565, toll free 800/851-4243. 27 rms. TV TEL

$ Rates Sun–Thurs single $30, Fri–Sat single $40. AE, DISC, MC, V.

The pleasant, economical, and centrally located Springs Inn features a popular hot tub and Jacuzzi. The three-story wood-frame inn offers rooms with king-size or two double beds. Free coffee is available in the lobby.

2. MINNESOTA VALLEY

U.S. Highway 169 extends from Minneapolis in a southwesterly direction through some of the state's most historic towns as well as those which have developed perennially popular tourist attractions of a more contemporary kind.

SHAKOPEE

Located some 30 miles from the Twin Cities, Shakopee offers stellar attractions, some seasonal, that draw great numbers of people from the Twin Cities and far beyond.

VALLEYFAIR, 1 Valleyfair Dr., Shakopee. Tel. 612/445-7600.

This 68-acre amusement park offers rides and attractions for fun seekers of all ages. Small children have a petting zoo plus games and rides appropriate to their age and size. Children can also dig for fossils in the **Dinosaur Pit,** climb **Spooky Old Tree,** and even test their computer skills in **Actual Factual's Museum.** For those who enjoy more hair-raising entertainment, there's a river-raft ride, a large Ferris wheel, a water-log flume, and four different roller coasters, among them Excalibur, which has convoluted curves and a 60-degree drop. There are some 50 rides and attractions in all. Also on site is an IMAX theater whose six-story screen displays entertaining as well as educational films.

Admission: $17.50 adults before 5pm, $9.95 after 5pm; $9.95 seniors and children under 4 feet in height; free for children under age 4. **Parking:** $3.50.

Open: Late May through Labor Day plus selected weekends in May and Sept, 10am to between 6pm and midnight, depending on circumstances.

MURPHY'S LANDING, Hwy. 101, Shakopee. Tel. 612/445-6900.

You can become part of America's past in this living history museum, where costumed interpreter-guides provide firsthand information on the day-to-day activities in this part of the country in the mid-19th century. Visitors watch residents shoe horses, bake bread over a hearth, or build a house. Horse-drawn trolleys take visitors past immigrant homesteads, each of which represents a different European ethnic group that settled in the Minnesota Valley between 1840 and 1890. Also present are the ancient burial mounds of Native Americans who lived here long before the white settlers arrived. Because many of the activities take place outdoors, visitors are reminded to dress according to the weather.

Admission: $7 adults, $6 seniors and students; free, children under 5.

Open: May–Christmas, Tues–Sun 10am–5pm.

RENAISSANCE FESTIVAL, 3525 W. 145th St., Shakopee. Tel. 612/445-7361 or toll free 800/966-8215.

This vivid re-creation of the 16th century surrounds visitors with the kinds of people and activities prevalent then. You can watch knights jousting, see strolling magicians and jugglers demonstrating their skills, and marvel at acrobats. Artisans are on hand, and vendors offer a wide array of delectables, none more impressive than huge turkey drumsticks. Ale, cider, and other beverages are available also.

Admission: $12.95 adults, $4.95 children 5–12; free, children under 5.

Open: 9am–7pm, weekends and Labor Day, mid-August through the last full weekend in Sept. **Directions:** Follow Hwy. 101 west through Shakopee to the point at which it turns into Hwy. 169. Follow Hwy. 169 about 2 miles beyond Hwy. 41 to the Renaissance Festival.

MYSTIC LAKE CASINO, 2400 Mystic Lake Blvd., Prior Lake. Tel. 612/445-9000 or toll free 800/262-7799.

This is the largest casino in Minnesota and also the busiest. Open 24 hours a day, seven days a week, it has about 2,300 slot machines that swallow every denomination of money from nickels to $5 tokens. You can also play live blackjack here, and, if bingo is your game, join many others in the ever-busy Bingo Palace. But you needn't gamble to keep occupied at Mystic Lake. Nine retail shops, two restaurants, and a gallery of Native American art will help you pass the time. So too will country-music performances from 9pm to midnight, seven nights a week.

Directions: Take I-35W to Hwy. 13 and proceed west on Hwy. 13 and Hwy. 101 to County Rd. 83, the first set of stoplights past Valleyfair. Turn south on Rd. 83 and follow it for about 5 miles to the casino.

NEW PRAGUE

Whether you're getting away for a day or a weekend or longer, you'll do well to consider New Prague, located just 35 miles southwest of the Twin Cities.

WHERE TO STAY

Expensive

SCHUMACHER'S NEW PRAGUE HOTEL, 212 W. Main St., New Prague, MN 56071. Tel. 612/758-2133. 11 rms. TEL

$ Rates: Fri–Sat $130–$155 double, Sun–Thurs $105–$125 double. AE, DISC, MC, V.

This remarkable hotel has been featured in such national magazines as *Gourmet, Good Housekeeping,* and *Better Homes and Gardens.* It was designed by famed architect Cass Gilbert, whose other work includes the U.S. Supreme Court Building in Washington, D.C., and the Woolworth Building in New York City.

Each of the guest rooms has been named for a month of the year and decorated in a manner consistent with that month and its season. TVs are available upon request. Czech glasswork and Bavarian folk art enhance the accommodations, along with antique wall sconces and chandeliers. Nearby attractions include golf, tennis, cross-country skiing, biking, canoeing, and, of course, shopping.

A favorite getaway for Minnesotans with an event to celebrate, New Prague is also famous for its cuisine. Innkeeper and head chef John Schumacher and his wife, Kathleen, offer a wide variety of authentic Bavarian dishes, featuring everything from paprikash and Wiener Schnitzel, to the house specialty, Czechoslovakian roast duck. Kathleen, a registered dietician, has added a "healthy heart" section to the menu, including dishes which are at once delicious and low in fat and cholesterol. Everything here is prepared to order from scratch, so special dietary requirements pose no problem. Lunchtime dishes are served with a choice of accompaniments which include dumplings, homemade sauerkraut, German potato salad, and the vegetable of the day. Dinner is served with hot or cold soup, German salad plate, choice of two Bavarian side dishes, and homemade kolache and rye roll. Reservations are required at this popular restaurant.

On your way to Le Sueur, the next stop on our Minnesota Valley getaway, take U.S. Highway 169 and continue south through Jordan, where you might want to visit **Sponsel's Minnesota Harvest Apple Orchard** (tel. 612/492-7753) in nearby Jordan. There's a wonderful array of fruit to be picked from the tree or from the bin. Minnesota Harvest's hours vary according to the season: In July, August, September, and October, hours are 9am to 7pm Monday through Thursday and 9am to 8pm Friday, Saturday, and Sunday; in November and December hours are 9am to 6pm daily; January and February hours are 9am to 5pm Friday, Saturday, and Sunday only. There's also an assortment of other attractions, including an animal farm, hiking trails, and, from time to time, helicopter rides.

LE SUEUR

This small Minnesota Valley town is notable as the birthplace of two world-famous figures, Dr. Will Mayo and the Jolly Green Giant. Actually the Green Giant gets more prominent billing on roadside signs as you approach the town, but the memorial plaque and the restored **Mayo House,** 118 N. Main St., hand built by the physician father of Drs. Will and Charles Mayo, are very much worth seeing. Costumed guides will show you the small home in which William Worrell Mayo, a native of Eccles, England, lived with his American-born wife and their small daughter before their first son, Will James, was born in 1861. The family later moved to Rochester, Minn., where, in 1864, a second son, Charles Horace, was born. Many years later, the Mayo brothers bought the small house that their father had built and presented it to the city of Le Sueur. It served as the town's library until 1967, then was restored and opened to the public in May 1974.

Another interesting local landmark is the **Le Sueur Museum,** 705 N. 2nd St., where a Green Giant display tells the story of the vegetable-canning industry. Other exhibits include a one-room school, an early post office, a veterinary room, and other reminders of this town's historic past. The bell that hangs in front of the museum was used to announce the end of the Civil War.

ST. PETER

The first thing you'll notice about the city of St. Peter is the extraordinary width of its main street, a fact that reminds us that political skulduggery was not born yesterday. It was certainly alive and well back in 1858 when a movement was underway to name St. Peter the capital of Minnesota. As capital, St. Peter would require an ample main thoroughfare, it was reasoned, and one was authorized. But a legislator named Joseph Roulette had other ideas. Representing the more northerly town of Pembina, Roulette wanted a capital considerably closer to home than St. Peter. He therefore stole the bill which needed only the governor's signature and didn't return it until after the deadline for signing had passed. Ironically, Roulette's home town of Pembina later became part of the new state of North Dakota.

St. Peter is known as the home of governors—no fewer than five Minnesota governors were born and brought up here. Another claim to fame is the fact that it's the home of **Gustavus Adolphus College,** whose Nobel Hall of Sciences is the site each year of an international gathering of winners of the prestigious Nobel Prize. Another notable name associated with Gustavus Adolphus is that of its resident sculptor Paul Granlund, whose work includes the remarkable statue of Charles Lindbergh at Le Bourget Field in Paris. A sculptural tour of the college is outlined in a pamphlet available to visitors; among the most recent sculptures installed is *Portrait of Srinivasa Ramanujan,* located near the mathematics department offices. (The 19th-century Indian theoretical mathematician whom it honors left no portrait of the kind usually used by a sculptor. Undaunted, Granlund settled for a passport photo.) Outside the Anderson Theatre, Granlund's *Masks of the Muses* displays representations of the Greek god of tragedy and comedy.

Primary among the significant sites to be seen in this historic area is **Traverse des Sioux Park,** along the Minnesota River where a natural ford served as a crossing for Dakota (Sioux) Indians. At this 5-acre site, the Treaty of Traverse des Sioux was signed in 1851, whereby the Indians ceded nearly 19-million acres of Minnesota land in exchange for annuities extending over a period of 50 years. The ultimate price per acre has been computed at 12.5¢. (Dissatisfaction with the provisions of this treaty was one cause of the Sioux uprising of 1862.) A new historical center serves as a repository for artifacts and documents related to the Native American presence here.

No knitter, weaver, or other kind of needlework enthusiast should leave town before visiting **Mary Lue's Knitting World & St. Peter Woolen Mill,** 101 W. Broadway (tel. 507/931-3702). Dating back to 1867, this is the oldest business in St. Peter and the only woolen mill in Minnesota. Owned and operated by the same family since it was founded, the mill specializes in the manufacture of wool-filled comforters and mattress pads. Forty-five-minute tours of the mill take visitors through the entire process of custom carding, a disappearing skill. An extensive assortment of specialty yarns is on display, as are the implements used in knitting, crocheting, weaving, quilting, and other handicrafts.

WHERE TO STAY

Inexpensive

PARK ROW BED & BREAKFAST, 525 W. Park Row, St. Peter, MN 56082. Tel. 507/931-2495. 4 rms.
$ Rates: $54–$69 double. DISC, MC, V.

Ann Burkhardt's Park Row Bed & Breakfast is a large and lovely yellow corner house. Actually a blend of two late-Victorian homes, one built in 1874, the other in 1903, this spacious house has become a popular home away from home for visitors to St. Peter. While some guests are in town for business or professional meetings, others have come to visit friends or family at nearby Gustavus Adolphus College or to celebrate special occasions—a birthday, an anniversary, or even a wedding. "I usually ask someone from the family to get the key ahead of time so the bride and groom can let themselves in at the front door after the dance," Ann declares. Many guests return simply because of the ambience and attention they remember so fondly. Known and admired throughout the state as a longtime food journalist for the Minneapolis *Star Tribune,* she is well suited personally and professionally to her role as innkeeper. "I want this to be a homey sort of place," she explains. "Like being at Aunt Harriet's but without Aunt Harriet breathing down your neck." Among the many antiques with which Ann has decorated Park Row, none is more widely admired than the dining-room centerpiece, a Victorian sugar spooner which served as a way of displaying the collections of spoons, sometimes inscribed, that were given to young girls as birthday or Christmas gifts. There are many such interesting antiques throughout the house along with as an abundance of books in virtually every room, including the kitchen, in which guests are welcome to browse through Ann's huge personal collection of cookbooks.

WHERE TO DINE

Moderate

THE COUNTRY PUB, State Hwy. 22, off U.S. Hwy. 169, 2 miles south of St. Peter, 8 miles north of Mankato. Tel. 507/625-5888 or 931-5888.
Cuisine: AMERICAN. **Reservations:** Recommended.
$ Prices: Appetizers $2.50–$8.95; main courses $10.95–$24.95.
Open: Lunch Mon–Fri, 11:30am–1:30pm; dinner Sun–Thurs 6pm–9pm, Fri–Sat 5–10pm; Sun brunch 11am–1:30pm.
Closed: Christmas, Memorial Day, New Years Day, Labor Day, July 4th unless it falls on a weekend.

This handsome restaurant is just far enough off the beaten path to make it a destination dining place with a faithful clientele of southern Minnesotans as well as with those from the Twin Cities who drive down for an end-of-the-week celebration or for the observance of special personal or professional events. There is, in fact, a special-occasion ambience here that's reinforced by a staff apparently determined not just to meet expectations but to exceed them. Chef Jeff Zernechel has developed a base menu to which he adds a main-course feature each night and frequently an appetizer feature as well.

Seafood is a specialty here, with favorites like Norwegian salmon, swordfish, mahimahi, and a relatively unfamiliar selection, Chilean sea bass, sweet and beautifully textured. Soft-shell crab, a seasonal delight with an ardent following of its own, is lightly battered and served in a delicate white-wine-butter sauce flavored with a touch of garlic. Chilean sea bass, sweet and beautifully textured, is served *au poivre*—patted with crushed pepper and grilled.

Unregenerate beef eaters find what they're longing for in the Country Pub's filet mignon or black Angus sirloin, dry aged for extra tenderness, while vegetarians have their own favorites, including fresh linguine with tomatoes, basil, and pine nuts. All main courses include a garden salad or fresh fruit cup, potato or rice, and vegetable du jour.

Originally a speakeasy during Prohibition, Country Pub was later turned into a supper club before assuming its present incarnation. Rusticity is supposed to be the opposite of sophistication, but in this instance, these qualities blend beautifully. General manager Jon Berg describes the cuisine here as "American with a French accent." Many memorable events have been observed at the Country Pub, including warm-weather weddings conducted on the expansive brook-side lawn and celebrated in the large brook-view room which overlooks it.

MANKATO

The name of the southernmost of our Minnesota Valley destinations is derived from the Dakota term *Mahkato,* which means "greenish blue earth." The name refers to the color of the clay here that lines the banks of the Minnesota River where it joins with the Blue Earth River. Now a business and commercial center, this city reflects the history of Minnesota in its historic buildings and plaques and in its abundance of antique shops, a dozen of which are listed in the interesting *Mankato Passport,* a visitors guide prepared for the **Mankato Visitors and Convention Bureau,** 112 Riverfront Dr., Mankato, MN 56002 (tel. 507/345-4519).

On the grounds of the city library, you'll find one of the most melancholy historic markers anywhere in this or any other area, a memorial of the largest mass execution in U.S. history. The story recounted on this large brass marker tells of the years of friction between white settlers and Indian hunters that finally culminated in the Sioux uprising of 1862 and the subsequent trial of several hundred Indian prisoners before a five-man military commission, which condemned 303 of them to death. Intervention by U.S. president Abraham Lincoln spared all but the 38 prisoners who were marched to a scaffold guarded by 1,400 troops in full battle dress. But the story doesn't end there. The final lines of the inscription tell of a reconciliation ceremony held on this site in 1975. It was an endeavor by Native Americans and the Mankato community to reach social change and equality through education and understanding.

Among local structures listed on the National Register of Historic

Places are the 1889 **Blue Earth County Courthouse,** 204 S. 5th St., constructed of local Mankato stone and occupying a full-block courthouse square; **Union Depot,** 112 N. Rivefront Dr., the only surviving railroad depot from the 13 Blue Earth County townships where railroads played a major role in the area's development; and **Seppman Mill,** Highway 60, south of Mankato, built in 1862, the first stone gristmill located on the edge of southern Minnesota prairie land.

3. ROCHESTER

Rochester, about 80 miles southeast of the Twin Cities, may be the most cosmopolitan community of its size in the entire country. That's because nearly a quarter of a million people from throughout the world arrive here each year to visit the famous Mayo Clinic.

The pleasant drive to Rochester from the Twin Cities takes you along U.S. 52 through some of the state's loveliest rolling countryside and luxuriant farmland. If you'd prefer to leave the driving to **Greyhound** (tel. 612/371-3311), the fare each way from the Twin Cities for the 2-hour trip is about $10. **Northwest Airlines** (tel. 612/726-1234) has a 30-minute flight from the Twin Cities to Rochester, with prices ranging from $52 to $135 each way.

WHAT TO SEE & DO

With a staff of more than 800 physicians, surgeons, and medical scientists, in addition to 1,500 medical trainees and more than 5,000 paramedical personnel, the **Mayo Clinic,** 200 1st St. SW (tel. 612/284-2511), is the largest and probably the most prestigious group medical practice in the world. It also maintains the largest graduate school of medicine in the world, with an international student body that adds further to the cosmopolitan atmosphere in Rochester.

How did so famous a medical complex happen to develop in a small midwestern city? The story began back in 1883, when a devastating tornado struck a then obscure farming community, leaving 26 people dead and the entire northern part of the town demolished.

Dr. William Worral Mayo was a local English-born physician who had practiced in Rochester for 20 years, after first coming here as an examining surgeon for the Union Army Enrollment Board. After the tornado struck, he worked with other Rochester doctors and with the nuns from the Convent of St. Francis to treat the injured, but their efforts were severely hampered by the lack of adequate medical facilities.

Shortly after the disaster, the mother superior at the convent suggested to Dr. Mayo that he head the medical staff of a hospital which the sisters were planning to build and maintain. At first reluctant, Dr. Mayo agreed, although he knew that hospitals then were frightening to the public, who viewed them as places where people went to die. When St. Mary's Hospital was opened in 1889, other local doctors refused to associate with it, leaving Dr. Mayo and his two physician sons, Will and Charlie, to serve as the entire medical staff.

Both Will and Charlie had been trained in the antiseptic methods introduced by Joseph Lister, and both began to practice the relatively new field of surgery as staff members of St. Mary's Hospital. Word soon got around that patients suffering from chronic ailments like ulcers, appendicitis, and gallstones were being made well again, quickly and permanently, by these young physicians.

Even as patients in Minnesota helped spread the word about Drs. Will and Charlie Mayo, physicians from around the country and even from Europe began coming to Rochester to see for themselves the kind of work that the young Mayos had described at medical meetings and written about in medical journals.

By the mid-1890s their growing practice made it necessary for the Mayos to enlarge their medical staff, and by 1914 they opened a building they called the Mayo Clinic. The group medical practice they established was unique in that it encouraged a sharing of knowledge among a group of medical specialists for the purpose of promoting more comprehensive care for patients. That remains the practice and the purpose of the Mayo Clinic to this day. Free tours of the impressive clinic facilities are available from 10am to 2pm Monday through Friday.

The **Mayo Medical Museum,** open free to the public, offers a variety of films and videotapes as well as exhibits that enable visitors to examine the human body and its functions, to learn about some of the illnesses and injuries that pose a threat around the world, and to become acquainted with some of the methods by which the medical profession deals with these problems. Hours are Monday through Friday from 9am to 9pm, Saturday 9am to 5pm, and Sunday from 1 to 5pm.

Perhaps the most beloved local attraction in downtown Rochester is the **Rochester Carillon,** in the tower of the Plummer Building. This set of 56 stationary bells of various sizes, sounded with levers pressed by a carillonneur's fist, was bought by Dr. Will Mayo during a trip to Europe in the 1920s. With a range of 4½ octaves, it's the most complete carillon in North America. Concerts are offered at 7pm on Monday and at noon on Wednesday and Friday. Additional recitals are held on holidays and for special events.

Mayowood, the splendid home of two generations of the Mayo family, was built in 1911 by Dr. Charles H. Mayo. He and his wife, Edith, brought up four daughters and two sons in this large, gracious home. Later, Dr. Charles (Chuck) W. Mayo, his wife, Alice, and their four sons and two daughters resided here. Perched on 3,000 acres overlooking the Zumbro River Valley, Mayowood has welcomed such famous figures as Helen Keller, Franklin D. Roosevelt, and Adlai Stevenson. Over 38 rooms are furnished in American, English, French, Spanish, and Italian antiques. The only way to get to Mayowood is via an Olmstead County Historical Society shuttle bus; phone 612/282-9447 for information concerning tours.

Another popular home tour is offered at the **Plummer House,** 1091 Plummer Lane (tel. 507/281-6160), once the residence of Dr.

Henry Plummer. Dr. Plummer joined the Mayo Clinic staff in 1901, and he is credited with having devised the pneumatic tube and the clinic's remarkable communication and recordkeeping systems. When he and his family moved into this Tudor-style mansion in 1924, they were the first in the area to make use of natural gas and the first to have burglar alarms. It's still notable for its exquisite rose garden and for its 11 acres of parkland, open to the public throughout the year from sunrise to sunset. House tours are available June through August on the first and third Wednesdays of the month from 1 to 5pm. The cost is $2 per adult and $1 per child or student; children under 5 are admitted without charge.

Perhaps the unlikeliest of all clinic-related attractions in Rochester are the hordes of giant **Canada geese** that winter here each year. They were first attracted by a small flock of geese donated by a grateful patient in 1947 and released in Silver Lake Park, at North Broadway and 13th Street. The following year, Rochester's new power plant began using Silver Lake for cooling water, with the result that the lake remained free of ice throughout the winter. The Canada geese stayed on that winter—and have ever since. Now numbering in the tens of thousands, these birds are welcomed in Rochester by people of all ages, who bring them bread crumbs, popcorn, and other goodies. Silver Lake Park has more than geese to offer, though. Paddleboats and canoes can be rented during the warmer months, and picnicking is popular then too.

Other outdoor activities can be enjoyed on the city's six 18-hole golf courses and 30 outdoor tennis courts. There's a popular 9-mile nature trail here as well. For sports information, phone 289-7414.

Cultural attractions in Rochester include the fine **Rochester Art Center,** 320 E. Center St. (tel. 507/282-8629), open Tuesday through Saturday from 10am to 5pm, and the highly regarded **Rochester Symphony Orchestra,** 109 City Hall, 200 1st Ave. SW (tel. 507/285-8076).

WHERE TO STAY

MODERATE

CLINIC VIEW INN, 9 3rd Ave. NW, Rochester, MN 55901. Tel. 507/289-8646. Fax 612/282-4478. 142 rms. TV TEL
$ Rates: $64.95 single, $74.95 double; $89.95 suite for one, $94.95 suite for two. AE, DISC, MC, V.
Another property with connections to the Mayo Clinic is the more modest Clinic View Inn. It offers a swimming pool, whirlpool, sauna, and restaurant and the choice of standard rooms or more luxurious suites, all at remarkably low cost.

KAHLER HOTEL, 20 2nd Ave. SW, Rochester, MN 55902. Tel. 507/282-2581 or toll free 800/533-1655. Fax 612/285-2775. 720 rms and suites. MINIBAR TV TEL
$ Rates: $56–$140 double. AE, DISC, MC, V.
Some of the most famous people in the world have stayed at Rochester's Kahler Hotel. Elegant enough for the most festive of

getaways, this hotel serves primarily as a comfortable home away from home for those who have come to Rochester to visit the Mayo Clinic.

Accommodations are comfortable and cheery, nearby medical facilities notwithstanding. Along with fine restaurants (see "Where to Dine," below) and shops, the Kahler offers a domed recreation center with swimming pool, sauna, and whirlpool.

The Mayo Clinic and the Kahler Hotel are very careful to protect the privacy of the hotel's visitors, but word does get around town when celebrities like Lady Bird Johnson, Bill Cosby, or Jim Nabors check in.

RADISSON PLAZA HOTEL, 150 S. Broadway, Rochester, MN 55904. Tel. 507/281-8000 or toll free 800/333-3333. Fax 612/281-4280. 212 rms and suites. TV TEL
$ Rates: $59–$129 double. AE, DC, DISC, ER, MC, V.

Connected by skyway 24 hours a day to the Mayo Clinic, the Radisson Plaza Hotel promotes other Mayo Clinic connections as well, with special rates and amenities for incoming clinic visitors. Complimentary shuttle service to the Mayo Clinic, St. Mary's, and Methodist Hospital, as well as complimentary hors d'oeuvres in the lounge from 5 to 7pm, are among the features here.

But some Radisson Plaza packages reach out to a clientele with no ties to the Mayo Clinic. For example, the Radisson Adventure Weekend is particularly popular among Twin Citians interested in combining privacy, elegance, and economy. For $59 you get a deluxe guest room, drink coupons, discounts on Friday Fish Fries, Saturday Shrimp Dinners, and Sunday Breakfast Buffets along with discounts at the Rochester Athletic Club, free movie passes, and more. If price is no concern you can emulate families from faraway places who arrive at the Radisson periodically, reserve the entire two top floors of the hotel, then receive certain dietary accommodations like lots of lentil soup and fresh lamb from a farm in nearby Spring Valley.

There are two excellent restaurants on site (see "Where to Dine," below), and a staff that couldn't be more helpful. "Our attitude," one of them explained, "Is 'The answer is Yes. Now what's the question?'"

WHERE TO DINE

MODERATE

ELIZABETHAN ROOM, at Kahler Hotel, 20 2nd Ave., SW. Tel. 282-2581.
Cuisine: AMERICAN. **Reservations:** Recommended.
$ Prices: Lunch $8.50–$11; dinner $15–$22.
Open: Lunch Mon–Fri 11:30am–2pm; dinner Mon–Fri 5:30–9pm, Sat 6–10pm; Sun brunch 10am–2:30pm. AE, DISC, MC, V.

You won't find a more elegant setting for a memorable dinner than the famous Elizabethan Room. The coats of arms on dark paneled walls, the stained-glass panels, the red velvet, and large, double-tiered wrought-iron chandeliers give a majestic ambience to this handsome room. A romantic air is provided by the Elizabethan Strings, strolling violinists who make a lovely musical contribution to your dining pleasure. The irresistible blend of impeccable service and fine fare—for example, breast of chicken or rack of lamb for two—make for a terrific evening out.

The adjoining Lord Essex Room is a perfect complement to the Elizabethan Room. Similar in decor but smaller in size, this room provides a delightfully intimate setting. Primarily a cocktail lounge, the Lord Essex becomes a small dining room during the Elizabethan Room's elaborate Sunday brunch. Overflow brunchers are directed to the Lord Essex Room, a very pleasant alternative indeed!

If you're interested in another cocktail lounge, try the Kahler's Penthouse, a delightful retreat where you can sink into overstuffed chairs amid towering plants and enjoy a commanding view of the city. And there's a third bar down on street level, the Greenhouse, with a terrarium, an aquarium, an oversize TV screen, and 2,000 hanging plants, all of them for sale.

McCORMICK'S, at Radisson Plaza Hotel, 150 S. Broadway. Tel. 612/281-8000.
   Cuisine: AMERICAN. **Reservations:** Not necessary.
$ Prices: Lunch $4.25–$7.95; dinner $4.95–$13.95. AE, DC, DISC, ER, MC, V
   Open: Mon–Sun 6:30am–11pm.

Everything about this handsome restaurant is comfortable, including the prices. The restful ambience of dark woods and an abundance of free-standing green plants is enhanced by unobtrusive classical music in the background. As many but not all diners here are outpatients of the Mayo Clinic, many but not all items on the menu are listed alongside symbols that indicate nutritional standards. Broiled fresh salmon, for example, receives a dietary blessing. If, however, you decide on chicken-fried steak smothered with pan gravy, you're on your own.

The range of items available to you afternoon or evening could hardly be wider. Prime rib au jus is a frequent request, and so is pecan dusted pork. But Mayo Clinic procedures sometimes intrude on selections. "We serve a lot of Jell-O here," one staff member noted. They also serve a lot of an item billed simply as "The Smallest Sundae in the World," a small scoop of ice cream with a topping of your choice, whipped cream, and a cherry, all of it served in a shot glass. Amazingly it provides satisfaction with a minimum of guilt.

THE MEADOWS, at Radisson Plaza Hotel, 150 S. Broadway. Tel. 612/281-8000.
   Cuisine: AMERICAN. **Reservations:** Recommended.
$ Prices: Dinner $12.95–$21.95. AE, DC, DISC, ER, MC, V.
   Open: Mon–Sat 5:30–10pm.

This is the Radisson Plaza's fine-dining restaurant, and your choices are many, varied, and sometimes surprising. Smoked goose breast complemented with a cranberry port glace is popular here; so is the mixed grill which combines lobster, port, and veal with the chef's specialty sauce. Radisson Plaza desserts are justifiably famed in these parts; consider a portion of homemade fruit cobbler or the glazed raspberries with sabayon sauce garnished with vanilla bean ice cream.

MICHAEL'S, 15 S. Broadway. Tel. 288-2020.

Cuisine: AMERICAN/MEDITERRANEAN. **Reservations:** Recommended.

$ Prices: Lunch $5.95–$7.95; early dinner (3:30–5pm) $7.95–$9.95, late dinner (5–10pm) $11.95–$14.95.

Open: Mon–Thurs 11am–10pm, Fri–Sat 11am–11pm.

No Rochester dining spot is better known than Michael's, a family restaurant started in 1951. Now six times larger than it was then, Michael's somehow manages to retain an air of intimacy and cordiality. But there's a cosmopolitan touch here as well. Although the decor in most of the rooms will remind you of an old English country home, one area, the Harkala Room, is decidedly Greek, as is the Pappas family that owns and runs Michael's. A section of the menu includes Greek dishes, but primarily this is an American steak-and-seafood spot. The food will please you, and so will the tab.

A recent remodeling of the lounge has added another dining room named Pappageorge Taverna in honor of Michael George Pappas, the adventurous young man who came to Minnesota in 1915 and founded the dining dynasty that is now in its fourth generation.

INEXPENSIVE

WONG'S CAFE, 4 Third St SW. Tel. 282-7545.

Cuisine: CHINESE/AMERICAN. **Reservations:** Recommended for parties of five or more.

$ Prices: $5–$9.95.

Open: Mon–Sat 11am–9:30pm, Sun 11am–9pm.

Another well-known family restaurant in these parts is Wong's Café. Now being run by second-generation owners, brothers Michael and Dennis Wong and their cousin Steve Wong, this restaurant was opened in 1952 by Ben and Mae Wong and Neil and Poya Wong. It was in 1982 that the second generation took over and two years later moved the restaurant into a remodeled 100-year-old bank building. (Just 50 feet from where the original restaurant stood, the "new" Wong's Café increased its seating capacity from 150 to 240.) Although American dishes occupy a prominent place on the menu seven days a week, Wong's is probably best known for its Chinese cuisine, particularly for such dishes as the ever-popular moo goo gai pan (sweet-and-sour chicken with pork-fried rice). Children have their own menu here on place mats that feature games and puzzles.

NEARBY PLACES TO STAY

Moderate

THE JAILHOUSE INN, 109 Houston 3 NW, Preston, MN 55965. Tel. 507/765-2181. 12 rms. TV TEL

$ Rates: Fri–Sat $69–$140, weekday $40–$109. DISC, MC, V.

If you're interested in spending the night in a bed and breakfast thoroughly different from any you've encountered before, Jailhouse Inn in Preston, about 35 miles south of Rochester, might be just what you're looking for. Each of the 12 beautiful rooms here is decorated differently, due in part to the fact that Marc and Jeanne Sather were professional designers before they became innkeepers. Working together in the field of restaurant and environmental design and getting ideas from the many bed-and-breakfasts and inns they'd visited, they decided it would be fun to try creating their own. The results have also been fun for their guests, who may find themselves spending the night in the Drunk Tank, a spacious room with king-size bed and access to the main floor porch, or in the Cell Block, actually an original cell block but improved now by the presence of a whirlpool and a walk-through shower.

Perhaps the most surprising room and also the most elegant is the Oriental Room with Eastlake furnishings and an antique painted slate fireplace. There was genuine interest in the Orient among Victorians, Marc Sather points out, so an Oriental Room is quite appropriate to this large 19th-century home.

You'll find the food here very good indeed, with late-afternoon hors d'oeuvres and beverages and, during the week, a hearty continental buffet of breakfast fixings. On weekends, the served dishes might include eggs Benedict, omelets to order, Belgian waffles, and other selections quite unlike what was probably offered before the jailhouse became the Jailhouse Inn. The breakfast room, by the way, is a cheerful place that's literally bathed in the sunlight which pours in through overhead glass windows.

Hostel and Campground

THE OLD BARN RESORT, CAMPGROUND, HOSTEL, & RESTAURANT, County Rd. 17, Preston, MN 55965. Tel. 507/467-2512 or toll free **800/552-2512. Directions:** 3 miles north of U.S. Hwy. 52.

$ Rates (hostel): $10 per person weekdays, $12 per person weekends. Discount for furnishing one's linens.

You'll be surprised by the sophistication of the cuisine at this large, sprawling, gleaming-white four-story barn, built in 1884, in which a 53-bed hostel now shares space with a fine restaurant, a well-stacked souvenir shop, and a gallery of authentic Amish handicrafts. There's also a campground featuring 80 developed sites, half of which have sewer hookups and all of which have water and 30 or 50 amp electrical service.

In the midst of this embarrassment of riches, you'll find a large rustic restaurant whose decor consists of country artifacts—everything from an old dog treadle to a cream separator to ice tongs to an interesting miniature lamp collection. Much of the woodwork done here in the dining hall, including the hand-hewed wooden pillars in the dining room, are the work of Amish craftsmen who bring their quilts and furniture and baskets and other works here for display and sale.

The menu selections include a long list of soups, sandwiches, salads, and, main dishes including shrimp pesto ($12.25), 10-ounce rib-eye steak with sautéed mushrooms ($11.50), and chicken San Michel ($11.50), all prepared by a young chef whose previous experience includes five years at the Rochester Country Club.

4. MANTORVILLE

About 65 miles south of the Twin Cities and 20 minutes west of Rochester, you'll find the historic town of Mantorville, whose entire 12-block downtown area is listed on the National Register of Historic Places. Limestone quarries were this town's claim to fame during the 19th century, and a great many important buildings throughout the country are constructed of "Mantorville stone," among them St. Mary's Hospital in Rochester. The Dodge County Courthouse, Minnesota's oldest operating courthouse, is also made of local limestone.

Among the historically significant buildings to be visited here are a 19th-century one-room **schoolhouse,** a recently restored **log house** (one of the earliest buildings in town), and the **Grand Old Mansion,** 501 Clay St., Mantorville (507/635-3231), an imposing Victorian building that serves today as a bed-and-breakfast remarkable not only for its fine cuisine but for its original woodwork, its hand-carved staircase, and the many antiques with which it has been furnished by owner/hostess Irene Selker. Rates range from $30 for a double-bed room with shared bath to $53 per couple for accommodations in a remodeled schoolhouse. (There's an $8 charge for each additional person.)

WHERE TO DINE

MODERATE

HUBBELL HOUSE, Hwy. 57, Mantorville. Tel. 507/635-2331.
   Cuisine: AMERICAN. **Reservations:** Recommended.
$ Prices: Lunch $5.95–$7.95; dinner $7.50–$29.95. AE, DC, DISC, MC, V.
   Open: Tues–Sat 11:15am–2pm and 5–10pm, Sun 11:30am–9:30pm.

Perhaps the most frequently visited old building in Mantorville is the Hubbell House, an old country inn established in 1854 and today one of the state's most famous restaurants. Its guests have included Sen. Horace Greeley, best remembered for his advice "Go west, young man. Go west . . ." Alexander Ramsey, Minnesota's first U.S. senator, dined here as well. So, more recently, did a variety of other luminaries, including circus impresario John Ringling North, Gen. Dwight D. Eisenhower, and baseball great Mickey Mantle. Facsimiles of their signatures and those of more than a dozen other famous guests decorate the place mats that have become popular as souvenirs.

Many Twin Citians regularly drive down for dinner at Hubbell House, where the elegant decor in no way detracts from the casual, comfortable atmosphere. The chateaubriand served here is justly famous. It's also reasonably priced, and comes with appetizer or soup, salad, vegetable, and potato. Jumbo shrimp slowly broiled and served over pasta and walleye pike amandine are other dinner specialties. Luncheons represent a particularly attractive buy, with dishes like stuffed pork chops or pasta seafood salad served with potato, vegetable or salad, and beverage.

5. MISSISSIPPI RIVER TOWNS

Follow the Mississippi south from the Twin Cities and you'll find a succession of quaint river towns that retain much of the architecture and atmosphere of bygone days.

Combine the historical interest of this area with the natural beauty of the surrounding Hiawatha Valley, add the unique attractions each community has to offer, and you'll see why Hastings, Red Wing, Lake City, and Wabasha are popular Twin Cities getaways for a day, an evening, a weekend, or longer.

HASTINGS

Just 25 miles from the Twin Cities, Hastings was one of the earliest river towns in Minnesota. A trading post was established here as early as 1833, and the town was incorporated in 1857. Three rivers—the Mississippi, the St. Croix, and the Vermillion—made Hastings readily accessible to other markets, and the spectacular Vermillion waterfalls provided power for the mills that made this one of the great wheat centers of the Northwest.

WHAT TO SEE & DO

Today, there are 63 buildings in Hastings that have been listed on the National Register of Historic Places. The newest is a contemporary work by Frank Lloyd Wright, who in 1957–59 built the dramatic **Fasbender Medical Clinic** at the southeast corner of Highway 55 and Pine Street. Situated on land that blends into an adjacent park, the clinic, which is largely submerged in the ground, is readily identified by its folded roof.

As part of the National Trust program known as "Main Street," all of downtown Hastings has been designated a historic district. See the helpful **Hastings Area Chamber of Commerce,** at 119 W. 2nd St., Suite 201 (tel. 612/437-6775), for a handy guide to a walking tour of these fascinating buildings, foremost among them the 1857 **Norrish octagon house** and the 1856 **LeDuc-Simmons Mansion.**

Alexis Bailly Vineyard, 18200 Kirby Ave., Hastings, MN

55033 (tel. 612/437-1413), was founded in 1973 and has since won more than a dozen awards from Wineries Unlimited, an international competition involving wineries all over the United States and Canada. From June through October the winery is open to the public from noon to 5pm Friday through Sunday. And in fact individuals and small groups are welcome to walk through the vineyards and to sample and purchase wines anytime during working hours. By the way, it was the original Alexis Bailly who selected the site for the trading post that would one day develop into the town of Hastings.

Carpenter St. Croix Valley Nature Center, 12805 St. Croix Trail S, Hastings, MN 55033 (tel. 612/437-4359), conducts a number of programs, including the rehabilitation of raptors (birds of prey such as bald eagles and hawks), the banding of birds, and the maintenance of orchards. It also organizes maple syruping in the spring, organic gardening in the summer, and animal tracking in the winter. The center is open to the public on the first and third Sunday of the month.

Other area attractions include Lock and Dam No. 2 on the Mississippi River, Vermillion Falls, Treasure Island Casino (5734 Sturgeon Lake Rd., Welch, MN 55089; tel. 800/657-6858), six golf courses, and two ski resorts.

WHERE TO STAY

Moderate

THORWOOD BED AND BREAKFAST, 649 W. 3rd St., Hastings, MN 55033. Tel. 612/437-3297 or toll free 800/922-INNS. 8 rms.

$ Rates (including full breakfast and evening snacks): $75–$225 double.

Thorwood is a reconverted 1880 mansion that's been turned into a delightful accommodation by Pam and Dick Thorsen. There are eight rooms here, some with fireplaces, some with whirlpools, and each with its own distinctive decor. Breakfast, brought to your door in an oversize basket, includes oven omelets, warm pastries, sausages, muffins, coffee or tea, and juice. Reservations are recommended.

A new bed-and-breakfast, also owned by the Thorsens, is **Rosewood Inn,** 620 Ramsey St., Hastings, MN 55033. There are seven rooms in this lovely home; the prices and telephone numbers are the same as those for Thorwood.

WHERE TO DINE

Moderate

MISSISSIPPI BELLE, 101 E. 2nd St. Tel. 437-5694.
    Cuisine: AMERICAN. **Reservations:** Recommended.
$ Prices: Lunch $3.50–$7.95; dinner $7.95–$18.95. AE, DC, DISC, V.
    Open: Tues–Sat 11am–1:30pm and 5–9pm, Sun noon–6pm.

Perhaps the best-known restaurant in Hastings is the Mississippi Belle, a replica of the side-wheel packet steamers that traveled the Mississippi during the golden era of riverboats, from 1855 to 1875. A perennially popular dinner main course here is baked seafood au gratin, which combines shrimp, scallops, crabmeat, and lobster in a sherry sauce. A smaller version is available at lunchtime as well. Oven-fried chicken, broiled center-cut pork chops, and Port of Hastings steak (a boneless New York cut) are among the items that have made Mississippi Belle a drawing card. The pies here are legendary, with apple, rhubarb, and pecan among the delicious offerings.

RED WING

As you continue your river-town ramble southward from the Twin Cities, you'll find Red Wing, a town whose beginnings date back to 1680, when Father Hennepin came upon an Indian village here. The town was later named in honor of the area's Sioux Indian chiefs, whose emblem was a swan's wing that had been dyed red. In 1837 white settlers came to Red Wing, and by the 1870s it had become a primary wheat market.

As railroads assumed a greater role in the transportation of products, Red Wing's importance as a shipping center began to diminish, even as the town's manufacture of two products, pottery and shoes, began to draw widespread attention.

WHAT TO SEE & DO

The Minnesota Stoneware Company, which began production in the late 1800s and eventually became known as Red Wing Pottery, made use of local raw materials and soon established a national reputation. In 1967, after nearly a century of operation, the company closed its plant as the result of a prolonged and bitter labor dispute. But the historic factory and salesroom have been turned into a major tourist attraction. At **Red Wing Pottery Sales,** 1995 W. Main St., Red Wing, MN 55066 (tel. 338-3562), you'll be able to find some remaining pieces of the original Red Wing pottery, along with collectibles from around the world. You can also browse among a variety of country items, and in the candy section you'll find such old-fashioned sweets as homemade fudge.

Winona Mills, 1902 W. Main St., Red Wing, MN 55066 (tel. 612/338-5738), one of a statewide network of factory outlet stores, offers a wide assortment of high-quality, reasonably priced apparel, all of it made in the United States, with one notable exception—the genuine Icelandic sweaters, which sell for much lower prices here than elsewhere.

And then there's **Loons and Ladyslippers,** 1890 W. Main St., Red Wing, MN 55066 (tel. 612/388-3562 or 800/228-0174), a delightful shop where you'll find a miscellany of gifts, crafts, and collectibles, all of them related in some way to Minnesota, whose official bird is the loon and whose official flower is the lady's slipper.

At nearby **Pottery Place,** 2000 W. Main St., Red Wing, MN 55066, you'll find a two-level mall containing factory outlets, specialty shops, and restaurants.

Theater

SHELDON MEMORIAL AUDITORIUM, 445 W. 3rd St., Red Wing, MN 55066. Tel. 612/388-2806 or toll free 800/899-5759.

You'll enjoy attending a production in this intimate 471-seat playhouse, believed to be the first municipally owned and operated theater in the United States. Built in 1904, the Sheldon served as a roadhouse for touring theatrical troupes before being damaged by fire in 1918. After being reconstructed, it was used to show motion pictures, which proved so popular that in the 1930s the theater was remodeled again to provide additional seating for movie audiences. In the early 1980s, local citizens overwhelmingly approved a bond issue to finance restoring the theater to its original 1904 appearance and using it as a showcase for local and national theater talent. Today the Sheldon's inner foyer area and horseshoe balcony are original to the 1904 building; so are the glue-chip glass panels which survived 50 years in storage before being returned to their original place beside the curved arches, gold-leaf stenciling, and theatrical masks. Light bulbs throughout the house are reproductions of Edison bulbs, which gives the theater's interior a distinctive golden glow.

WHERE TO STAY

Moderate

CANDLELIGHT INN, 818 W. 3rd St., Red Wing, MN 55066. Tel. 612/388-8034. 4 rms.

$ Rates (including full breakfast and snacks): $75–$135 double. MC, V.

Heritage and hospitality are what Mary and Bud Jaeb offer at Candlelight Inn, a Victorian home built in 1877 and listed now on the Minnesota Historical Register. Restful shades of burgundy, green, and blue predominate throughout the house; original Quesal lighting, five unique fireplaces, and beautifully crafted woodwork in all the rooms combine to impart an abiding sense of heritage. The hospitality derives in large measure from Mary's prior experience in the Twin Cities, where for fifteen years she owned and operated a very successful catering business. The bountiful breakfast served here each morning typically includes some combination, all of it homemade, of baked french toast, quiche, caramel rolls, scones with Devonshire cream, wild rice cakes, and, of course, fresh fruit and coffee. Summertime breakfasts are served on a screened-in porch.

GOLDEN LANTERN INN, 721 East Ave., Red Wing, MN 55066. Tel. 612/388-3315. 4 rms.

$ Rates (including full breakfast and snacks): $79–$125 double. MC, V.

This luxurious Tudor Revival house, built during the early 1930s, was home to three presidents of the Red Wing Shoe Company before becoming a bed-and-breakfast in 1993. An unusual and popular feature here is the backyard hot tub, which accommodates eight people. Guests have a choice of breakfast in the dining room, the three-season porch, or in the privacy of their own rooms. The full breakfast typically includes a combination of some of the following: juice, an egg dish, french toast, sausage patties or links, bacon, ham, muffins, hash browns, fruit cup, and coffee or tea. Guests are welcome to enjoy the comfort of the large living room with its fireplace, spinette, large white sectional, and limited-edition paintings as well as the library, which contains books, couches, a fireplace, and a TV.

ST. JAMES HOTEL, 406 Main St., Red Wing, MN 55066. Tel. 612/388-2846. Fax 612/388-5226. 41 rms. TV TEL
$ Rates: $100–$155 double. AE, DISC, DC, MC, V.

After making a national name for itself as the manufacturer of fine leather products, the Red Wing Shoe Company took a step in an entirely different direction in 1977, when it bought the 100-year-old St. James Hotel. The subsequent restoration was meticulous and skillfull.

The 60 original guest rooms were reduced to 41 in order to accommodate private modern baths and facilities. Each room is individually decorated with period wallpaper, period pieces, and coordinated handmade down quilts. In a discreet bow to modernity, handcrafted Victorian wardrobes open to reveal television sets. Delightful examples of Victorian workmanship have been displayed throughout the corridors.

A popular gathering place at the St. James Hotel is **Jimmy's Pub,** which offers not only a fine fifth-story view of the city, but a warm, friendly ambience enhanced by antique stained-glass panels, old English hunting scenes in antique frames over the oak bar, and upholstered armchairs facing the massive fireplace. Jimmy's Pub should really be called Jimmy's Bar—no food is served in this otherwise hospitable room. But you can get a bite at breakfast or lunchtime at the delightful **Veranda Restaurant,** with its lovely view of the Mississippi. You have your choice here of a table in the cheery informal dining room or on the adjoining enclosed porch.

WHERE TO DINE

Moderate

PORT OF RED WING, in St. James Hotel, 406 Main St. Tel. 388-2846.
   Cuisine: AMERICAN. **Reservations:** Recommended.
$ Prices: Lunch $5.50–$7.95; dinner $16.95–$19.95.
   Open: Lunch Mon–Sat 11am–2pm; dinner daily 5–9:30pm. AE, DC, DISC, MC, V.

Only an hour from the Twin Cities, this restaurant is close enough for a lunch or dinner date. Port of Red Wing, the St. James's major restaurant, retains its original limestone walls and a variety of period antiques, which have been put to ingenious use. The original safe-deposit vault, for example, serves now as a fine wine cellar. Port of Red Wing offers a traditional American menu, with specials every evening.

A perennial dinner favorite here is filet of fresh salmon sautéed with shallots, garlic and white wine, then finished with a basil cream sauce. Grilled tenderloin of lamb and bacon-wrapped veal tenderloin are popular choices also. Your main course will be accompanied by a large dinner salad and huge popovers.

LAKE CITY

Picturesque bluffs overlook Highway 61 as you approach Lake City, situated on Lake Pepin, the widest expanse on the Mississippi River. Lake City takes pride in the fact that the sport of waterskiing was invented here back in 1922, when 18-year-old Ralph Samuelson steamed and then bent into shape two pine boards. His theory was that if people could ski on snow, they could also ski on water, and the corroboration of that theory put Lake City on the map and enabled millions of men, women, and children throughout the world to ski, if not walk, on water.

This small city features a variety of activities that center on its major claim to fame, the largest marina on the Mississippi River. Following a recent expansion, 625 sailboats can now be docked here, while a 90-foot breakwater makes **fishing** possible from three 60-foot platforms. Northerns, walleyes, crappies, and bass are among the varieties most often caught in these waters. But fish are not the only wildlife that draws tourists to Lake City. There are also the majestic bald eagles that have made their home in the bluffs overlooking Highway 61, south of Lake City at Read's Landing. These imposing birds can be seen from time to time swooping down onto the open water for food, and as the season progresses they do their ice fishing on the shoreline before it too freezes over.

WHERE TO STAY

Moderate

RED GABLES INN, 403 N. High St., Lake City, MN 55041. Tel. 612/345-2605. 5 rms.

$ Rates (including full breakfast and twilight wine and hors d'oeuvres): $68–$89 double.

It was while stationed with the U.S. Army in Germany that Doug DeRoos and his wife, Mary, and two daughters began visiting bed-and-breakfasts as a way of learning about new places and people. Following his retirement from the army after a stint at Fort Snelling in St. Paul, the idea of starting a bed-and-breakfast of their own seemed like a good idea. Now firmly established as the proprietors of this Victorian bed-and-breakfast the DeRooses aim to recapture here in Lake City the romantic spirit of the Victorian age. Built in 1865, Red

Gables Inn has been painstakingly restored, with even the wall coverings and trim duplicated as examples of the period. Bicycles are available to guests, who are encouraged to familiarize themselves with the local area and attractions. Red Gable's savory breakfast buffet includes juices, fruits, home-baked breads and pastries, along with special egg dishes, jams, jellies, and coffee and tea.

WHERE TO DINE

Moderate

WATERMAN'S, 1702 N. Lakeshore Dr. Tel. 345-5353.
  Cuisine: ECLECTIC. **Reservations:** Not accepted.
$ **Prices:** Dinner $5.95–$16.95; sandwiches and burgers $2.50–$6.50. Sun morning breakfast $5.45–$5.95. MC, V.
  Open: Bar weekdays 11am–10:30pm, 11am–11:30pm week-ends; restaurant weekdays 11am–9:30pm, weekends 11am–10:30pm. **Closed:** Christmas, Thanksgiving Day, Tues mid-Oct to Memorial Day.

As its name proclaims, this restaurant started as a place for those who live and work and relax in or near the water. In Lake City, with the largest marina on the upper Mississippi, the number of water men is great; and when you count the ones that hail from other river towns in Minnesota and Wisconsin as well as a great many Twin Citians who regularly make their way down to these parts, you understand the need for the large dock right outside the picture windows here at this famous dining place. A major reason for the success of Waterman's is the remarkable skill with which fine dining has been combined with casual comfort. You won't find linen tablecloths here; paper napkins are part of the table settings even at dinnertime. There's no dress code; boaters tend to dress casually. But the ambience is somehow luxurious in addition to being warm and comfortable. Service is of paramount importance to proprietors Mark and Shayna Fayette. "We want the time spent here to be relaxing," Mark explains. "We don't want customers to feel they're being rushed through. This isn't a getting-out-in-a-hurry place."

In addition to impeccably prepared meat and fish dinner main courses, including lamb chops, grilled salmon, and boneless, skinless chicken parmesan, vegetarian dishes are great favorites. Consider vegetable Alfredo or shrimp, broccoli, and wild mushroom pasta. And above all, don't forget to save room for one of the thoroughly delicious desserts prepared daily right on the premises.

WABASHA

You'll be visiting the oldest city in Minnesota when you arrive in Wabasha. Named for Indian chief Wapashaw, a peacemaker during the Sioux Indian uprising of 1862, Wabasha was by the 1880s a center of lumbering, milling, and boat building. Many of the buildings of that period, constructed of local materials, still stand today. In fact, Wabasha's entire downtown business district has been placed on the National Register of Historic Places. There are two marinas here, offering 400 open slips and 200 closed slips, and the city dock provides launching to the public as well. Many sailors take advantage of the shuttle service provided at the docks by the Anderson House, the state's oldest operating hotel.

If you're in these parts between November and March, you may get a look at some of the bald eagles that spend the winter in the Wabasha area. In fact, if you make your way to Pembroke and Lawrence Boulevard, you'll find an observatory staffed by volunteers during the November-March period. A wind shelter has been installed there to protect visitors and volunteers from the wind, and another amenity has recently been installed as well—a handicapped-accessible spotting scope, which makes a closer view of our national symbol easier for everyone. By the way, the reason for the presence in this area of birds that are considered "endangered" in most states and "threatened" in all the others has to do with the open water just north of town where the Chippewa River empties into the Mississippi. The fish that inhabit this open water are fair game for eagles, who either catch the fish themselves or steal them away from other birds. You'll remember that Benjamin Franklin thought the turkey should be our national symbol rather than the bald eagle because of the eagle's habit of intercepting other birds on their way to feed their young. "The bald eagle pursues him and takes the fish," Franklin declared, condemning this "injustice." Oh, well, no birdy's perfect, and despite his moral failings, the bald eagle has made a majestic symbol for more than 200 years. Moreover, as you may see for yourself when you come to Wabasha, the bald eagle isn't bald at all. He just looks that way because at maturity the top of his head is covered with white feathers. (The Old English word for "white" is "balde.")

NEARBY TOY STORE

L.A.R.K. TOYS AND MEADOWLARK SHOPS, City Rd. 88, off Hwy. 61, Kellogg, MN 55945. Tel. 507/767-3387.
Open: Mon–Fri 9am–5pm, Sat–Sun 10am–5pm.

If you're in Wabasha, you're close enough to drive six miles to the small town of Kellogg for a stop at unique L.A.R.K. Toys. Here you'll find Don and Sarah Kreofsy, two former schoolteachers who started making toys when their own children were small and by now, with a staff of 16, produce more than 100,000 toys and games a year. But these are no ordinary playthings, as an explanation of their acronym indicates: Lost Arts Revival by Kreofsky. With child-safe coloring and no metal parts, the toys created on these premises are hand cut from knot-free pine and constructed with nontoxic glues. Larger rocking toys—rocking horses, rocking rabbits, and more—are hand carved from basswood. More recently, carousel-size creatures have been added to the creations here—a dragon, a giraffe, a moose—all in one stage of development or another can be viewed by visitors who line up at the glass windows behind which handicrafters do their painstaking and magical work. Of course the browsing is great fun in the Meadowlark Shops, in which L.A.R.K. toys are for sale along with others from all over the world. Yet another attraction in another part of the complex is GIP, a potbellied pig (G-I-P is *pig* spelled backward) that has a home of his own and a growing fan club as well.

WHERE TO STAY

Moderate

ANDERSON HOUSE, 333 N. Main St., Wabasha, MN 55981. Tel. 612/565-4524 or toll free 800/862-9702. Fax 612/565-4003. 27 rms (19 with bath).

$ Rates: $49–$59 double with shared bath, $59–$99 double with bath, $104–$120 suite. DISC, MC, V.

Run by the members of the same family since it first opened in 1896, Anderson House has received national TV, magazine, and newspaper coverage as the Minnesota hotel that gives new meaning to the term "cathouse." Here guests can reserve a complimentary overnight cat when they register for a room; a feline, its food, and even a litter box will be delivered to their door that evening. Daytime visits can also be arranged—usually at nap time for children or their elders.

There are other homey touches at the Anderson House as well. Home-baked cookies are available in a large jar on the front desk 24 hours a day. Heated bricks are provided for those who opt for that sort of bed warmer. Guests with the sniffles can have a mustard plaster delivered to their door. And those who remember to leave their shoes outside the door at night will find them there brightly shined the next morning.

Besides its meticulous services, Anderson House is also famous for its home cooking. Grandma Ida Hoffman Anderson brought her Pennsylvania Dutch recipes from Lancaster, Pa., at the turn of the century, and the family has been using them ever since. Today Ida's granddaughter Jeanne Hall and great grandson John share the operation of the Anderson House. They've also shared authorship of a number of cookbooks for those who want to try their hand at this kind of fare.

The cinnamon and praline breakfast rolls at Anderson House are massive, and so is the selection of home-baked breads and rolls that waitresses bring to your table at dinnertime. Main dishes include Dutch oven steak, Pennsylvania Dutch beef rolls, and batter-fried cod, as well as such standbys as roast turkey and dressing, baked ham, and barbecued ribs. And then there's the Friday-night seafood buffet, an all-you-can-eat selection of seafood gumbo, shrimp, deep-fried pike, crab sections, oven-baked cod and whitefish, along with potato and vegetable and, of course, the bread tray, all for $6.95. Lunches here, served from 11am to 3pm, range from $5.50 to $8.95. Dinners, served from 5 to 8:30pm, range from $10.95 to $15.95. Never mind that the river recreation is top-notch in Wabasha. Anderson House itself is reason enough to visit this historic river town.

NEARBY PLACES TO DINE

Moderate

HARBOR VIEW CAFE, 100 Main St., Pepin, WI 54759. Tel. 715/442-3893.

Cuisine: SCANDINAVIAN. **Reservations:** Not accepted.
$ Prices: Dinner $9–$19. Checks but not credit cards accepted.
Open: Lunch Thurs–Mon 11am–2pm; dinner Thurs–Mon 5–9pm, Sun noon–7:30pm. Open weekends during the spring and after the leaves fall. **Closed:** Thanksgiving Day–Mar.

Harbor View Café is a very small restaurant with a very great reputation. Diners arrive by boat and by car from river towns on both the Minnesota and Wisconsin sides of the Mississippi. Twin Citians too come in great numbers, a fact that's all the more surprising when you remember that reservations are not accepted here and that waiting for a table comes with this territory. Once their names are put on that evening's list, diners generally get an idea of how long the wait will be and then take off for a pleasant walk along the waterfront or the nearby woods. Others stroll around the town of Pepin, whose population numbers something under 1,000. Clearly the residents of Pepin itself could hardly be credited with the runaway success of the Harbor View, particularly because some local folks seemed apprehensive back in 1980 when this eating place first opened in the building which for more than 100 years been known primarily as a bar. But from the very start, April Fool's Day 1980, business here has been brisk. Boaters from Wabasha, Winona, Lake City, Rochester, and beyond came early and often and helped immeasurably in spreading the word. Soon even the Twin Cities started to take notice. And not once during all the intervening years have the co-owners of this café—Paul and Carol Hinderlie and Tom Ahlstrom—ever advertised. Word of mouth has done the job for them.

Lamb and fish are served often here, in dishes with names like "farikal" and "klippfisk" which sound characteristically Scandinavian; what's uncharacteristic, though, is the degree to which garlic is used at Harbor View for a cuisine which chef Paul Hinderlié describes as "bourgeois" and "forward" and "full-bodied." It's also very healthful. A large majority of the foodstuffs come from local sources—produce from nearby gardeners; eggs, cream, and unsalted butter from local farms; flour which is milled in Winona, Minn.; and lamb from Spring Valley, Wis. The emphasis here is not on nuances or what Paul Hinderlie calls "devotional eating." "Everything is simply made," he explains. "Our coq au vin is made with the wine on hand—burgundy or whatever. Our cooking is not for people with jaded palates. We want them to come hungry and leave full."

Inexpensive

JENNY LIND CAFE & BAKERY, 114 Spring St., Stockholm, WI 54769. Tel. 715/442-2358.
Cuisine: ECLECTIC/WHOLESOME. **Reservations:** Not accepted.
$ Prices: Sandwiches $2.55–$4.45; soup $2.50–$2.95; burritos, quiches, pizza, salad $2.75–$4.75. No credit cards.
Open: Memorial Day–Oct Mon, Wed, Thurs 9am–4pm, Fri 9am–6pm, Sat–Sun 8am–6pm. **Closed:** Tues.

This tiny dining and take-out restaurant, in the heart of the tiny river town of Stockholm, Wis., attracts devotees from throughout the area, including the Twin Cities. Ruth Raich, whose mother came from

Sweden, opened her café in 1990 and enlarged it in 1993, gladdening the hearts and palates of fans of homemade kolaches, focaccia, cardamom braids, limpa, scones, biscotti, muffins, and a great deal more. For those who want to break bread right on the premises, Ruth also offers a variety of homemade soups, salads, sandwiches, burritos, pizzas, and more—some of them vegetarian. But it's the fresh-baked pastries that first put Jenny Lind on the map of Minnesota. Folks come a long way for them—with very good reason.

WINONA

Almost every Minnesota schoolchild knows the sorrowful story of Maiden Rock, the precipice overlooking Lake Pepin from which a lovely Indian girl leaped to her death because she was not permitted to marry the handsome young man of her choice. Not so widely known, though, is that her name was We-no-nah and that the river town of Winona was named in her honor. A statue of We-no-nah stands in one of the many parks in this historic city, which, during the 19th century, gained significance as a place where pioneers could secure supplies before heading west. At that time this was a booming prosperous city thanks to two major industries, lumbering and milling. By the turn of the century, though, the supply of lumber had greatly diminished and the milling industry had gone elsewhere.

What remains today is the considerable success of this city's determined efforts to retain and maintain its historical legacy and to provide for its citizens a quality of life that makes Winona particularly appealing to visitors. Twin Citians regularly book a place for themselves and their bikes on the Amtrak line that connects St. Paul to Winona; the number and beauty of the trails here make for spectacular outdoor fun. Other visitors are delighted with this lovely river town as well for reasons that extend from its beautiful natural scenery to its affordability (the very best hotel room in town costs just $95 a night) to the serenity and sense of safety that prevail here.

At the same time, Winona enjoys cultural benefits locally as the home of Winona State University, St. Mary's College, and the College of St. Teresa and wide recognition for a variety of products. **Winona Knits** (tel. 507/454-1724) produces and markets a popular line of sweaters, scarves, blankets, and other knitted goods. **Hauser Art Glass** (tel. 507/457-3500) and **Conway Universal Studios** (tel. 507/452-9209) are known widely for the stained-glass windows that are designed and created here, then sent to distant destinations. Also widely known and enjoyed are **Gummy Bears** (tel. 507/452-3433), a special favorite with youngsters. These multicolored chewy confections made a far-flung name for themselves after having originated right here in Winona, Minn.

WHAT TO SEE & DO

CONWAY UNIVERSAL STUDIOS, 503 Center St. Tel. 507/452-9209.
You can tour workshops in which you watch staining, cutting,

trimming, and etching of windows that will be shipped to homes and churches throughout the world.

JULIUS C. WILKIE STEAMBOAT CENTER, Levee Park. Tel. 507/454-1254.

This full-size replica of a Mississippi steamboat includes an area on the first deck where you can examine artifacts of river history and miniatures of other steamboats. Visit the Grande Salon on the second deck to savor the splendor of the Victorian era. And while you're here in Levee Park, seek out the lovely statue of We-no-nah.

C. A. ROHRER ROSE GARDEN, Lake Park. Tel. 507/457-8258.

At another of Winona's many city parks, enjoy a visit to one of the largest rose gardens in the Midwest. Founded in 1957, this rose garden features over 3,000 plants and about 250 varieties, presenting an exquisite display of color.

J. R. WATKINS ADMINISTRATION BUILDING, 150 Liberty St. Tel. 507/457-3300.

Home of the line of Watkins' products that includes everything from spices to personal-care items. This two-story block-long building combines Viennese classical elements with local ornamental imagery in the manner of the Prairie school.

6. DULUTH

About halfway between the Twin Cities and the Canadian border is Duluth, the third largest city in Minneapolis, but second to none in its importance as an international inland port. Ships from all over the world arrive and depart each day from April to December, imparting a truly cosmopolitan air to this northeast Minnesota city.

Like Minneapolis and St. Paul, Duluth is linked to a "twin"—in this case one in a different state. Superior, Wis., and Duluth, Minn. have always shared a natural harbor on Lake Superior, the huge inland sea that Henry Wadsworth Longfellow immortalized in 1855 as the birthplace of Hiawatha: "By the shores of Gitche Gumee, By the shining big-sea water. . . ."

Like any siblings, these cities have disagreed at times, most memorably perhaps one April weekend in 1871, after Duluth had decided to do something about the 6½-mile sandbar, Minnesota Point, around which its fishing ships had to travel before reaching open water. The city of Superior enjoyed a natural advantage because Wisconsin Point, less than 3 miles long, gave its boats readier access to the lake.

On this April day in 1871, Duluth officials authorized the digging of an artificial channel through Minnesota Point. A steam shovel had already started work when Superior officials contacted Washington, D.C., with a request that the excavation be halted. Word reached

Duluth on a Friday afternoon that an army engineer was on his way with an injunction to halt the excavation. By the time he actually arrived early on Monday, the entire town had bent to the task, working ceaselessly throughout the weekend and finishing the entry-way in time for a little tugboat, *Fero,* to toot its way through while Duluthians cheered.

In 1873 the federal government assumed control of the canal and the harbor, and 10 years later named it the Duluth-Superior Harbor. Today an aerial lift bridge oversees the nearly 40 million tons of domestic and international cargo that passes through each year.

These international ships carry grain to Europe and beyond, while more boats take on taconite for shipment to cities in the American East. And of course the presence here of ships from all over the world has become a prime tourist attraction for the city of Duluth.

WHAT TO SEE & DO

One of the musts in any visit to Duluth is a drive along **Skyline Parkway,** a 26-mile strip of city that hugs the crest of a hillside at the western end of town. Day or night, winter or summer, this is a beautiful drive, looking out on Lake Superior, St. Louis Bay, and many residential areas. Part of the route goes through another sightseeing attraction, **Hawks Ridge Nature Reserve,** a place where bird-watchers gather each fall to watch the migratory flights of hawks and eagles.

At the other end of town, **Spirit Mountain** (tel. toll free 800/247-0146) has been bringing ever-increasing numbers of skiers to Duluth during the past decade to enjoy such innovations as the 444 Express, a chair lift that raises four skiers in a bubble-domed quad to a height of 4,000 feet in just four minutes. The first of its kind in Minnesota, the 444 Express is one of only three or four similar lifts in the entire country. Work is constantly under way not only on lengthening and improving existing runs, but also on developing programs for individual skiers and families. One of the most notable events at Spirit Mountain takes place each New Year's Eve when instructors and members of the ski patrol lead a torchlight parade down the slopes before fireworks erupt into the cold, clear winter sky.

One of the long-range development plans here is to extend runs as far as the **Lake Superior Zoological Garden,** at 7th Avenue West and Grand Avenue (Highway 23; tel. 218/624-1502), which boasts more than 500 animals from around the world, including a variety of "night animals" that recently took up residence in their own newly constructed nocturnal building. Another popular spot here is the **Children's Zoo Contact Building,** where children, under staff supervision, are invited to touch and pet a variety of animals. Admission to the zoo from April 15 to October 15 is $1.50 for adults, 75¢ for children 6 to 12. Zoo hours during this period are 9am to 6pm seven days a week. There's no entrance fee during the rest of the year, when the zoo is open from 9am to 4pm. Closed Thanksgiving Day, Christmas, and New Year's Day.

Another favorite sightseeing attraction, for children and grown-ups alike, is the **Depot,** 506 W. Michigan St. (tel. toll free

800/438-5884). An interesting series of exhibits and museums leads visitors through two centuries of local history, with an early stop at the Immigrants' Waiting Room. Elsewhere along the way, children enjoy the two-story walk-through Habitat Tree, and visitors of all ages admire the wonderful mid-19th-century collection of Ojibwa Indian portraits by Eastman Johnson. Elsewhere at the Depot you'll find a fascinating assortment of antique trains, glassware, and furnishings. Open daily from 10am to 5pm during the summer months. During the winter, the hours are Monday through Saturday from 10am to 5pm and on Sunday from 1 to 5pm.

And then there's **Glensheen,** a most popular attraction. This magnificent mansion, at 3300 London Rd. (Highway 61 North), was donated by the wealthy Congdon family to the University of Minnesota and stands in the lakeside neighborhood where logging and mining barons built lavish homes nearly a century ago. Glensheen features a dazzling array of exquisite architecture, interior design, art, and horticulture. You'll find your visit to this 39-room Jacobean manor house one of the highlights of your visit to Duluth. Call 218/724-8863 for recorded information regarding hours, and admission charges, or 218/724-8864 for reservations and additional information. Glensheen is open year-round.

For information about other attractions, call or write the **Duluth Convention and Visitors Bureau Information Center,** 5th Avenue West and the Waterfront, Duluth, MN 55802 (tel. 218/722-6024 or toll free 800/862-1172 in Minnesota).

WHERE TO STAY

Theoretically, you could make a 1-day excursion from Minneapolis to Duluth, but since the drive takes about three hours each way, I strongly suggest that you spend the night. There's a lot to see and do in this lovely city.

EXPENSIVE

THE MANSION, 3600 London Rd., Duluth, MN 55804. Tel. 218/724-0739. 10 rms.
$ Rates: (including country breakfast): $95–$195 double. MC, V.
Just two doors away from Glensheen, the Mansion was from 1929 to the early 1930's the 13-bedroom home of another member of the Congdon family, Majorie Congdon Dudley, and her husband, Harry C. Dudley. Accommodations here are named for the color of the rooms and the view they command.

A hearty country breakfast, served in the formal dinining room, is included in the rates. So is access to the oak-paneled library, the pine-paneled living room, and sun porch and dining room, and the third floor trophy room. As of this writing, the Mansion is open to overnight guests only from Memorial Day to October 15 and most winter weekends, with certain other periods available by special arrangement. For the doctor's family that runs it, this beautiful and gracious home has become a labor of love, and you'll find all kinds of delightful reasons to come back again.

MODERATE

FITGER'S INN, 600 E. Superior St., Duluth, MN 55802. Tel. 218/722-8826 or toll free 800/726-2982. Fax 218/727-8871. 48 rms and suites. TV TEL

$ Rates: Peak season $84.95–$104.95 double; off-season $79.95–$89.95 double. AE, CB, DC, DISC, MC, V.

Another notable place to stay is Fitger's Inn. Listed on the National Register of Historic Places, this restored 19th-century structure offers individually styled rooms, some of them with a view of Lake Superior and some with original stone walls from the days when the building served as a famous Duluth brewery.

INEXPENSIVE

BEST WESTERN EDGEWATER WEST MOTEL, 2211 London Rd., Duluth, MN 55804. Tel. 218/728-3601. Fax 218/728-3727. 280 rms. A/C

$ Rates: $54–$115 double. AE, MC, V.

Very comfortable accommodations are available here and at another location, Edgewater East, 2330 London Rd., Duluth, MN 55804 (tel. 218/728-3601). Rates include breakfast delivered to your door. The more expensive rooms, not surprisingly, are those that look out on Lake Superior. Edgewater East, the original lakeside complex, faces Edgewater West, located on the other side of busy London Road. A new lakeside building also has rooms.

WHERE TO DINE

MODERATE

GRANDMA'S SALOON AND DELI, 522 Lake Ave. S. Tel. 727-4192.
Cuisine: ITALIAN/AMERICAN. **Reservations:** Not necessary.
$ Prices: $5.95–$14.95. AE, DISC, MC, V.
Open: Winter daily 11:30am–10pm; summer daily 11am–11pm.

Grandma's is something of an institution throughout the state because of both its food and its decor. You'll find absolutely everything hanging on the wall or from the ceiling at Grandma's. That means antique neon signs, stained-glass windows, brass beds and cribs, and even a stuffed black bear (the one, supposedly, that ran into the Hotel Duluth some years ago and thereby achieved immortality). The food is Italian American—equal proportions of each, actually—and all of it well prepared and reasonable in cost.

PICKWICK, 508 E. Superior St. Tel. 727-8901.
Cuisine: AMERICAN. **Reservations:** Recommended.
$ Prices: Lunch $2–$7.50, dinner $8–$30. AE, MC, V.
Open: Mon–Sat 11am–11pm.

The family-owned Pickwick has been serving fine food at reasonable prices since 1914. The decor here is 19th-century German, the cuisine is primarily American, and the beer is imported from a number of European countries.

The service will make you think of an earlier, more gracious time; so will the across-the-board senior citizens' 10% discount, which may account for the somewhat advanced average age here. Or the explanation may be that older folks know value when they run into it and return because of it. At any rate, the Pickwick is a beautiful, unique, and very popular Duluth tradition.

INDEX

Now Save Money on All Your Travels by Joining
FROMMER'S ™ TRAVEL BOOK CLUB
The World's Best Travel Guides at Membership Prices

FROMMER'S TRAVEL BOOK CLUB is your ticket to successful travel! Open up a world of travel information and simplify your travel planning when you join ranks with thousands of value-conscious travelers who are members of the FROMMER'S TRAVEL BOOK CLUB. Join today and you'll be entitled to all the privileges that come from belonging to the club that offers you travel guides for less to more than 100 destinations worldwide. Annual membership is only $25 (U.S.) or $35 (Canada and foreign).

The Advantages of Membership

1. Your choice of *three* free FROMMER'S TRAVEL GUIDES (any *two* FROMMER'S COMPREHENSIVE GUIDES, FROMMER'S $-A-DAY GUIDES, FROMMER'S WALKING TOURS *or* FROMMER'S FAMILY GUIDES—plus *one* FROMMER'S CITY GUIDE, FROMMER'S CITY $-A-DAY GUIDE *or* FROMMER'S TOURING GUIDE).
2. Your own subscription to **TRIPS AND TRAVEL** quarterly newsletter.
3. You're entitled to a **30% discount** on your order of any additional books offered by FROMMER'S TRAVEL BOOK CLUB.
4. You're offered (at a small additional fee) our **Domestic Trip-Routing Kits.**

Our quarterly newsletter **TRIPS AND TRAVEL** offers practical information on the best buys in travel, the "hottest" vacation spots, the latest travel trends, world-class events and much, much more.
Our **Domestic Trip-Routing Kits** are available for any North American destination. We'll send you a detailed map highlighting the best route to take to your destination—you can request direct or scenic routes.

Here's all you have to do to join:
Send in your membership fee of $25 ($35 Canada and foreign) with your name and address on the form below along with your selections as part of your membership package to **FROMMER'S TRAVEL BOOK CLUB, P.O. Box 473, Mt. Morris, IL 61054-0473.** Remember to check off your *three* free books.
If you would like to order additional books, please select the books you would like and send a check for the total amount (please add sales tax in the states noted below), plus $2 per book for shipping and handling ($3 per book for foreign orders) to:

FROMMER'S TRAVEL BOOK CLUB
P.O. Box 473
Mt. Morris, IL 61054-0473
(815) 734-1104

[ ] **YES.** I want to take advantage of this opportunity to join FROMMER'S TRAVEL BOOK CLUB.
[ ] **My check is enclosed.** Dollar amount enclosed_____*
(all payments in U.S. funds only)

Name_____
Address_____
City_____ State_____ Zip
All orders must be prepaid.

To ensure that all orders are processed efficiently, please apply sales tax in the following areas: CA, CT, FL, IL, NJ, NY, TN, WA and CANADA.

*With membership, shipping and handling will be paid by FROMMER'S TRAVEL BOOK CLUB for the three free books you select as part of your membership. Please add $2 per book for shipping and handling for any additional books purchased ($3 per book for foreign orders).

Allow 4–6 weeks for delivery. Prices of books, membership fee, and publication dates are subject to change without notice. Prices are subject to acceptance and availability.

AC1

Please Send Me the Books Checked Below:

FROMMER'S COMPREHENSIVE GUIDES
(Guides listing facilities from budget to deluxe,
with emphasis on the medium-priced)

	Retail Price	Code		Retail Price	Code
☐ Acapulco/Ixtapa/Taxco 1993–94	$15.00	C120	☐ Morocco 1992–93	$18.00	C021
☐ Alaska 1994–95	$17.00	C131	☐ Nepal 1994–95	$18.00	C126
☐ Arizona 1993–94	$18.00	C101	☐ New England 1994 (Avail. 1/94)	$16.00	C137
☐ Australia 1992–93	$18.00	C002	☐ New Mexico 1993–94	$15.00	C117
☐ Austria 1993–94	$19.00	C119	☐ New York State 1994–95	$19.00	C133
☐ Bahamas 1994–95	$17.00	C121	☐ Northwest 1994–95 (Avail. 2/94)	$17.00	C140
☐ Belgium/Holland/ Luxembourg 1993–94	$18.00	C106	☐ Portugal 1994–95 (Avail. 2/94)	$17.00	C141
☐ Bermuda 1994–95	$15.00	C122	☐ Puerto Rico 1993–94	$15.00	C103
☐ Brazil 1993–94	$20.00	C111	☐ Puerto Vallarta/ Manzanillo/Guadalajara 1994–95 (Avail. 1/94)	$14.00	C028
☐ California 1994	$15.00	C134			
☐ Canada 1994–95 (Avail. 4/94)	$19.00	C145	☐ Scandinavia 1993–94	$19.00	C135
☐ Caribbean 1994	$18.00	C123	☐ Scotland 1994–95 (Avail. 4/94)	$17.00	C146
☐ Carolinas/Georgia 1994–95	$17.00	C128	☐ South Pacific 1994–95 (Avail. 1/94)	$20.00	C138
☐ Colorado 1994–95 (Avail. 3/94)	$16.00	C143	☐ Spain 1993–94	$19.00	C115
☐ Cruises 1993–94	$19.00	C107	☐ Switzerland/ Liechtenstein 1994–95 (Avail. 1/94)	$19.00	C139
☐ Delaware/Maryland 1994–95 (Avail. 1/94)	$15.00	C136			
☐ England 1994	$18.00	C129	☐ Thailand 1992–93	$20.00	C033
☐ Florida 1994	$18.00	C124	☐ U.S.A. 1993–94	$19.00	C116
☐ France 1994–95	$20.00	C132	☐ Virgin Islands 1994–95	$13.00	C127
☐ Germany 1994	$19.00	C125	☐ Virginia 1994–95 (Avail. 2/94)	$14.00	C142
☐ Italy 1994	$19.00	C130	☐ Yucatán 1993–94	$18.00	C110
☐ Jamaica/Barbados 1993–94	$15.00	C105			
☐ Japan 1994–95 (Avail. 3/94)	$19.00	C144			

FROMMER'S $-A-DAY GUIDES
(Guides to low-cost tourist accommodations and facilities)

	Retail Price	Code		Retail Price	Code
☐ Australia on $45 1993–94	$18.00	D102	☐ Israel on $45 1993–94	$18.00	D101
☐ Costa Rica/Guatemala/ Belize on $35 1993–94	$17.00	D108	☐ Mexico on $45 1994	$19.00	D116
☐ Eastern Europe on $30 1993–94	$18.00	D110	☐ New York on $70 1994–95	$16.00	D120
☐ England on $60 1994	$18.00	D112	☐ New Zealand on $45 1993–94	$18.00	D103
☐ Europe on $50 1994	$19.00	D115	☐ Scotland/Wales on $50 1992–93	$18.00	D019
☐ Greece on $45 1993–94	$19.00	D100	☐ South America on $40 1993–94	$19.00	D109
☐ Hawaii on $75 1994	$19.00	D113	☐ Turkey on $40 1992–93	$22.00	D023
☐ India on $40 1992–93	$20.00	D010	☐ Washington, D.C. on $40 1994–95 (Avail. 2/94)	$17.00	D119
☐ Ireland on $45 1994–95 (Avail. 1/94)	$17.00	D117			

FROMMER'S CITY $-A-DAY GUIDES
(Pocket-size guides to low-cost tourist accommodations
and facilities)

	Retail Price	Code		Retail Price	Code
☐ Berlin on $40 1994–95	$12.00	D111	☐ Madrid on $50 1994–95 (Avail. 1/94)	$13.00	D118
☐ Copenhagen on $50 1992–93	$12.00	D003	☐ Paris on $50 1994–95	$12.00	D117
☐ London on $45 1994–95	$12.00	D114	☐ Stockholm on $50 1992–93	$13.00	D022

FROMMER'S WALKING TOURS
(With routes and detailed maps, these companion guides point out the places and pleasures that make a city unique)

	Retail Price	Code		Retail Price	Code
☐ Berlin	$12.00	W100	☐ Paris	$12.00	W103
☐ London	$12.00	W101	☐ San Francisco	$12.00	W104
☐ New York	$12.00	W102	☐ Washington, D.C.	$12.00	W105

FROMMER'S TOURING GUIDES
(Color-illustrated guides that include walking tours, cultural and historic sights, and practical information)

	Retail Price	Code		Retail Price	Code
☐ Amsterdam	$11.00	T001	☐ New York	$11.00	T008
☐ Barcelona	$14.00	T015	☐ Rome	$11.00	T010
☐ Brazil	$11.00	T003	☐ Scotland	$10.00	T011
☐ Florence	$ 9.00	T005	☐ Sicily	$15.00	T017
☐ Hong Kong/Singapore/			☐ Tokyo	$15.00	T016
Macau	$11.00	T006	☐ Turkey	$11.00	T013
☐ Kenya	$14.00	T018	☐ Venice	$ 9.00	T014
☐ London	$13.00	T007			

FROMMER'S FAMILY GUIDES

	Retail Price	Code		Retail Price	Code
☐ California with Kids	$18.00	F100	☐ San Francisco with Kids		
☐ Los Angeles with Kids			(Avail. 4/94)	$17.00	F104
(Avail. 4/94)	$17.00	F103	☐ Washington, D.C. with		
☐ New York City with Kids			Kids (Avail. 2/94)	$17.00	F102
(Avail. 2/94)	$18.00	F101			

FROMMER'S CITY GUIDES
(Pocket-size guides to sightseeing and tourist accommodations and facilities in all price ranges)

	Retail Price	Code		Retail Price	Code
☐ Amsterdam 1993–94	$13.00	S110	☐ Montréal/Québec		
☐ Athens 1993–94	$13.00	S114	City 1993–94	$13.00	S125
☐ Atlanta 1993–94	$13.00	S112	☐ Nashville/Memphis		
☐ Atlantic City/Cape			1994–95 (Avail. 4/94)	$13.00	S141
May 1993–94	$13.00	S130	☐ New Orleans 1993–		
☐ Bangkok 1992–93	$13.00	S005	94	$13.00	S103
☐ Barcelona/Majorca/			☐ New York 1994 (Avail.		
Minorca/Ibiza 1993–			1/94)	$13.00	S138
94	$13.00	S115	☐ Orlando 1994	$13.00	S135
☐ Berlin 1993–94	$13.00	S116	☐ Paris 1993–94	$13.00	S109
☐ Boston 1993–94	$13.00	S117	☐ Philadelphia 1993–94	$13.00	S113
☐ Budapest 1994–95			☐ San Diego 1993–94	$13.00	S107
(Avail. 2/94)	$13.00	S139	☐ San Francisco 1994	$13.00	S133
☐ Chicago 1993–94	$13.00	S122	☐ Santa Fe/Taos/		
☐ Denver/Boulder/			Albuquerque 1993–94	$13.00	S108
Colorado Springs			☐ Seattle/Portland 1994–		
1993–94	$13.00	S131	95	$13.00	S137
☐ Dublin 1993–94	$13.00	S128	☐ St. Louis/Kansas		
☐ Hong Kong 1994–95			City 1993–94	$13.00	S127
(Avail. 4/94)	$13.00	S140	☐ Sydney 1993–94	$13.00	S129
☐ Honolulu/Oahu 1994	$13.00	S134	☐ Tampa/St.		
☐ Las Vegas 1993–94	$13.00	S121	Petersburg 1993–94	$13.00	S105
☐ London 1994	$13.00	S132	☐ Tokyo 1992–93	$13.00	S039
☐ Los Angeles 1993–94	$13.00	S123	☐ Toronto 1993–94	$13.00	S126
☐ Madrid/Costa del			☐ Vancouver/Victoria		
Sol 1993–94	$13.00	S124	1994–95 (Avail. 1/94)	$13.00	S142
☐ Miami 1993–94	$13.00	S118	☐ Washington,		
☐ Minneapolis/St.			D.C. 1994 (Avail.		
Paul 1993–94	$13.00	S119	1/94)	$13.00	S136

SPECIAL EDITIONS

	Retail Price	Code		Retail Price	Code
☐ Bed & Breakfast Southwest	$16.00	P100	☐ Caribbean Hideaways	$16.00	P103
☐ Bed & Breakfast Great American Cities (Avail. 1/94)	$16.00	P104	☐ National Park Guide 1994 (Avail. 3/94)	$16.00	P105
			☐ Where to Stay U.S.A.	$15.00	P102

Please note: if the availability of a book is several months away, we may have back issues of guides to that particular destination. Call customer service at (815) 734-1104.